How To Get More
For Your Money
in
RUNNING YOUR HOME

Merle E. Dowd

Author of:

How to Save Money When You Buy and Drive Your Car
How to Live Better and Spend 20% Less

Parker Publishing Company, Inc.   *West Nyack, N. Y.*

To My Mother

who always made a house a home

and

To My Wife

who carries on the same tradition

How This Book Will Help You

This book is dedicated to saving you money on housing. You already know that the cost of a place for you and your family to hang your collective hats bulks large in your spending plan. Shelter, or housing, is a basic necessity—but one open to discretionary spending—within a fairly wide range of dollars. Families can—and do—spend a big chunk of their income on their houses because they want to. You have probably noticed the family whose home in the middle of the block is really a HOME. The lawn is neat, no weeds grow among the shrubs, the windows are clean, if there's a fence, it is stained or evenly painted, and the house appears to radiate a feeling of well-being. Further, the family spends a lot of time really living in their home. You may also have noticed the families who live in pitifully inadequate shelters. Their houses are a mess, and they spend little time around the premises. Such families would rather spend their too-few bucks on something else—like a new car every year, long vacation trips, or a continued flurry of away-from-home activities—or maybe they fritter away their resources.

Who's right?

Both families could be right. It all depends on their HOUSE-POWER. That is, how they FEEL about their home. Because how a family feels about their home affects their spending pattern for housing. But, whether you spend a lot or as little as possible on housing, you'll find this book helps you to choose from alternatives. For example, you might—

- Spend the same number of dollars, but buy a bigger, better house to serve your purposes from what you learn about buying.
- Buy just the house you need and want—but for fewer dollars, so you have more money left over to spend on other activities.
- Buy the furnishings you've been holding off buying because you thought you needed more cash, but you buy them for less right away.
- Buy the appliances and home equipment you really want instead of doing without or going into debt—using the limited number of dollars you have available—through aggressive spending.
- Keep your house, lawn, and garden looking better for fewer dollars.

All of these ideas—and more—are analyzed chapter by chapter with one idea in mind—to help you and your family achieve the best mix of housing values at least cost. Both ideas together—best value and least cost—add up to cost effectiveness. This book will help you achieve maximum cost effectiveness for every element of shelter costs—buying, selling, and operations day in and day out.

You'll learn how big business manages its housing costs for plants and offices—and how you can apply many of these same principles to the management of your housing expenses, such as—

- Learning how to analyze repetitive costs, how minor savings each day add up to a budget-boosting cost reduction over a year.
- Learning how to examine the cost-saving alternatives for major expenditures, such as buying a house, spending big money for remodeling, and buying major items of equipment.

With families on the move these days, selling a home happens oftener today than 20 years ago. How much you get for your home when you sell impacts your housing costs, your savings account, and your ability to start with a gain from the exchange—rather than a loss. You'll learn how to prepare your house for sale and how to get the best value from it.

When you learn how to manage your housing expenses, you'll learn to enjoy your home more.

Contents

v

How's Your Housepower?

Trying to put a price tag on your house and home may seem almost sacrilegious. Yet, how much housing you get for your money depends, at least in part, by how you FEEL about your house. Nostalgia, the "bit of earth and stone that is mine" concept of defending one's own, pure living space, the "living machine" approach to housing — all become wrapped up in instinct and emotion. Some families obviously develop greater "housepower" than others. How's your housepower? To find out, let's look at—

- *Your housing personality — how it affects your choice of a house.*
- *Your housing interests — in-home oriented vs. out-of-home oriented?*
- *Where you and your family are in your life cycle.*
- *Special needs that impact design and cost.*
- *Pocketbook power and the effect of "sweat equity."*

So, you're going to buy a house! What kind?

Families buy homes for the cockeyedest reasons! How many corny movies can you remember where the romantic couple planned their life in a "rose-covered cottage?" Why a rose-covered cottage? Or a Cape-Cod cottage?

Let's take another tack — If you buy a new, shiny car every year or two, do you compensate by living in a 200-year-old house? Antiques obviously affect some people emotionally — and the biggest antique of all may be a house whose primary attribute is its age. It was built during the Revolutionary war — or Washington slept there! Or, maybe you drive an old car and live in a sparkling new, steel-framed, big-glass living-machine of a house?

You may not buy a house *just* because it is old. Maybe the old, stately manor commands an exciting view. Maybe the old house is close to mother's house — or is just like the one you grew up in.

Practical reasons may tip the scale toward an older house. Older houses tend to be bigger, so you get more space per buck than you can buy in a new house — and your family needs space — space — space.

Possibly, you buy an old house because you like old houses. They have charm. They're your tie to tradition. They develop a lump-in-the-throat feeling of nostalgia.

Families that select colonial houses may be searching for a secure base. They may be hanging onto the old because they are afraid of the new. They may also be carrying on a long-standing and comfortable habit. Say a family moves from New England to California. No longer is a steep roof needed to shed heavy snows. The need to conserve heat with a second story is gone. Yet, this family may look at the full range of homes from sprawling ranch-type, one-floor models to adobe-style, Spanish-influence homes — and then select a two-story colonial that some smart builder erected to attract the Eastern immigrants. The family was comfortable in the colonial, was used to the arrangement of rooms with its center hall and stairway, and felt "at home" in a house like the one they grew up in.

Just as extreme is the family from California that searches out a rambling ranch house on a large tract in New England. Maybe they have to build one because none exists to buy. There, they pay an exorbitant price for enough land to site their large-area ranch house properly, pay heavy taxes on the large lot, spend hours every day commuting from open country to the city, and grouse about the heating bills and uncomfortable drafts in winter and the electric bills for air-conditioning in summer.

Probably more than anything else you buy (except, possibly, a "fun car"), you FEEL about a house. Your home is a personal, emotional part of your being. A man may put up with leaky plumbing and ceilings 14 feet high without a murmur — yet scream like a cat with a run-over tail at the simplest malfunction in his car. You LIVE in your house. It's your castle — your bit of territory that you guard as jealously as a male swan guards his nest. You're a part of your house — and it, in turn, affects your style of living. It's this emotional attachment for your house and home that I term "housepower." It's the emotional power your house exerts on you and your family. Housepower affects your spending plans, your living pattern, and your parent-child relationships. With so many subjective factors affecting your housepower, let's explore a few—

What's Your Housing Personality?

Builders and realtors find it easier to build or find a house that suits a buyer's personality than to try to change their personality to suit a specific house. What kind of house suits your personality?

You're Likely to Prefer a Stately, Traditionally Styled, Two-Story, Colonial-Type House if you —

- Prefer to work for a prestige company rather than develop a business of your own that entails considerable risk.
- Lean toward law, sociology, art, or other subjective occupations rather than objective finance, physics, mathematics, or statistics.
- Enjoy vicarious adventure, reading about trips or exotic Tahiti, for example, good music, literature, rather than attending a football game in 10° weather, or playing baseball in an inter-department league at your plant.
- Buy on credit and keep your cash in a bank savings deposit — or in stocks as a guard against emergencies. You have enough confidence in your ability to manage money that you don't have to pay cash.
- Tend to vote conservative rather than liberal.
- Enjoy a cocktail party with good lively talk more than a gathering with active party games, and prefer a formal dance with black tie to a quiet, informal picnic.

You're Likely to Prefer a Modern House with big windows and an open, interior plan with modern materials, low profile and enclosed yard if you —

- Enjoyed subjects like physics, mathematics, chemistry when you were in school.
- Prefer to work by yourself, sell on commission, or to take the risk of building a business of your own rather than work at a steady salary for a mature, established company.
- Enjoy outdoor sports, such as hunting and fishing. You also prefer to attend spectator sporting events, football, baseball, etc., in preference to opera or the symphony.
- Would rather play competitive contract bridge than compare birdwatching "captures" or judge a flower show sponsored by a garden club.
- Abhor stupidity and clumsiness among your friends or business associates.
- Prefer to dream about being a cowpoke in "Marlboro Country" rather than a cloak-and-dagger operator or correspondent with a double-breasted trench coat and crushed hat at a jaunty angle.

- Tend to plow ahead on a predetermined plan regardless of difficulties and obstacles rather than to readjust your plan when it runs into trouble.
- Consider as your heros, inventors, scientists, the first man in space — rather than a politician, artist, or writer.
- Are likely to plunge into a subject you know nothing about and become an expert or at least knowledgeable about the subject rather than hire a qualified artisan to handle a specific task for you.

So, how do you qualify? Maybe you prefer the informal, modern house while your wife's personality and upbringing causes her to lean toward the stately, nostalgic colonial — or vice versa. Then, you may have problems you don't know how to solve because you can't identify the emotional thorns that keep sticking you both.

How about living near the heart of a big city, close to the cultural life it affords? Do you like a house that fits naturally into the atmosphere of a circle of gregarious and entertaining friends — where parties tend to be formal rather than "come as you are?" Or, do you prefer an easy-to-care-for, informally planned house in the deep woods or with open space all around — your own hide-a-way where you can retreat from contact with so many, many people, where you can get close to your family — where you can, for a while, shut out the world? Few families would admit to being 100 per cent in either direction. Look at these attributes and see which house your personality would guide you to.

You Are Likely to Prefer a Colonial-Style townhouse, possibly with pillars and a big living room adapted for entertaining, if you —

- Plan your family finances but don't worry much about living closely within your budget, are not likely to know how much change you have in your pocket, and avoid going into debt.
- Prefer to study French, German, Spanish, sociology, and world history rather than statistics, bookkeeping, mathematics, or physics.
- Remain flexible in your plans and are able to readjust to problems as they come up, are less likely to get upset if you don't complete work on time or according to some preconceived plan.
- Operate as a manager on the job, prefer to delegate jobs and tasks rather than do them yourself, radiate confidence and lack of fear about friends' thoughts or concerns.
- Prefer to work on a commission basis rather than be stuck on a specific salary — a further indication of self-confidence.

 • Tend to like the kinds of houses occupied by most of your friends.

You're Likely to Prefer the Modern Hide-a-Way far out in the suburbs, possibly in a wooded landscape or in the middle of large acreage, possibly on a city-farm, if you —

 • Enjoy hunting, fishing, and other participation sports away from your house.
 • Are budget-conscious but buy on credit with the idea of keeping cash in the bank as a guard against emergencies.
 • Seldom approve of the houses friends live in — at least you wouldn't build one like those most of your friends own.
 • Prefer honest, unassuming friends rather than those who might appear snobbish or depend on "position."
 • Are likely to be daring in planning for business or personal finances — yet suggest that families ought to use more caution in their plans.
 • Prefer to tackle jobs yourself rather than manage or delegate them to others.
 • Like the study of science — biology and physics, rather than modern languages or the humanities.
 • Are likely to believe your wife's family meddles too much in your family's activities.
 • Are little concerned with "position" in the community and are not likely to participate in community activities, belong to service clubs, or enjoy cocktail stand-arounds with much small talk.

Many other personality quirks influence home buyers' decisions. Two other categories are the "home oriented" and "out-of-home oriented." You may find some of these personality barbs sticking out of the lists above, but look at them distinctly for a moment. How you FEEL about your house is reflected by what you DO in your house.

Is Your Family Home Oriented? Does your wife like to spend time around the house? Sew her own and the children's clothes? Make her own curtains and drapes? Spend hours on end in the kitchen cooking up goodies for the family? Then your wife is truly home oriented — with well-developed nesting instincts.

If you are the wife reading this, does your husband work in a basement shop to make furniture, rebuild broken toys, and buy tools with his spending money? Is he constantly adding new shelves, rebuilding closets for more efficient storage, and constantly on the alert to keep the house leak-tight and the paint in good shape both inside and out? How about the lawn and garden? Is he a compulsive weed puller, is he constantly spreading fertilizer, spraying weeds or insects on shrubs, and mowing the lawn — both directions and crosswise to get rid of streaks? Then, your husband is home oriented. He enjoys being in, around, and working on his and your home.

Is Your Family Out-of-Home Oriented? Does your family prefer to travel or spend time away from home? Bowling, attending sporting events, going to the movies? If you are the wife, do you work regularly because you get bored staying home? Do you prefer to volunteer for club and fund-raising activities, if you don't work, just to get out of the house? Do you get "cabin fever" frequently during winters when weather keeps you inside?

If you are the husband, do you spend as much time as you can find at hunting, fishing, sailing, skiing, or one of the other outdoor activities that get you out of the house? Would you rather hire someone to paint the house, fix the cabinets, mow the lawn, and clean up the basement? Do you and your wife eat out at restaurants, clubs, or parties frequently? Would you rather go out to a movie than entertain friends at home — or watch TV with your children? If your interests lie mainly outside the walls of your home, then you are probably out-of-home oriented.

Only you can decide what home orientation means to you. How does your housepower rate?

Housepower Affects Your Spending

How you FEEL about your house and home and what you DO in your home largely determine how much you spend on housing. If your family is home oriented, you will build a bigger home, furnish it more lovingly, lavish TLC on every part, and generally spend a larger share of your available money resources on things and activities associated with your home.

If your family is out-of-home oriented, your house and home are likely to be only a base of operations, a place to sleep, a place to change clothes in, and to eat in when necessary. The money you spend on your house is "grudge money" — even if you don't recognize it. You're likely to spend as little of your money resources as possible on your home because you believe the money you spend painting the house could better be spent buying a new outboard motor for your boat — or any one of dozens of things you prefer doing — outside your home.

Your HOUSEPOWER reflects quite definitely your orientation

toward a home. If you are home oriented, you've got great house-power. If you prefer out-of-the-home activities, your housepower is weak.

What's Your Age and Family Position?

Your HOUSEPOWER is also a function of where you and your family are in your life cycle. You obviously need less house when you're single than when you're married with a passel of kids underfoot. Our ideas change as we pass from one stage of life to another — and our ideas about housing also change. Let's look at the progression —

Single Status — As a single girl or man out of college or living away from your family, you probably couldn't have cared much about where you lived — for several reasons. If you were a single girl, clothes soaked up a large share of your income. Probably your income failed to cover all the demands on it — so, you shared an apartment with other single girls to cut housing costs to the bone. If you were a single man, you probably rented a furnished room or shared an apartment. You probably didn't care or think much about housing — except how to spend as little as possible. You spent money instead on entertaining friends and yourself, on a sleek, sporty car, and clothes.

Just Married — Immediately after a couple returns from its honeymoon, frequently before, housing suddenly assumes importance. Setting up housekeeping calls for a lot of decisions on where to live, how much to spend, and plans for the future. Latent nesting instincts in the female forge to the surface. Instead of bits of string, feathers, and grass, the newly married female of *homo sapiens* begins collecting furniture, drapes, carpeting, kitchen equipment and utensils, and the hundreds of other items necessary to furnish the nest (read house). Two other factors may cloud issues and impair objectivity —

• Prior living standards — When young birds leave an established nest, the change from living in a large, smoothly running household to something considerably more austere can be an eye-opening shock. Newlyweds may forget how many years of planning and how much money spent over years went into their parents' homes. Instead, they wish to continue living at or near their accustomed standard right from the beginning. Usually, the young husband's income simply won't support such an affluent level of housing. Three alternatives are available —

1. One or both parents may give the young couple a home and money to furnish it with.

2. The newlyweds swallow hard, adjust their sights to a standard of housing they can afford, and plan to build their nest gradually as income permits.

3. The young couple immediately plunges deep into debt for a mortgage on a bigger house than they need and a flock of conditional sales contracts for furnishings to go with the house.

Alternative No. 1 doesn't happen along often. A couple that follows alternative No. 3 frequently finds the load too heavy. Smart, forward-looking couples choose alternative No. 2

• Pressure from contemporaries — When recently married couples attend parties at their friends' homes, they may suffer the pangs of status. A couple logically wishes to entertain friends in comparable quarters. So, there is a push to upgrade their quarters. Such social pressure may continue throughout a couple's life. Actually, inner drives for a bigger house, better furnishings, and a prestige location can be a powerful incentive. That's HOUSEPOWER too.

A young couple just starting on the long road of married life could advantageously live in a small apartment. Frequently, the young wife works, at least until she is well along in pregnancy with her first child. While she is working, her earnings might be stashed away entirely with two thoughts in mind: 1) Build a fund for a down payment on a house — some day. 2) Learn to live on one income, looking ahead to the time when she will not be working. When talking to a mortgage banker, there is no substitute for down payment money. But, rather than use the cache to reduce interest costs by borrowing less, the couple should at least consider using their nest egg to buy a bigger, better house in a neighborhood likely to grow — along with their family. Changing houses to upgrade size, quality, location, and status can become an expensive exercise — as detailed in Chapter 12. Instead, look ahead, plan how and where you can get the housing you need for a growing family.

A House for the Children — A family needs more space as children arrive. Affluence affects family attitudes here too. Children used to sleep two, three, possibly four to a room, sometimes doubled up in beds. But, no longer. Now, children feel deprived if they don't have a room of their own. And, it costs anywhere from $14 to $18 per square foot of livable floor area to provide that space. Builders have become quite adept at providing extra living space in attics, in basements or lower levels, or in space generally reserved for the family car. But, any way you slice it, a growing family needs a bigger house.

Housing needs begin to conflict with doctor bills, a need to straighten Janie's teeth, and children-related activities of all kinds. How does your HOUSEPOWER withstand these many and varied demands?

One big way to get the room you need to raise a family is to make a big jump all at once. Most young men just establishing a family can look forward to a rising income. Spending a higher-than-average amount on housing at first, when you jump from a small apartment, might pinch the budget for a few years, but be a reasonable percentage of a higher income later. So — look ahead — plan! Consider the savings if you jump from that small apartment into a house that will satisfy your needs for many years. Maybe you hedge against the future by buying an expandable house — one that you can add onto later.

A Home for Grandchildren — As first one and then another of your children fly away, you no longer need as much space as when they were all around. This is the time to replace much of your "interim" furniture and redo your home in stages. The extra rooms may not be needed full time. For a while they serve as a base of operations for children away at college or serving in the military, the Peace Corps, or testing their wings alone. Your home may have a hollow ring during some of these years, but you still need the space. Later, grandchildren visit — and you have the pleasure of little children again without the worry and responsibility. Your big, homey, comfortable home becomes the grandmother's house that the younger generation travels "over the hill and across the river" to.

Retirement — A Home for Less Active Years — Entertaining grandchildren is great for a few years. Then, they don't come so often. Or, young families move away as opportunities open up in other parts of the country. Soon, you find yourselves visiting your children's homes instead of vice versa. You no longer need the old family home. The space and extra rooms become a chore to maintain. Or, as your joints become less flexible, the weeds and insects appear to become stronger, tougher, and more numerous. When you're away on trips, the house is a worry — burglars pick on unoccupied homes, storms may damage a part of your house or blow a tree over, and the lawn and garden suffer from neglect. You have several choices, but two are worth considering —

• Sell the big, old house to a young family that badly needs space. Move into a smaller home that will be easier to care for and less of a worry. If your housepower is still up, you'll find an outlet for cooking and keeping a garden in the old ways.

• Move from the big, old house into one of the comfortable apartments or condominiums. Your HOUSEPOWER has ebbed and you satisfy your needs with less housing.

Special Housing Needs

Seldom are the choices and the plans so straightforward as those just noted. Everything from heavy family responsibilities to unique requirements can clobber the best-laid housing plans. Consider how your HOUSEPOWER is affected by —

A Parent Who Must Live With You — Despite Social Security, company retirement plans, and annuities, young families may still care for aged parents during part of their lives. Usually only one parent, frequently the mother because of her greater durability, lives with her children. Such an arrangement calls for special planning. "Grammy" wants and needs a small in-house, self-contained apartment of sorts. She needs her own bathroom, possibly a separate entrance, space to watch her choice of TV programs, and room to entertain her friends away from your young family. If you are faced with such a situation and are building or remodeling a home, consider how you can provide this specialized housing. How the rest of your house "lives" will depend on how successfully you answer the special needs of a parent who lives in.

An Office at Home — Space is expensive for the professional practitioner. Office space at home conserves cash while the lawyer, dentist, doctor, real estate salesman, manufacturers' representative, accountant, writer — or what have you, gets started. You know, of course, that the cost and maintenance of business space in a home becomes a valid deduction from personal income tax at reporting time. Sometimes the home office is little more than a converted bedroom or den wired for a telephone and fitted with office equipment. But, if you happen to be a doctor or dentist, you need special lighting, possibly extra wiring for equipment, several different examining rooms, a private entrance with a waiting room, and possibly separate space for a receptionist or technician. Converting a normal house for such special use can be quite expensive. How long you plan to operate from the home area, the cost of alternative space in a clinic complex or professional building, and how long you will be practicing in the locality — all affect your decision.

Special Hobby Provisions — Suppose you're a sculptor. You would prefer to work under even light flooding in through enormous north windows. If you go for the big stuff, you might even have to reinforce the floor of your studio. If your wife dabbles in ceramics, you might run afoul of the local fire authorities if you try building a kiln in your bathroom. Not all hobbies can be relegated to the basement shop — or accommodated out of a built-in cabinet in the family room. If you ride a special hobby, should you remodel your present place? Build a new house? How will special provisions, such as an inclined north wall of glass, affect the tax valuation and resale values of your house? Again, planning and the consideration of alternatives from the dollar view may keep you from making an expensive mistake.

Housepower and Your Pocketbook

Selecting a house, deciding whether to buy or rent, and how much you spend on housing are much like a businessman's decision to build a new plant. Both are long-term propositions. If you make a mistake, you may live with it for many years.

"You have to build at least three houses before you get the one you want!" according to many frustrated homeowners. Experience is a wonderful teacher — but mighty expensive. Families that built three houses to get the one they wanted didn't take the time to plan — to search out what they really wanted in a house, or to discover the elements that would make a house "work" for them. Maybe they bought a house from habit, mistaken ideas about "status" rather than family needs, or hastily because a specific house appeared to be the only one available. Examine your motives, aspirations, long-term goals — then fit them into a housing plan that withstands searching analysis from every viewpoint.

How Much Money Should You Spend for Shelter? — We've already examined how your personality affects the kind of house you buy. Where you are in your life cycle also affects shelter spending. But, even more important is — How much house do you really want? If yours is a home-oriented family, you can reasonably expect to spend more on housing and less on out-of-home entertainment, clothes, and cars. But, if yours is an out-of-home-oriented family, you'll pinch the bucks you spend for housing so you can spend more on fishing trips and football tickets.

Today's family spends more of its income on housing — both as a per cent of income and in absolute dollars — than formerly. Houses are bigger, include more rooms, two garage spaces instead of one, more bathrooms, a family room, and higher quality as measured by everything from insulation and sound-conditioning to air-conditioning and built-in appliances. During the last 10 years, the average family's housing expenditures increased by about 65 per cent. Inflation accounts for much of the increase. But, if you and your family are feeling the pinch for better housing, consider yourself in good company — so are many of your friends and contemporaries.

When Your "Dream" House Costs Too Much — Many young couples won't settle for the house they can afford. They want much more house than any amount of income-shifting will cover. They have a dream — their housepower is great. So, they supply the "sweat equity" needed to build or remodel themselves. But, building your own house from scratch — even finishing a shell house, takes guts and stick-to-itiveness. If you decide on the "sweat equity" approach, make sure you have the extra "housepower" necessary to pull you through the sticky parts. You've got to give up something — like quiet evenings glued to that "purveyor of mental waste," the TV; week end picnics, and summer vacations at the shore. Instead, you dash home after work to use available daylight and good weather in summer, rest up on the job during the week from 14-hour week ends of labor at "the house," and schedule vacations for handling tough parts of the construction — or when you can con a brother or friend into helping out.

But, sweat-equity housepower pays off in grand style. Instead of spending $14,995 on a peoplecoop, the same number of borrowed dollars plus your labor can buy an $18,995 shell house with up to 50 per cent more floor space ready for you to finish. Or, you can start from scratch, build with materials purchased from current income and spend the same number of dollars for a house that might sell for $40,000 when finished. But, finishing might take five years — or ten.

Sweat equity really pays off big in remodeling! Suppose you buy a run-down, inadequately small existing house and move in. You may rebuild part of the plumbing, replace an aged and inefficient heating system, and fix up the quarters for reasonable living. All the while you are planning and saving cash for materials. Finally, you're ready. You may push out the roof and build in dormer rooms upstairs. Or, you add on a whole new wing off the back hall. Maybe you convert the garage into a family room and add a carport out front. You upgrade the electrical system, then you tie all of the additions together with a completely new exterior treatment, landscape the yard and grounds, possibly add a fence for privacy, and paint the whole place a new color. Result — you convert a "cabin" that cost $12,500 into a new

$35,000 house that's modern and efficient. And, all the while you were living in your own place. You weren't paying rent on a place to live while you built a house from scratch.

If your housepower is up to it, sweat equity is one sure way of building a nest egg. When you take your sweat equity out of the place you build yourself — it's all yours. And, if you reinvest in another house soon (see Chapter 16), you don't pay income tax on your gain. Where else can you earn a bundle and not pay income tax on it?

It all depends on your housepower. How's yours?

SUMMARY

How we FEEL about our home determines in a large way how much money, time, and effort we spend on it. All of these emotional values, childhood influences, and basic instincts can't be separated from your pocketbook — that is, how much money you spend for a house. Wrap all of these subjective and objective interests together and you've got HOUSEPOWER. In helping you rate your housepower, you were introduced to such ideas as —

- *How the house you select reflects your personality, your job values, and your way of living.*
- *How outdated and outmoded habit patterns may be affecting how much money you spend to acquire and maintain your house.*
- *How you relate housing needs to your life cycle position.*
- *How you can manage housing expenditures according to your in-home, out-of-home orientation.*
- *How you can turn your personal housepower into a bigger and better house for your family through a "sweat equity" investment plan.*

2

How To Control Expenses
For Heating And Cooling

Cuddly warmth in winter or refreshing coolth in summer! Comfort, sure — and you're probably paying too much for it. Rather than blow your stack about bills, resolve to use less heat and generate the heat your need for less money. Look at the heat balance in your house like a pan of water under a faucet. As you tip the pan, the water flows out. Then, by adjusting the faucet, the incoming flow exactly balances the outflow. If you tip the pan so the outflow is rapid, you need to adjust the faucet for more inflow to maintain the level. Now, consider that instead of water, you are balancing the heat inflow and outflow in your house to maintain a constant temperature. The more heat that escapes, the more you have to add to keep the comfort level up. So, your best way to control the heating bill — whether for gas, oil, electricity, or some other fuel — is to keep as much heat as possible from escaping. Just the reverse is true for air-conditioning. You try to keep as much heat as possible out of your house. Other cost-cutting ideas you'll find here include—

- *How to compare costs of different fuels for heating your house.*
- *Figuring how cold (or warm) the weather really is.*
- *Heat-saving insulation — how to install it all over your house.*
- *Getting more heat from your heating system for less cash.*
- *How to balance your heating system — two ways.*
- *Practicing heat-saving tactics to cut your fuel bill still further.*
- *How to bargain for fuel oil.*
- *How to have more fun with your fireplace.*
- *How to keep your house cooler in summer for less money.*

Utilities are the nitty-gritties of running your house. You'd like to spend less, but the oil or gas bills and the water bills just keep coming in — higher all the time, you figure. Or, maybe you figure the money spent for heating, cooling, water, electricity, sewer service, rubbish removal, and telephone is fixed. Nonsense! Neither are such expenses much fun. So, let's figure ways to spend as little cash as possible on these necessities.

Trade-offs in Fuel Types and Costs

You might pick the type of heating system (hot air, electrical panels, hot water, or steam) and the fuel if you are building a new house. Otherwise, you're stuck with the black monster in the basement. You can, within limits, change the type of fuel burned. For example, millions of coal-burning furnaces have been converted to natural gas or oil. Many oil furnaces have been converted to gas.

Properly installed and maintained, any of several systems will keep your home warm. Also, given any specific fuel at the same price and a house with a certain U factor (a measure of heat loss), any distribution system will keep your home warm for close to the same cost. But, major differences show up when comparing fuels burned in a central furnace. To compare costs, you need a common denominator. The one commonly used is the Btu (for British thermal unit). One Btu will raise one pound of water one degree Fahrenheit. That's not much heat. A typical house in the Midwest or East may require 80,000 to 100,000 Btu's each hour of a winter day to keep a house warm. So, the unit, therm, for 100,000 Btu's was invented.

Efficiency also enters into any comparison. A furnace actually produces less heat than a fuel's potential heating value. Natural gas normally burns in a furnace at an 80 per cent efficiency. This simply means that each therm of gas (100,000 Btu's) delivers about 8/10 therm (80,000 Btu's) of heat to the house. So, in any comparison of fuel costs, you are really interested in the cost of *usable heat*. Units might be cents per therm of usable heat. A formula for figuring this cost is:

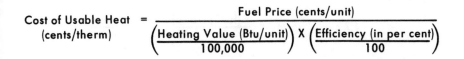

$$\text{Cost of Usable Heat (cents/therm)} = \frac{\text{Fuel Price (cents/unit)}}{\left(\frac{\text{Heating Value (Btu/unit)}}{100,000}\right) \times \left(\frac{\text{Efficiency (in per cent)}}{100}\right)}$$

According to various university and government tests, oil burners operate at 70 to 80 per cent efficiency, gas at 80 per cent and electricity at 100 per cent. Heating values of average fuels are as follows: electricity, 3,413 Btu per kilowatt-hour; natural gas, 1,000 Btu per cubic foot; manufactured gas, 535 Btu per cubic foot; home heating oil, 141,000 Btu per gallon; and coal, 13,000 Btu per pound. One factor to remember is that gas is usually priced on a sliding scale. That is, the minimum bill per month may be $1.50 and includes one therm. The next 49 therms used per month may be 14 cents per therm. All therms used over 50 may be priced at 11 cents per therm. For a valid comparison, use the average cost of a therm each month.

Suppose you want to compare fuel costs. For example, compare gas at an average price of 12 cents per therm with heating oil at 16 cents per gallon. Using the formula above—

$$\text{Natural Gas Cost (cents/therm)} = \frac{12\text{¢/therm}}{\left(\frac{100,000}{100,000}\right) \times \left(\frac{80}{100}\right)} = \frac{12}{.80} = 15\text{ cents/therm}$$

$$\text{Fuel Oil Cost (cents/therm)} = \frac{16}{\left(\frac{141,000}{100,000}\right) \times \left(\frac{80}{100}\right)} = \frac{16}{(1.41)(.80)} = 14.2\text{ cents/therm}$$

In this example, natural gas would be 8/10ths of a cent or 5.6 per cent higher in cost per therm than fuel oil. This difference could amount to $11.20 over a heating season that called for $200 in normal fuel costs. But, regular maintenance of the oil burner and furnace is required to maintain the 80 per cent efficiency. So, higher maintenance cost for the oil burner could wipe out a small difference in fuel costs.

Electrical heat is gaining popularity for two reasons — 1) clean heat without any burning in the house itself, and 2) lower installation cost. If you are building a new house, you may be interested in the trade-off between lower installation cost and fuel cost for a number of years. Look only at fuel cost if you are buying a used house with electrical heat. Using the 14.2 cents per therm noted above for oil, what would the cost of electricity need to be for the same fuel cost? Figure it as follows:

$$14.2\text{ cents/therm} = \frac{x \text{ (fuel price per kilowatt-hour)}}{\left(\frac{3,413}{100,000}\right) \times \left(\frac{100}{100}\right)}$$

$$14.2 = \frac{x}{\left(\frac{3.413}{100}\right)}$$

$$x = (14.2)(.003413) = .484\text{ cents/kw. h.}$$

Since fuel costs and burning efficiencies vary widely, the chart in Fig. 2-1 will give you a quick check on comparative fuel costs.

How Much Heat?

Weather complicates any comparison of heating costs, either between systems or fuels. Obviously, you burn more fuel during a cold winter than a mild one. With air-conditioning, the hotter the weather, the more electricity goes for cooling. Weather bureaus compute degree-days as a measure of "coldness" or "hotness." It works like this. First, the high and low temperatures for a 24-hour period are averaged. Second, this average number is compared to the figure 65. If the average 24-hour temperature is lower than 65, the difference is noted as degree-days.

For example, suppose the high temperature is 72 and the low is 36 for a 24-hour period. The average day's temperature would be 54 (72 + 36 divided by 2). Then 65 − 54 = 11 degree-days. Fuel dealers know from experience how much fuel oil your system burns each degree-day. By keeping track of the degree-days recorded, they know when it's time to refill your tank.

Insulation — For Fuel Economy

Insulation cuts heating expenses, reduces air-conditioning costs, and increases the comfort level inside your house.

How Much Insulation? — How much insulation do you need? How cold are the winters? How hot and muggy the summers? You need lots of insulation where winters are frigid or where summers are steamy. On the basis of a 1,000-square-foot home, 6-inch-thick attic insulation for these extreme zones might cost as much as $150, but would save $80 to $95 worth of heat in one season. You'll save most with ceiling insulation because of heat's natural tendency to rise. But, don't overlook the savings possible from insulating outside walls, installing storm windows and doors, and weather-stripping doors and windows. The kind of wall construction and the amount of insulation combine to affect heat loss (see Fig. 2-2). The effectiveness of storm windows, storm doors, and weather stripping also varies according to the wind.

Insulation has such an effect on home heating that you save two other ways:

• Smaller heating plants can be installed originally in a home with full insulation. With less heat escaping, less make-up is needed — so,

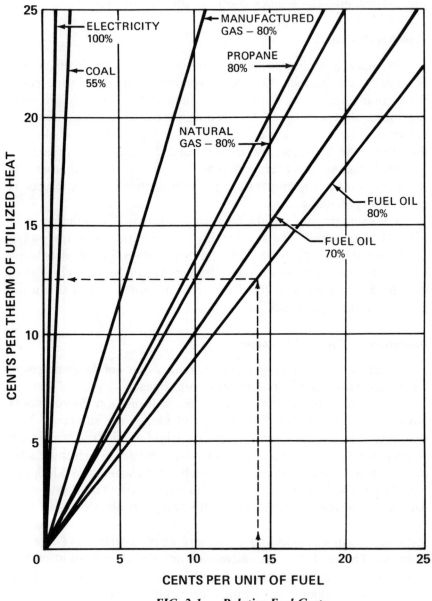

FIG. 2-1 — Relative Fuel Costs

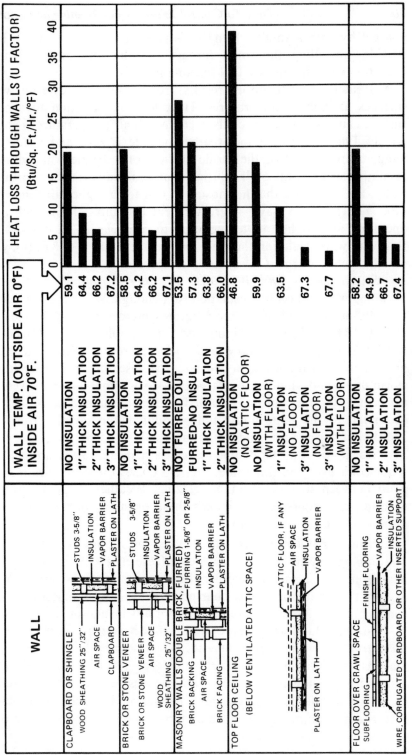

FIG. 2-2 — Heat Loss Through Various Types of Walls

19

you get by with a smaller furnace. Savings accrue two ways — less cost for installing the small furnace initially and more efficient operation with the furnace ON for long periods.

• Greater room comfort results from insulating exterior wall surfaces at higher temperatures. Heat loss by radiation to a cool surface can make you feel chilly even though air temperature is above 70° F. For example, if the weather outside is zero and inside air temperature is 70° F, the inside surface of a frame wall without insulation will be only 59 °F. Sitting near cool walls is uncomfortably chilly. So, you raise the thermostat to call for a higher air temperature. You lose two ways — greater heat loss through the wall and operation at a higher air temperature to compensate for cold walls. But, with wall insulation the inner wall temperature is 67° F. So, you save by feeling warm at lower room temperatures.

Storm Doors and Windows, Weather Stripping — Simply installing wall and ceiling insulation isn't enough. When the difference between outside and inside temperatures increases to 50 degrees or more (72° F inside and 22° F outside, for example), your house needs two layers of glass at windows and doors to prevent heat loss and for protection from the wind. In one extensive research program, adding storm doors and windows to a large two-story colonial house saved 22 per cent of the fuel normally burned in the uninsulated house. When compared to the same house fully insulated, the savings from the addition of storm doors and windows was about 15 per cent.

Storm windows or double-glazed sash decrease the amount of water condensing on the inside. Fig. 2-3 charts the difference in dew point between single and double glazing. Weather stripping around windows and doors simply makes these openings tighter and their insulation value more effective.

How and Where to Insulate — Most insulations depend on bulk — trapping tiny pockets of air which effectively block the passage of heat from one surface to another. Insulating an attic is simple. You can lay thick batts or simply pour pelleted loose wool material in the spaces between joints. But, remember, for any insulation, a vapor seal is important. Batts will incorporate a vapor barrier to be installed on the *warm* side of the ceiling or wall. When pouring loose wool, lay a plastic film barrier next to the ceiling before pouring in the wool. Hire a specialist to blow loose wool into the spaces between vertical studs. Here, you will need to apply a vapor barrier on the inside of the walls (two coats of aluminum paint in a varnish base under decorated oil-

The probability of moisture condensing on windows depends on the temperature of the glass and the amount of water vapor in the air within the house. The chart shows the point at which condensation occurs on the room-side surface of single-glass and double-glass windows for various percentages of indoor humidity and various outdoor temperatures. The humidity must be kept below this point to avoid condensation.

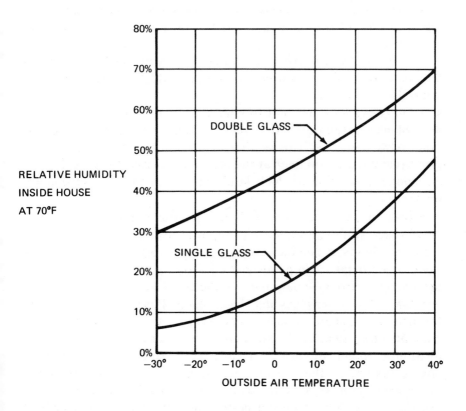

Reprinted by permission of the University of Illinois Small Homes Council from its copyrighted publication, Circular F 11.2, Insulating Windows and Screens.

FIG. 2-3 — *Moisture Condensation on Single and Double Glass*

base paint will do). Install batts with their own vapor barrier between studs in a new house before installing plaster or plasterboard.

Storm windows and doors are readily available. If you are building a new house, consider the added cost of double-glazed windows against potential fuel savings and the task of putting up and taking down storm windows each season. Double-hung storm windows or three-pane windows with movable sash provide the advantages of storm windows without having to remove and install separate windows each year. Weather stripping, too, is easily installed, and materials are inexpensive.

Some of the heat-saving insulation tricks you may not be familiar with can save real money over several years. Most of these you can do yourself:

• Don't overlook the door to your attic., Cover a lift-up attic door with blanket insulation and increase a counterweight to balance the door. Also, seal edges with weather stripping just like an outside door. For a regular, walk-in door at the top of a staircase to the attic, tack on blanket insulation or thick insulating siding to the attic side and weather-strip.

• Insulate the underside of floors. If your house is built over a crawl space, install insulation with vapor protection from two sides — the warm floor side and the damp ground side. If the ground under the floor is continually damp, cover it all with a plastic vapor barrier to prevent water from evaporating into the crawl space.

• Cover hot-water pipes and hot-air ducts. Pipes and ducts that run through unheated areas, such as a crawl space or attic, lose significant amounts of heat before the hot water, steam, or air reaches the room distribution point. Builders frequently leave off these niceties because few buyers notice. But, the increased operating cost bites the homeowner every year. Cover pipes with an asbestos-fiber cellular coating, and seal joints with wrapped asbestos fiber tape. Cover the outside of hot-air ducts with slabs of semi-rigid fiber glass and tape joints.

Check and Adjust Your Heating System

Any central heating system, whether steam, hot water, or hot air, works best only when properly adjusted. If you are mechanically inclined and have the time, check your library for service manuals and books on the exact details for tuning up your furnace blower and burner. Otherwise, hire a professional to tune up your heating system.

Adjusting the Furnace — Between calls by a professional furnace repairman, you can adjust your heating system to generate more heat for your home for fewer dollars by some or all of these tactics:

• Check chimney for draft — Chimneys should be free of soot and not plugged with something that may have fallen or blown into the chimney. Check the draft damper. It will be in the smoke pipe between the furnace and chimney. Open the lightly weighted valve and blow cigarette smoke a foot or two from the entrance. The smoke should be drawn into the valve and up the chimney. If not, some plugging is possible. If the furnace is heavily sooted, hire a professional to clean it with the proper tools. Also, a heavily sooted chimney clues you to a problem in combustion. A flame burning efficiently will not generate enough soot to clog a chimney.

• Keep filters clean — In a hot-air system, return air is filtered on the inlet side of the furnace. Loosely packed glass fiber filters strain the biggest particles of dirt and lint from the air. A sticky film on the fibers attracts fine particles. But clogged filters slow airflow. With less air flowing, less heat is transferred in the furnace and more heat escapes up the chimney. So, during the winter, open the access door and remove the filter packs. Vacuum the incoming air surface and then blow through from the back side. However, over a period of a heating season (possibly two in temperate areas), the sticky surface of individual fibers is covered with fine particles. So, replace the filter packs at least once each heating season.

• Remove loose soot from firebox — Even the best oil or gas furnace deposits small amounts of soot during starting or stopping. Soot is an insulator that slows the flow of heat from the fire box to air being circulated. An additive can be mixed with burner oil to remove soot by combustion. Check with your supplier. If his oil does not contain the additive, ask him to supply enough for a shot once or twice a season.

• Adjust furnace flame and air mixture valves regularly — Oil furnaces work themselves out of adjustment more easily than gas furnaces. Unless you are fairly expert, hire a burner serviceman to adjust your furnace to peak burning efficiency, preferably at the beginning of really cold weather. By waiting, you will be assured of getting the most heat from every drop of oil when you need the heat the most, through the cold months of November through March. Gas flames can usually be adjusted once a year without regard to season because only the gas-air mixture is involved. However, if simple adjustments in the air intake don't keep the gas flame burning with a clear blue consistency, burner jets may need cleaning.

• Check steam and hot-water systems — Single-pipe steam systems operate effectively only if the inlet valve to each radiator is fully open to permit water to flow back to the boiler. Check too the slope of steam lines. Usually, a low spot that collects water will announce itself with a regular banging of pipes. Check too for water level in the boiler for both steam and hot-water systems. Remove caked soot from around water tubes to improve heat transfer to water or steam systems.

• Adjust fan controls on hot-air system — On a hot-air system, the fan that forces hot air through the duct system operates on a different cycle from the burner. The fan comes on after the burner has warmed air in the plenum to a comfortable level. Frequently, controls turn the fan on between 130 and 150 degrees and shut if off again when plenum temperatures drop to 115-120 degrees. These temperatures are unnecessarily high when you realize that room temperature averages 72° F. Instead of waiting until the plenum temperature reaches 135 (average setting), adjust the thermostatic switch to turn the fan on when the air temperature reaches 110° F and to shut the fan off when air temperature falls to 95° F. You'll find the fan switches on a control box near the firebox end of the furnace. Such settings will keep the fan on for longer periods (it may never stop during cold weather), but you'll be getting a larger share of the heat generated in the furnace.

• Check steam vents and radiator valves — Leaky vents or valves that permit air to enter radiators can cause inefficiencies. Extract both water and air from radiators at the beginning of each heating season. Check also the valve to the water system that adds make-up water; otherwise, a leak may flood the system.

Turn Down the Thermostat at Night? — Logically, reducing the temperature differential between inside and outside should reduce the heat flow from warm to cold temperatures. Cooling times, heat make-up time in the morning, and possible discomfort during morning hours while the house picks up heat — all are factors. Tests conducted at the University of Illinois determined that turning back the thermostat by 11° F. with a hot-air system reduced fuel costs by about 9 per cent in the test house. Tests on a hot-water system indicated no savings in fuel cost without an unacceptable comfort level in the morning hours. The reason? Hot-air systems respond quickly to changes in temperature. In the test house air temperature quickly built up each morning after the house had cooled down during the night. With a hot-water system, the house stayed warm longer at night and took longer to build back heat the following morning. So, with hot-air systems you can expect to save as much as 6 to 10 per cent of a season's fuel by turning back the thermostat from 10 to 12 degrees.

Balancing Your Hot-Air Heating System — One centrally located thermostat controls the heating cycle in most homes. Only the air temperature in that one room will remain relatively constant unless you balance your heating system to provide just the right amount of heat to each room. You may prefer higher temperatures in bathrooms and lower temperatures in bedrooms. You can adjust the heat to provide just the right temperature for each room — within limitations. Here's how you can correct imbalances — and save heat — and dollars.

• Balancing air flow between rooms — Take each step in turn and change damper or register valve positions gradually. When you reduce air flow to one room, the air automatically flows to another room. You may need to recycle the balancing several times before all rooms receive the desired amount of heat. Remember, once balanced, all rooms receive heat in response to the thermostat in one room (unless your home is equipped with multiple-zoned controls).

1. Pick a cold day with little wind.

2. Calibrate several cheap thermometers by lining them up near your thermostat. After 15 to 30 minutes, note the temperature indicated on each. Mark the difference between the thermostat thermometer and each of the individual thermometers directly on the case. Cheap thermometers may indicate an error, but the error will repeat itself quite accurately. So, if No. 1 thermometer registers 70° when the thermostat thermometer registers 72°, you know the No. 1 reads two degrees low and you can allow for it.

3. Hang a calibrated thermometer near the center of each room at chair height — about 4 feet from the floor. Air must circulate freely around the room thermometers.

4. Adjust the room thermostat to 72°.

5. Check room registers to make sure they are free from obstructions and that furniture does not interfere with hot air distribution.

6. After the system has operated for half an hour or so, read each of the room thermometers. If wide variations are noted between rooms, write down the readings, because several tries will be needed to balance heat flow throughout the house.

7. Work on the hot rooms first. If ducts to each room are

accessible in the basement or crawl space, check for a damper in each duct. A damper is simply a valve that turns inside the duct. A handle and pointer indicate valve position. Partly close the damper to restrict the flow of hot air to the register in the hot room. Or, you may find a damper in the register for each room. Some registers can be adjusted to a partly open position and still permit opening and closing for night cooling. Allow the house to adjust to the new heat-flow pattern for at least an hour. Then read the room thermometers again.

8. Cool rooms require just the oposite treatment — more hot air. Check duct dampers and room registers for position. Open them gradually if they are partly closed. Some systems include dampers in major outlets from the plenum at the furnace. In such cases, you may need to adjust as many as three dampers in series to achieve the heat balance you prefer.

9. After adjusting duct dampers and room registers, you may find that one or more rooms still won't reach a comfortable temperature without overheating other rooms. The cold room may be too far from the furnace, the duct may be too small, or the hot air may be cooled before it reaches the room. Try insulating the duct to prevent heat loss. If that doesn't work, you may need to add a small electric or gas heater to the cool room for supplementary heating during really cold weather.

Basement rooms may be particularly difficult to keep warm. Many builders leave heat outlets in the basement ceiling to cut their costs. Heat from the ceiling registers rises, and the floor remains cold. The only real solution here is to extend the ducts in the wall down to floor level, preferably around exterior walls. Then, adjust register so that heat flows out along the floor and rises naturally. If ducting hot air to the floor is not practical, check with a heating contractor for possible installation of supplementary electric baseboard heating around exterior walls.

• Adjusting total air circulation through the furnace — Unless airflow through the furnace is right, you will either lose heat up the chimney (and increase your costs), or distribute too little heat through your house. You will need to adjust the fan or blower only once, unless you change the burning rate of the furnace or add additional rooms. Take each step in turn:

1. Open all ducts and registers to full open. If you have previously balanced room distribution, mark position of dampers or

registers before opening, so you can move them close to balance position again.

2. On a cold day, move the room thermostat higher than normal or high enough to keep the furnace operating continuously.

3. Drill or punch a small hole in the main warm-air outlet duct and the return air duct near the furnace. Insert a cooking thermometer in each hole to enable you to measure the temperature of the cool inlet air and the warm outlet air. Check the limit control on the furnace to make sure it is set at the 200-degree safety limit. Wait 15 or 20 minutes for the system to stabilize. Read the temperature of the return air and the outlet air.

4. Note the difference in temperature between the return air and the warm air. If the difference is greater than 85 to 95 degrees, the blower should be adjusted to push more air through the furnace. If the difference is less than 85 degrees, the blower should push less air through the furnace.

5. Adjust the volume of air moved by the blower by changing the ratio of pulleys between motor and fan. How you change this ratio will depend on your blower. To increase volume, use a larger pulley on the motor or a smaller pulley on the fan. If the fan pulley is adjustable, increase fan speed by decreasing the pulley diameter. To decrease blower volume, do the reverse — that is, increase pulley diameter at the fan or decrease pulley diameter at the motor. Make all adjustments only with the heating system turned OFF. Several tries may be necessary before achieving just the right air flow. Close the holes punched in the ducts with short pan-head sheetmetal, self-tapping screws.

Balancing a Hot-Water System — Much the same step-by-step procedure can be used to balance hot-water systems. Depending on the design, you may be able to adjust valves in the piping systems to each room radiator. Or, dampers in enclosed radiators can be adjusted to increase or decrease the amount of air that is drawn in the bottom and allowed to flow out the upper grills. Steam systems can be adjusted at each radiator by changing the vents — do not attempt to regulate heat at steam radiators by partly opening the main valve. This valve must be fully closed or fully open to allow water to flow back to the boiler. Hot-water systems change temperature much more slowly than hot-air systems. So, you may need to change valve or vent positions gradually over several days. Note the instructions for boiler operation to determine the best temperature between return water and hot water at the outlet of the boiler.

Heat-Saving Tactics

Regardless of the kind of heating system installed in your house, you can cut fuel costs by practicing all or most of the following heat-saving tips and tactics:

• Close off rooms not used — Sun rooms, unused bedrooms, and storage rooms that are not occupied should be closed off and the heat to those rooms shut off. How much heat this tactic saves depends on the room location and how effectively you isolate the room. A bedroom on a second floor over the room where the house thermostat is located will remain partly warm even if the register is closed or radiators shut off. A room relatively remote will stay cool and save heat. When closing off a room, pad the air gap at the bottom and weather-strip around doors to keep cold air from escaping into the rest of the house.

• Keep doors and windows closed — Don't attempt to heat all outdoors by leaving a window open with the heat on. If you prefer to sleep in a cool bedroom, shut off the heat at the register or radiator, then open the window a crack. Train your children to close doors quickly and tightly. Weather-strip or seal off cracks or openings to attic or unheated spaces.

• Check room thermostat temperature — Sometimes the thermostat controls house temperature to a different degree than indicated. For example, you may set a thermostat at 72°, but the temperature may actually hover close to 74°.

• Keep temperatures as low as comfortable — Tests have indicated that for each degree house temperature is set below 70°, the furnace burns 3 per cent less fuel. While temperatures much below 70° can be uncomfortable, similar additional costs are incurred for each degree above 70°. So, if the thermostat is set for 72°, your furnace is likely to burn 6 per cent more fuel than if the thermostat is set for 70°. These other ideas will allow you to control air at lower temperatures without affecting comfort—

1. Pull drapes across windows to reduce the effect of cold glass surfaces. Your body loses heat to such cold surfaces by radiation. In really cold climates, insulating drapes save a remarkable amount of fuel when covering large view windows. A lining of reflective, insulating cloth or foam will reduce actual heat loss to windows and help you feel warmer.

2. Keep humidity levels up by adding moisture to heated air. An automatic humidifier in a hot-air furnace or a mechanical atomizer

replaces the moisture frozen out of air as it cools outside. When such dry air is heated, relative humidity drops even lower. Dry air contacting your skin dries surface moisture and cools you in the same way that a breeze evaporating perspiration keeps you cool in summer.

3. Acclimatize your body to a lower temperature. Instead of turning the heat up to 72 ° or higher as soon as temperatures drop in the fall, allow your body to get used to lower temperatures. After your body adjusts to a 70 ° temperature, you will feel just as comfortable as you might otherwise feel at 72 ° or 74 °.

• Install a reflective, insulation barrier between radiators and an outside wall. An aluminum foil layer over a one-inch thickness of insulation prevents as much as 35 per cent of the radiator heat from escaping through the wall. Reflective foil radiates the heat out into the room.

• On warm, sunny days, open curtains and turn on a circulating fan to distribute the solar heat that streams into south-facing rooms. Distributing this heat saves later on fuel. As soon as the sun disappears, draw the curtains or drapes to prevent a reverse flow of heat to the outside.

• Close damper when fireplace is not in use. Cold air flows down the chimney and spreads out over the floor as a cool draft unless damper is closed.

• Install an outside air vent to the furnace if possible. Air used to burn fuel is usually drawn from the house. As this warm air burns and is exhausted up the chimney as smoke and carbon dioxide, an equal amount of cold air must be drawn in from outside and heated. Drawing air directly from outside through a separate duct permits the furnace to burn cold, outside air. So, less make-up air must be heated; thereby saving fuel.

• Add a radiant panel or heat lamp to bathroom. Since we all wear fewer clothes in a bathroom, temperatures must be higher to maintain comfort levels. However, instead of ducting extra heat to the bathroom 24 hours a day, consider installing a supplementary heat lamp in a strategic position to maintain warmth only when needed.

• Keep hot-air registers and radiators free of obstructions. Don't place furniture directly over ducts or in front of radiators and expect them to work effectively. Don't stack magazines on ducts or on top of radiators to interfere with hot-air flow.

• Turn down the thermostat to 55 ° degrees any time you will be away from the house for a full day or more.

Bargain for Your Fuel Oil — Electricity and gas are monopoly, controlled-price fuels. But, if you burn oil, shop around for a supplier who will sell oil at 10 to 15 per cent less than the so-called "standard price." The money you save is yours to spend elsewhere. As a starter, try these leads:

• Ask your friends, neighbors, and fellow workers where they buy oil. Someone will have a line on a discount oil dealer.

• Inquire of discount houses, big mail-order stores, or watch for ads to locate a low-cost supplier.

• Work through your union or combine your orders with others to get a group rate.

• Ask for a volume discount if your oil tank holds more than 300 gallons.

• Negotiate with several dealers for a lower price. Just for the asking, one or more dealers may break the price barrier. The "standard price" isn't fixed. If your present supplier believes he may lose you as a customer, he may reduce the price rather than lose your volume. Or, a new supplier may cut his price to gain a new customer.

Increase Your Fireplace Fun

Reactions to fireplaces run from "that stinky hole in the wall" to a "nostalgic remembrance of campfires on fishing trips" and the like. Certainly with central heating, fireplaces have lost most of their functional value. To gain the most enjoyment from a fire and spend the least cash, remember these tips—

• Locate your furnace thermostat away from the fireplace, preferably in some other room. Otherwise, the additional warmth created by the fireplace affects the thermostat and prevents the furnace from keeping the rest of the house up to temperature.

• Where fireplace wood is scarce and/or expensive, roll newspapers into a form with air spaces between the sheets and burn them instead of logs. You'll need a special device to roll the newspapers, and ties to keep the roll together while it burns. You not only build "logs" for your fireplace, but you dispose of old newspapers.

• Burn substitute logs made from compressed sawdust. These clean, uniform cylinders of sawdust compressed with a binder are available in many areas for considerably less than natural cordwood.

• Check with road and street departments in your city for downed trees. If you can spend an hour or so sawing up trees that have been removed for some purpose, you can get your logs for nothing.

Telephone and power companies also remove many large limbs from trees menacing their precious wires.

• Instead of buying neatly split cedar kindling, roll newspaper sheets into a 1-inch roll and tie them in a loose knot for use as fire starters. Or, split any wood packing boxes you may pick up at furniture stores into kindling.

• Add your own inexpensive coloring chemicals for a multihued fire. Dissolve the indicated quantity of chemical in one gallon of water. Work outside and handle chemicals with rubber gloves — just to be safe, although none of the chemicals is considered dangerous. Use only plastic, wood, or glass containers for the chemical solutions. Wood to be soaked in the chemicals should be dry. To treat logs, stand them on end in the solution and allow them to soak for three to four hours for each end. Then, remove the logs onto a rack or other logs where they can dry thoroughly. Keep the logs out of rain. Mark the color on each log with a crayon as you finish treatment.

Flame Color	Chemical	Quantity*
Red	Strontium nitrate or Lithium chloride	1/3
Purple	Potassium chloride	1
Blue	Copper sulfate	1
Orange	Calcium chloride	1
Green	Boric acid	1

*Number of pounds of chemical per each gallon of water.

On cold days limit operation of your fireplace. Air for burning and for lifting smoke up the chimney comes from the room. As hundreds of cubic feet of warm room air sweep up the chimney, equal quantities of cold air must be drawn in from outside, heated, and distributed within the house.

Cooling and Air-Conditioning (A-C)

All of the things said about insulation, weather stripping, and calking in the earlier part of this chapter apply even more strongly to air-conditioning. The cost of keeping the inside of a whole house cooled to 75 ° F when the outside temperature is 95 ° F is several times more expensive than keeping the same house warmed to 70 ° F when the temperature outside is only 50 ° F. Several factors account for this difference — air-conditioning systems use electricity for "fuel," the cooling cycle is a complex mechanical-chemical process, and much of the energy goes for condensing water vapor out of the air to maintain comfort. Normally, houses centrally air-conditioned use insulation twice as thick as homes to be heated in moderately cold areas. The extra insulation definitely pays off.

Save Money on Air-Conditioning — Basically, when you buy air-conditioning you are buying comfort — cooler temperatures and reduced humidity. How much comfort you buy affects the cost of air-conditioning. If you buy only a single-room unit for sleeping comfort, you will obviously spend less than if you keep your whole house cool with a central unit. These tips for getting more cooling comfort save money primarily by using fewer kilowatt-hours of electricity. If you are considering a central unit, practicing these tips will enable you to get by with a smaller, more economical unit. Any item that keeps heat outside the house permits you to get the same cooling inside with a smaller unit and for less electricity.

• Leave storm windows and doors installed for the summer. Any kind of double glazing increases insulation value — keeping hot air out in summer is even more important than keeping cold air out in winter.

• Paint a reflective aluminum coating on your roof. Special paints (many in color) contain millions of tiny aluminum flakes that reflect the sun's radiant heat. Temperatures inside the house can be 10 degrees lower by simply using your roof as a reflector rather than an absorber of heat.

• Install an attic fan. Preventing heat build-up under the roof reduces the heat load on any air-conditioning unit. Where temperatures are not extreme, an attic fan may be all that's needed to keep your home reasonably comfortable, particularly for sleeping.

• Check local restrictions for using water as a coolant for A-C condenser. Single A-C units work in reverse to your household refrigerator, the heat extracted from your house must be transferred to some medium outside the house. If excess heat is transferred to air, the A-C unit must work harder (use more electricity) when you need it most; that is, during extremely hot weather. Also, an air-to-air unit operates less efficiently than an air-to-water unit.

• Spraying roof with water reduces heat load and may provide enough cooling to avoid need for-air conditioning. Roof spraying works best if the attic is uninsulated or on flat or low-slope roofs. Roof water works two ways — by absorbing heat and carrying it away in the runoff or by evaporative cooling. As much as 250 gallons of water per hour may be needed for effective roof-spray cooling. If water is expensive in your area, added insulation and a bigger air-conditioner may be less costly.

Evaporative cooler replaces air-conditioner in dry areas. In Arizona, New Mexico, and other dry-climate states, circulating air that has been drawn through a wet pack of excelsior provides low-cost cooling. These units operate almost entirely by evaporative cooling. The circulated air is moist as a result. Evaporative coolers will not work effectively unless the hot, outside air is dry because: 1) Unless the air is dry, little water will be evaporated, thereby reducing air temperatures only slightly. 2) Addition of evaporated moisture to air already humid simply increases humidity discomfort and reduces evaporative cooling on the skin.

Operate Air-Conditioning for Less — Whether you have room A-C units or a central system, a number of tips will save on cooling and reduce your electrical bill:

• Shades, awnings, and trees keep sun's direct light and heat off the house. Windows, particularly, need to be shaded to keep the sun's heat from streaming through the glass. Remember, once the sun's radiant heat gets into the house, it will not radiate out again. Roll shades on the outside of the house, for example, are much more effective in keeping your house cool than curtains or drapes inside the house.

• Plantings and screen walls are needed along western exposures to block the sun's heat. By the time the sun gets around to the west during the hottest part of the day, the sun's rays are almost horizontal. Only a vertical wall away from the house or a thick hedge of plants can keep the low-angle rays out. A wide overhang is effective along south-facing windows because of the high angle of the sun during the middle of the day.

• Reflecting insect screens effectively block sun from entering windows. Instead of wires, reflecting screens are built with many tiny strips of metal canted to reflect the sun without blocking vision.

• Exhaust cooking heat and shower or dryer steam. Use a range-top exhaust fan to carry both cooking heat and moisture out of the house. If your bathroom is not vented with an exhaust fan, set up a portable fan to blow hot air and steam out through an open window.

• Schedule house cleaning chores that release lots of moisture to the air, such as floor mopping, washing windows, and laundry, early in the morning or postpone them to cool days. Don't leave wet clothes to dry in a kitchen, laundry, or bathroom, as this moisture must be removed by the dehumidifying section of the A-C unit or system. Ironing clothes also releases considerable moisture into the air, particularly if you use a steam iron. Moisture, once it gets into the house air, must then be extracted or the cooled air feels clammy.

• Begin air-conditioning early in the day. A small unit will keep a house cooler if you anticipate the heat load and keep the house cool from morning on. Otherwise, you may be tempted to buy a big unit to handle the heat load after it builds up.

• Set indoor temperatures at about 15 degrees cooler than outside or at about 76-78 ° F. Greater differentials increase operating costs and encourage summer colds.

• Close hot-air registers in any room where a window A-C unit is operating, to prevent cooled air from draining into the duct system. Also, close the room door unless you wish cooled air to circulate through the rest of the house.

• Clean the unit fans and radiators frequently to keep them free of dust and lint. Efficient heat transfer depends on air movement, so make sure the air passages and the filter are not plugged. Also, blow out or vacuum the cooled metal areas; lint and dust act as insulators.

MONEY SAVERS FOR CUTTING HEATING AND COOLING COSTS

Managing expenses for heating and cooling falls in the repetitive category of looking for the small differences every day. A small saving repeated daily mounts to a really big saving over a year. You know, of course, you're going to keep your house fairly comfortable. But how much money you spend to keep it comfortable could range from 25 to 35 per cent lower or higher than an expected average. How you manage these heating and cooling expenses makes the big difference. The cost-cutting ideas to keep costs down while keeping comfort up were detailed as —

- *Choosing the right fuel when you build or remodel.*
- *Cost-effectiveness of insulation, storm doors, and windows.*
- *Getting the most heat from your furnace and distribution system.*
- *Balancing your heating system for comfort at a saving.*
- *Whether to turn your thermostat down at night or not.*
- *Heat-saving tactics you can practice every day.*
- *Buying your fuel oil for 10 to 15 per cent under the market.*
- *Having more fun with your fireplace.*
- *Cash-saving tactics to use for cutting air-conditioning costs.*

3

How To Achieve Regular Savings
On Water And Lights

Just because something is cheap doesn't give you a license to waste it. Both electricity and water are pretty inexpensive — at least in many areas. Electricity varies widely in cost, but it's still one of the best bargains you'll find for running your home. Despite the steady price rise of most home expenses, electricity has actually gone down in price as efficiency outpaced inflation. Water is so cheap most homeowners waste it without a thought. Availability, rather than cost, limits use in some areas. But, you can still save enough on these two utilities over a year to buy a few days' extra vacation, a new pair of skis, a shotgun, sewing machine, several new dresses, or some other fun things you've been wanting. Cost-saving ideas you'll find useful include—

- *Learning how to figure electricity costs.*
- *Practicing electricity-saving habits that pile up the penny savings every day. Most of the waste occurs because you don't realize it.*
- *Picking and using the right kinds of light bulbs.*
- *Saving water by reducing the need for sprinkling and watering.*
- *Reducing the water you use in your house.*
- *Saving on a water softener.*

Two other utilities, water and electricity, regularly drain a variable amount of cash from your money pool. Wasteful or unknowing habits in using both can increase your cost. Even President Johnson made a point of economizing on White House expenditures by regularly turning out lights not in use. You may consider there is little you can do to save on either water or electricity usage. Not so — and the repetitive savings each month add up to a sizable sum by year's end.

Electrical Savings

Despite the ever-increasing trend of most prices, electricity has either stayed close to the same price it was 20 years ago or dropped slightly. Also, prices for electricity vary greatly around the United States. For example, according to figures compiled by the Federal Power Commission, the cost for 500 kilowatt-hours (KWHR) of electrical energy used by a household in one month for a Seattle homeowner was only $5 in 1965. The same 500 KWHR cost a homeowner $10.61 in Monterey, California; $13.88 in Bismarck, North Dakota; $13.51 in Urbana, Illinois; $9.98 in Chicago, $12.04 in Tampa, Florida; $14.82 in New York City, and $6.03 in Rossville, Georgia.

How to Figure the Cost of Electricity — When you get your electric bill, you may wonder why it varies from period to period and how electricity is priced. First off, if you have any questions, the public informant at your local power company will happily answer your questions. Power companies are monopolies, and they are anxious to preserve their image of helpfulness and to discourage any rumor that, as a monopoly, they are taking advantage of consumers — so ask away. But generally, you can figure your bill this way—

• The kilowatt-hour (KWHR) is the basic unit of power. It is a two-part term — Kilowatt is simply one-thousand watts. One watt is the rate of energy flowing through a circuit defined as one ampere at one volt flowing through one ohm of resistance. So, one watt for one hour equals one watt-hour; one kilowatt-hour is simply 1,000 watt-hours. For example, a 100-watt light bulb burning for one hour consumes 1/10 kilowatt-hour of electrical energy.

• Your electric meter computes wattage by measuring the flow (amperage) and pressure (voltage). It integrates these factors and presents a dial reading of the number of kilowatts used. You can read the dials yourself and check consumption. But, unless you read the dials at the same instant as the meter-reader, your computation of electricity consumed will not equal the billed amount.

• Quantity discounts apply. The first kilowatt-hour (KWHR) may cost you $1.50. The cost of each block of power after the minimum usually goes down and the block size goes up. Over a specific quantity the price per KWHR remains the same. Individual homeowners pay more per KWHR than heavy industrial users of electricity.

• Electric bills frequently arrive only once every two months. So, if you are comparing monthly rates, don't forget to divide by two.

• Recognize seasonal differences. Homes used to use more electricity during winter months than in summer because lights were burned longer, motors that operated heating systems operated more often, you cooked more meals indoors, and watched more television. In most areas the pattern is now reversed. More electricity is now used in summer than in winter for one reason — air-conditioning. Heavy loads occur on hot days. It was these peak demands that led to power blackouts in the eastern United States.

How Much Electricity Do You Use? — Table 3A lists the common appliances and electrically powered items around a household. Notice that the heating appliances use electricity in big chunks. Appliances powered by electric motors are also big users of power. Other items are almost negligible in comparison. Use this consumption table as a guide to saving electricity. For example, since cooking units may use as much as 2 KWHR, don't leave them on carelessly.

Tips for Reducing Electrical Costs — Learn to practice these power-saving ideas regularly for maximum savings. How much you save depends on power rates in your area—

• Use less electricity for heating water by estimating closely the exact quantity you need. For example, if you are heating a cup of water for instant coffee or tea, heat only a cup — not a teakettle full. Also, heat only fresh water. Before heating water in a teakettle, swish any remaining water around before pouring it out. Rinse the teakettle with a half-cup of fresh water and pour it out before filling to the level needed. Heating only fresh water and habitually rinsing the teakettle prevents the build up of lime deposits that effectively insulate the teakettle from the burner, thereby increasing power costs.

• Hot-water tanks heated electrically use large quantities of power. In areas where electric rates are high, homes may use some alternate fuel—

• Hot-water tanks heated electrically use large quantities of power. In areas where electric rates are high, homes may use some alternate fuel — natural gas or a heating coil as part of an oil-burning furnace. Regardless of the fuel you use, saving on hot water pays off. Note these ideas —

1. Keep faucet washers in good condition. Hot-water faucets tend to drip more frequently than cold because washers deteriorate quicker at hot-water temperature. A steady drip can waste hundreds of gallons each month.

2. Insulate hot-water pipes that run considerable distances from

the heater. You probably allow the hot-water tap to run for several minutes in a distant bathroom before the water warms up. Electricity used to heat this water that cooled in the pipe is wasted. Insulation helps two ways — it keeps the water from cooling between uses and it delivers water hotter at the tap so you can mix more cold water with it for normal use. So, using less hot water in a mix saves electricity.

3. Use preset mixing faucets cautiously and knowingly. If you have a one-handle faucet in a bathroom, for example, you may leave it at a middle position. This calls for a mixture of roughly half hot and half cold water. If there is a lag in hot-water delivery, you may be using as much as half hot water without realizing it. Such small but repetitive uses simply draw more hot water into piping where it cools between uses.

• Keep lint filters cleaned regularly on clothes dryers. Plugged lint traps prevent a free flow of air, so the dryer must operate for longer periods to dry clothes.

• Plan your opening of refrigerator and freezer doors. Any time an upright freezer door is open, cold air flows out the bottom because cold air is heavier than air at room temperature. The refrigerating unit powered by an electric motor must then recool the air. Train children to open a refrigerator only when necessary and to keep the door open as short a time as possible. The hotter the room air, the greater the loss from refrigerator or freezer door openings.

• Turn lights off when they are not needed. Despite the obvious fact that a single light bulb burns little "juice," electricity burned by all the light bulbs in a house forms a sizable part of the monthly bill. While one light bulb may use only 100 watts, you may have as many as ten bulbs burning regularly in a house. So, consumption is one KWHR. Lights burn longer than appliances operate. So, you have many small consumers of electricity operating for long periods; the total quantity of electricity is substantial. You don't need to play Abraham Lincoln and read by flickering firelight — just follow these common-sense rules—

1. Get in the habit of turning lights off when you leave a room. Follow a teen-ager around the house at night, and you'll see that he or she leaves a trail of lighted lamps and room lights. Turning a light off when you leave a room should become as automatic as closing an outside door in the winter.

2. Eliminate as many hidden lights as possible. A light left on in a closet or furnace room may burn for days before it is discovered. A

tiny red lamp, for example, can be hitched to a furnace-room light to tell you when it is on.

3. Use low-cost fluorescent lamps where light is needed for long periods. Fluorescents generate more light per watt than incandescents. If you leave lights on all night on a porch or in a garage, a fluorescent will save money over the long run.

4. Use lights in a basement only when absolutely necessary, as for reading. During daylight it's hard to remember to turn out lights when leaving a basement. If your basement includes window wells, line them with aluminum foil to reflect more daylight into the basement.

• Use only as big a bulb as needed. In hallways, closets, or for exterior general lighting, size the bulbs to the minimum light really needed. Use plenty of light for reading lamps, for example, but save at other locations.

Which Kind of Light Bulbs? — Why do light bulbs burn out so quickly? You and millions of other Americans have wondered. For two years the Government Activities Subcommittee studied the problems of light-bulb life and issued a report — "The Short Life of the Electric Light Bulb." Some of the conclusions and data reported include—

• Lives of "standard" bulbs are too short.

• Standard 100-watt bulbs, the most popular size for use in American homes, were designed to burn 800 hours in 1908, 1,000 hours in 1910, and 750 hours from April 1, 1933, to date.

• Federal agencies, by switching to a specially selected series of "extended service" and 130-volt bulbs (in 120-volt circuits) are saving an estimated $2 million yearly.

• Design life for 100-watt light bulbs could be doubled at a minimal cost to consumers.

• Dollar costs alone indicate an increase in bulb life is feasible. Convenience and safety, although unmeasurable in dollars and cents, are major factors also. Two safety factors are — 1) Changing burned-out bulbs frequently calls for climbing on rickety ladders or makeshift boxes to reach outlets. 2) Burned-out bulbs that are not replaced over stairways or in dark basements or halls lead to stumbles and falls over unseen obstacles.

• There is no such thing as the perfect incandescent electric light bulb that will give the largest possible amount of light, burn for extended periods, and use little electric power. Efficient bulb design requires a proper balance between these three factors.

• About one billion light bulbs are sold in the United States each year.

Without getting into excessive detail about the relationship between bulb cost, power consumption, and light output, the subcommittee's findings established that, as efficiency goes up, bulb life decreases; as bulb life increases, light output decreases; and as both bulb life and light output increase, power consumption increases. For example, for an 8-to-10 per cent decrease in brightness, the life of a bulb can be doubled. Also, for a minor increase in bulb wattage, bulb life can be significantly extended. The cost of electric power affects this three-way equation too. As a part of this study, National Bureau of Standards scientists developed a "rule of thumb" for evaluating electric light bulb economy. This "rule of thumb" states that optimum economic balance is achieved when the cost of electric power needed to supply the bulb to "burnout" is equal to six or seven times the cost of the bulb. On this basis, Table 3B defines the power cost for various sizes of bulbs. For comparison purposes, Table 3B uses 25 cents as the average cost of a light bulb and 2 cents per KWHR as the cost of electricity. Several practical facts are quickly apparent from analyzing this table—

• Bulbs at 60 watts and less could be designed for much longer lives without increasing over-all costs to a householder — plus adding convenience. So, for bulbs of 60-watts and less, you could economically buy extended-life or 130-volt bulbs.

• Only the 100-watt bulb appears to be in balance, if you disregard convenience or safety factors. However, either an increase in bulb cost or a decrease in average cost of electricity would favor an increase in the life of 100-watt bulbs.

Further data from the report indicates that, while the optimum life for a 100-watt bulb may be 750 hours, doubling the life expectancy of the 100-watt bulb would increase electricity cost during its life by only 2.5 per cent. Using these same criteria, the average cost to a consumer would be about 4.5 cents per year if bulbs were designed for 1,500 hours of use. The subcommittee concluded — "that double-life bulbs would be well worth this minimal cost."

What To Do—

With this information in mind, use these ideas for reducing light bulb and electricity costs—

• Buy extended-life bulbs designed to operate for up to five years

TABLE 3A Wattage Consumption of Household Appliances

FIXED APPLIANCES	APPROXIMATE WATTAGE RATINGS
Kitchen	
Refrigerator	200-250
Refrigerator-freezer combination	300-475
Food freezer	250-400
Range (single or double oven?)	12-18 kw
Oven, built-in (single or double?)	3.8-7.6 kw
Cooking top, built-in	5.8-9.5 kw
Vent fan	75-200
Dishwasher (built-in or portable?)	1,000-1,500
Waste disposer	350-900
Wall clock	2-10
Laundry	
Water heater(s)	3,000-9,000
Clothes washer (automatic)	700
Clothes dryer (automatic)	4,000-5,800
Combination washer-dryer	4,600-5,800
Ironer	1,200-1,650
Utility (heating, cooling, etc.)	
Furnace fan (for gas, oil, or elect.)	250
Electronic air cleaner	75
Air conditioner	1,600
Room air conditioner	1,350-3,350
Attic fan	375
Dehumidifier	250
Heater (bathroom)	1,000-1,650
Vent fan (bathroom)	75-200
Heat cables	Variable
Incinerator	600-800
Miscellaneous	
Intercommunication system	10-20
Water pump	350
Timed sprinkler system	
Garage door opener	125
Central vacuum system, built-in	1,000
Portable Electrical Appliances	
Bed covering	130-200
Blender-liquifier	300-450
Bottle warmer	300-500
Broiler-rotisserie	700-1,650

TABLE 3A Wattage Consumption of Household Appliances (Continued)

FIXED APPLIANCES	APPROXIMATE WATTAGE RATINGS
Casserole	500-1,250
Clock	2
Can opener	90-175
Coffee maker (automatic)	600-1,150
Coffee maker (party server)	1,000-1,250
Corn popper	450
Cooker, egg	500
Fan (circulating, portable)	150-375
Fire starter	625
Floor polisher	200-400
Fruit juicer	350
Fry pan or skillet	1,100-1,250
Hair dryer	300-800
Heater, radiant, portable	900-1,650
Heating pad	50-75
Heat lamp (infra-red)	250
Humidifier	65
Ice crusher	200
Knife sharpener	50
Mixer (food)	100-200
Radio	100
Razor (electric)	12
Roaster	1,250-1,650
Sewing machine	75
Slicing knife or charger unit	7-85
Steam and dry iron	1,000-1,200
Sun lamp	300-500
Tea kettle	1,500
Television (black and white)	250
Television (color)	350
Toaster	850-1,500
Vacuum Cleaner	350-800
Waffle baker	1,000-1,250
Warming tray	300-500
Workshop (should have branch circuit box)	

TABLE 3A Wattage Consumption of Household Appliances (Continued)

FIXED APPLIANCES	APPROXIMATE WATTAGE RATINGS
Drill (¼-in.)	100
Sander	746
Portable saw	1,500
Band saw	250
Table saw	560
Multipurpose power tool	746

TABLE 3B Light Bulb Cost Comparisons

WATTAGE	LUMENS	HOURS	COST OF POWER .02 CENTS/KWHR	6 TIMES COST OF BULB
10	80	1,500	0.30	$1.50
15	142	1,200	.36	1.50
25	262	1,000	.50	1.50
40	464	1,000	.80	1.50
50	665	1,000	1.00	1.50
60	834	1,000	1.20	1.50
75	1,155	750	1.13	1.50
100	1,630	750	1.50	1.50

for small bulbs and for large bulbs to be used in outlets difficult or hazardous to reach.

• Shop around for the best buys in extended-life or 130-volt bulbs. About 95 per cent of the bulbs sold are the standard, 750-hour bulbs. Only a few small manufacturers make long-life bulbs, although the big manufacturers (General Electric, Westinghouse, and Sylvania) do market some types of long-life bulbs. Because the volume in these special bulbs is small, prices are high, running up to as much as 69 cents each. Read the labels carefully to make sure you understand what you are buying.

• Buy bulbs in bunches. Watch for specials by discount houses and loss-leader sales by drug and hardware stores.

• Consider buying bulbs from mail-order sources. You can determine from the catalogue descriptions exactly what you are buying, and when you buy a pack of four or six, savings can be substantial. Typical prices from one source are 36 cents for two 1,000-hour bulbs or 51 cents for two bulbs with a 50 per cent longer life.

• Pick up free replacement bulbs at some utility company offices. In Chicago and Detroit, for example, burned-out bulbs can be exchanged for new ones on a one-for-one basis.

Saving On Water

Fresh, potable water is becoming scarce and expensive throughout the United States. A major reason for both trends is the wasteful practices among homeowners and industries alike. Water is so cheap in places it is used without much thought. A higher price per 1,000 gallons or 100 cubic feet (usual units for pricing) would put a premium on water conservation. In fact, many observers have remarked that our country's water problems would disappear if reasonable pricing practices were adopted. Water may be inexpensive or costly in your area. In either case, you can reduce usage and cost by one or more of the following practices:

Reduce Sprinkling and Watering of Lawns, Shrubs, and Gardens — Using the business principle that big money savings are possible only on big money expenditures, look to reduction in water costs where large volumes of water are required. Keeping lawns green and gardens healthy requires thousands of gallons during dry summer months in most areas. Follow these water-saving practices around your home—

• Prepare lawn beds with an idea to water saving. A deep seed bed encourages deep root growth and access to the water contained naturally in a larger volume of soil. Properly prepared seed beds for lawns can eliminate watering entirely. See Chapter 11 for detailed directions on how to build a labor-and cost-saving lawn.

• Soak lawns occasionally when watering is required. Deep watering pays off two ways — 1) Enough water is laid on for it to soak deep below the surface, and 2) Grass roots are encouraged to grow deeper when the surface layers of soil dry up between watering. Rather than hurting a lawn, deep watering every week or ten days rather than shallow watering every two or three days builds a better lawn. Frequent sprinkling encourages grass roots to seek water near the surface and deep roots never develop. Frequent watering simply allows much of the sprinkled water to evaporate.

• Don't attempt to keep your lawn a verdant green all summer. When soil temperatures get too hot, perennial grasses turn dormant to survive, much as they do when soil temperatures become too cold to continue growth throughout the winter. Later, when cool weather and moisture are present, the grass begins growing again and turns green.

• Apply mulching around shrubs and flowers to help the soil retain natural moisture. Leaves, ground bark, sawdust, ground corncobs, and other mulching materials not only save moisture by insulating the soil surface from dry air, but aid in keeping weeds under control. Properly mulched shrubs, trees, hedges, and other plants will continue to grow without watering in many areas throughout the hottest, driest summers.

• Select drought-resistant plants for your landscaping if normal conditions require regular watering during a part of the year. Note the descriptions of plants before selecting them for indications of "drought resistant," "grows on dry ridges," and similar words. Also, scout around for plants indigenous to your area. These plants have naturally selected themselves to survive in the water and temperature conditions around your home. See Chapter 11 for hints on how to find plants that fit your growing conditions best.

• Use waste water for growing whenever possible. Hot, dry weather is commonly associated with areas where air conditioning is common. If your system uses a water-cooled condenser, use the effluent to water plants or lawn. Also, you may design the gutter and downspout system of your house to permit diverting rain water during summer showers to a cistern or well or directly onto lawn and garden areas. Thus, you conserve rainwater rather than allowing it to escape down a storm sewer.

Reduce House Use of Water — Most of the water used in your house flows almost immediately down the drain. You can cut water usage by—

• Installing a half-flush toilet bowl mechanism. By one count, about 43 per cent of the water used in a house flushes down the toilet. Most of these flushes require considerably less than the usual six to ten gallons used. So, install a mechanism that flushes only half of the bowl water when a full flush isn't necessary — and save the water.

• Use a control valve in the shower head to slow the rush of water while soaping or while washing hair. Then, when a rush of water is needed, simply open the valve for a full flow. Reducing the flow when it is not necessary not only saves on water, but saves on electricity or gas to heat the hot water that is otherwise wasted.

Water Softeners — In many areas of the country water distributed through mains contains more than 10 parts per million (ppm) of minerals. Usually, these minerals are calcium and magnesium compounds. When used with soap, these hard-water minerals form insoluble curds that end up as the "ring" around the bathtub. Similar unsightly particles are left in the clothes you wash in soap and hard water. Detergents were developed to substitute a sulfate chemical as part of the soap to eliminate much of the curd-forming action of soap. However, "hard" water is still a problem for bathing, detergents sometimes cause skin irritations, and more detergent is needed for every wash.

Water softeners are attached to the central water system or may be hooked into only the hot-water system on the theory that only hot water or mainly hot water will be used for washing clothes, dishes, or people. If water conditions dictate a water softener in your area, you can save by—

• Not buying a water softener unit from a door-to-door salesman. These peddlers make a very high markup on units. You will spend less money at an established store, plumbing shop, or mail-order source and probably come out with a better unit.

• Not buying a fully automatic system. Recharging a water softener takes only a few minutes every week or so. The added complexity of an automatic system not only requires more maintenance but may prevent you from getting full effectiveness from the recharging.

• Plumbing a bypass around the water softener for all of the cold water that may be used for sprinkling or watering the lawn or garden. If the softener is hooked into only the hot-water system, such a bypass isn't needed.

• Conditioning the resins used for the softening to assure full utilization of the salt. Unless the resin bed is mechanically stirred during the backwashing, the water begins flowing through channels and much of the resin is undisturbed during a backwash. Break the sediment crust at the top of the resin bed with a stick through the access hole; then turn on the backflush valve. When the water reaches the hole, replace the cap and backflush as usual.

• Buying salt in large quantities. But don't buy the cheapest rock salt unless your softener includes a brine tank that permits the salt to dissolve before it is charged into the softener. Or, you can dissolve the rock salt in a separate container and use the brine for recharging.

• Eliminating a system water softener entirely. Instead, if the water in your locality is only marginally hard, add a water conditioner to the laundry water used for washing delicate fabrics, to hand dishwashing water, and to bath water. New detergents adequately control the hard-water problem for most other needs.

MONEY SAVERS FOR WATER AND LIGHTS

Are expenses for water and electricity fixed? Not at all. Both of these utility expenses can be controlled, mainly with a change in habit patterns. Some of the money-saving ideas detailed for you in this chapter included —

- *Locating the big power users in your house and limiting their use.*
- *Learning where the big wasters of both hot water and electricity are around your house — then shutting off the waste.*
- *Buying light bulbs with the lowest **total** cost — electricity use and bulb cost — then buying them for less.*
- *Planting your lawn and garden so you use less water during dry seasons.*
- *Getting the most service from a water softener for less money.*

4

Buying Home Insurance Right
To Get More Protection
For Less Cash

Insurance for your home against the multitude of natural hazards is another of those so-called "fixed" expenses. Don't you believe it! There's nothing fixed about the cost of home insurance. You can control the costs within a wide range. Sure, you pay more for more protection. Just be sure you don't pay more for the same — or less — protection. To make sure you don't, learn how to —

- *Package up your policies into one kit bag at an overall saving.*
- *Pick the level of protection you need — and buy all the insurance from your choice of company — not your mortgage company's choice.*
- *Tailor the coverages you need for your house in your locality rather than buy an all-purpose policy for everyone everywhere.*
- *Use the insurance comparator for figuring cost differences.*
- *Add specific coverage riders to package policies for cost-effectiveness.*

You must buy insurance for your home. In fact, if your house is mortgaged, the lender will insist on enough coverage to protect his investment. But, that insurance isn't enough for you. The lender will require fire protection coverage up to the amount of the loan. In addition, you need protection for your equity and protection against losses on contents, liability, and theft.

If you are buying four separate policies to get full protection or if you are only buying one or two of the four, you're behind the times. Now, instead of buying four different policies, you put them all together and buy them in a "homeowner" package. And, the package costs you about 25 per cent less than buying the same protection in separate policies (see Table 4A). Or, price it another way — with a package policy you get full four-way protection for the same cost as part protection with two or three policies. So, your first consideration is to satisfy the mortgage company with a homeowner policy that covers its interests and yours. Here's how to get your best buy — Don't buy your homeowner policy from the mortgage lending institution *without shopping*. Housing insurance is relatively standard in most states. In fact, the actual wording of insurance contracts is dictated by some state insurance departments to assure uniform coverage by all companies writing insurance in that state. But costs may vary widely. Use the insurance comparator (Fig. 4-1) while shopping for coverage to compare costs and coverages. If you are

TABLE 4A — Cost of Separate Vs. Homeowner Policies

Costs are typically representative of insurance policies written for a face value of $20,000 on a frame house in a median neighborhood, Town Class 6, within 1,000 feet of fire hydrant. Applicable for comparison only.

Type of Coverage	Homeowner Package				Separate Policies		
	Standard		Deluxe				
	Full Coverage	$50 Deductible	Full Coverage	$500 Deductible	Basic Fire	Extended Coverage	Added Extended Coverage
House							
Basic Fire Protection	x	x	x	x	$25.90	$25.90	$25.90
Extended Coverage			x	x		10.00	10.00
Added extended Coverage							10.00
House Contents & Personal Property							
Basic Fire Protection	x	x	x	x	16.30	16.30	16.30
Extended Coverage			x	x		4.00	4.00
Added Extended Coverage ($8,000 limit on contents)							4.00
Theft ($8,000 Limit)	x	x	x	x	15.00	15.00	15.00
Family Liability ($25,000 Limit)	x	x	x	x	9.90	9.90	9.90
Total without Deductible	$50.20		$69.80		$67.10		
Total with $50 Deductible on fire, glass breakage & extended coverage		$30.10		$35.50		$81.10*	$95.10**

* $50 deductible on wind and hail only.
** $50 deductible on all coverages.

renting, a tenant's package covers three of the four policies, excluding protection on the house itself.

When you find the company that provides the coverages you need at least cost, assign the policy to the lender — up to the extent of his financial interest. The insurance company sends the original copy to the lender as the primary insured and a copy to you for reference. Most lenders will accept an assignment of interest from a homeowner policy as sufficient coverage.

Homeowner Package Policies

Nothing is simple any more. Insurance companies have kept pace with the complexity parade — just to confuse buyers, you might suspect. So, you can now buy one of five different homeowner policies. The lowest-cost packages may be variously designated as Standard, A, or No. 1. The highest-cost packages may be designated "all risk," C, or No. 5. Unless you know what is covered in each package, how can you compare coverages and prices? Generally, the make-up of these packages is —

Basic Fire Protection — This primary coverage protects your house from damage by fire and lightning. Broad coverage in these basic policies also protects you from losses to your house as a result of windstorm, hail, smoke, explosion, glass breakage ($50 limit), damage from vehicles (except when driven by someone in your own family), or from aircraft, civil commotion, or riot. Coverage also extends to outbuildings up to 10 per cent of the amount for the main house.

Extended Coverage — In addition to the basic fire protection, extended coverage includes protection against losses by vandalism, accidental leakage or overflow of plumbing, full cost of glass breakage (unless a deductible applies), damage by vehicles driven by someone in your own family, falling trees or other objects, living expenses while house is being repaired (up to 10 per cent of major coverage amount), bursting of hot water tank or heating system, collapse from weight of ice or snow, electrical injury to applicances and wiring (except TV picture tube), and sudden accidental smoke damage from a fireplace.

Added Extended Coverage or Special Form — Sometimes called, erroneously, an "all-risk" policy, this added-cost coverage protects you from practically all losses except those specified as exempt in the policy. Previous coverages specify what is covered; the "all-risk" policy covers all losses except those specified — "If it isn't excluded, it's covered." Typical of the added coverages found in most "all-risk" policies are — damage to a wall if you accidentally knock a hole in it while you are moving furniture, damage to the porcelain of a bathtub if you drop a hammer on it, a damaged ceiling due to rain seeping in under the roof, and many others. Theft coverage is liberalized, but there are still limits on coverage for "mysterious disappearance" and for things of value that are easy to sell, such as jewelry. With such broad protection, you can expect the premium to be high — and it is.

Specifically not covered in most A, B, and C homeowner package policies are losses from termites, smog, earthquake, flood, water backing up through sewers, nuclear radiation, war, and cracks or damage due to earthslides, settling, or water. However, usual coverages offer some protection as a secondary feature. For example, earthquake protection is either unavailable or prohibitively expensive as a named-risk coverage. But, if an earthquake should break windows in your house, you could collect under glass-breakage coverage.

Contents and Personal Property — Your family's property is protected at home or, under limited conditions, away from home, under the contents portion of the homeowner package. Mainly this coverage applies to burglary, holdup, pickpockets, or sneak thieves. This coverage protects against theft of furniture, appliances, clothing, and most personal property. Excepted are such items as money, bullion, coin and stamp collections, bills, bank notes, deeds, securities, and stock certificates. Depending on the coverage purchased, liability for payment on some or all of these normally excluded items may be limited to stated amounts. For example, a policy may agree to pay up to $100 for loss of money, bank notes, bullion, and coin collections. The liability limit may be increased to $500 for accounts and bills payable, deeds, etc. A $1,000 limitation may apply to manuscripts lost by fire or theft. Theft protection applies also to such items as boats (not including trailers), outboard motors, and marine craft furnishings up to a stated limit. Specifically deleted from coverage by theft or fire are animals and birds, automobiles, property of roomers not related to the insured, and samples.

Theft protection for personal property extends to the continental United States and Canada, except losses by theft from an unlocked car, among others. A recent addition to policies extends protection against loss of credit cards, usually up to a specified limit. For example, if your all-purpose bank-issued credit card should be lost or stolen, charges against the card up to $1,000 (or some other limit figure) would be covered, if you notify the bank and the insurance company of the loss as soon as discovered.

Liability Protection — This is the coverage that pays off if your mailman slips on icy steps and breaks a leg. If your child accidentally breaks a window while playing in the neighbor's yard, liability coverage pays the full cost of replacing the window. If a neighbor's child falls out of a tree on your property, you may be judged liable, and your liability coverage protects you. Under this coverage your family is protected from lawsuits arising out of injuries to others while on your property and for damage to others' property by some member of your household. Coverage is not limited to your house and environs but protects your family on vacation, at a vacation house, or while traveling anywhere in the world.

Over the years a considerable body of common law has developed around the general idea of liability. One is the "attractive nuisance" or protection extended to children. Suppose you are building an extension on your house and have not yet backfilled around a foundation. While you're away, a neighbor's child slips into the hole while playing and is injured. You are likely to be judged liable and directed to pay damages. Of course, you can argue that the child should not have been on your property playing around something that was obviously dangerous. Too bad; you lose — the principle of "attractive hazard" will usually apply. But, your liability policy protects you and your family.

Many nuances of the law apply to your liability. For example, your liability varies according to the reason for a person's presence on your property. Social guests are invited, but they must still assume some risk for their presence. The law doesn't require you to provide more care for them than you do for your own family. But, if a visitor slips on loose stair carpeting, you may have to pay. If you and your family knew the carpeting was loose and didn't tell your visitor, chances are you would lose in court. If you could prove that you and your family didn't know the carpeting was loose, then you did not know more about the hazard than the visitor, and you might not be required to pay. Some liability policies include volunteer medical payments that permit you to pay medical costs for an accident to a visitor without establishing negligence.

Visitors on business with a legal or reasonable right to be on your property must be protected from dangers you know about, such as a basement stairway under repair. Here, a barrier or warning that the stairway is unsafe constitutes reasonable care in preventing injury. Rented property coverage varies also. For example, if you rent a vacation cottage and a guest is injured, your liability coverage protects you just as well as if the property were owned by you. However, if you borrow a lawnmower and damage the blades by running over rocks, your liability coverage will not pay for the cost of repairing the lawnmower because it was under your control when the damage occurred.

Insurance Costs

Ordinarily, the premium on a homeowner package policy will cost you from about .3 per cent to nearly 1 per cent of the house value per year. Your cost will vary according to a number of things — some of which are under your control, others of which are not under your control.

Risk Ratings — When pricing homeowner package policies, insurance companies rate your residence mainly according to its fire risk. Applicable risks are assessed from two sources — 1) Independent rating bureaus that supply information to insurance companies on such factors as fire department efficiency, and — 2) Insurance companies' own loss records that determine which kinds of houses, conditions, localities, and families are greater risks than others. Some of the risk-rating factors that apply are:

• Fire department efficiency — Your community's organized fire department will be rated for efficiency on such things as number of full-time paid firemen, equipment available, and performance. A volunteer fire department cannot respond as quickly to a fire call as a full-time, on-location crew. The time lost while volunteers are assembling and before they can effectively control a fire raises the loss rate. So, risks — and premiums — are higher. Ordinarily, big-city fire departments rate higher than those in suburban or sparsely settled areas. Big-city fire departments include equipment needed to fight industrial fires and fires in high-rise buildings. The added capability of this equipment permits quicker and more effective control of fires, so losses — and premiums — are less.

• Distance of your house from fireplug and firehouse — Again, time is a factor. The first few minutes are critical. Unless control measures limit the initial spread of a fire, a house may become a total loss. So, if your house is more than 1,000 feet from a fireplug, your risk-rate — and premium — are figured at a higher rate. Also, if your house is more than two miles from a firehouse, you may pay more than the same house within the two-mile limit. Because suburban or unincorporated areas already carry a higher rate, the distance from your home to the firehouse may extend up to five miles without extra cost in some cases.

FIG. 4-1—Homeowner Insurance Cost and Coverage Comparator

COVERAGE	Company A		Company B		Company C	
	Coverage Limit	Dollar Cost	Coverage Limit	Dollar Cost	Coverage Limit	Dollar Cost
Basic Fire Protection—House and Contents						
Fire						
Lightning						
Family property off premises						
Windstorm and hail						
Deductible amount						
Smoke or smudge						
Exclusions						
Explosion						
Exclusions						
Glass breakage						
Deductible amount						
Riot, vandalism, civil commotion						
Aircraft damage						
Vehicle damage (not owned or operated by family members)						
Others						
Theft						
Personal property						
Exclusions						
Off premises						
Exclusions						
Damage by thieves						
Other						

• House construction — Brick or masonry houses ordinarily carry a lower risk rate than frame houses. Formerly, the type of roof also affected the rate. However, while insurance companies still note the roof construction, rates are the same for most policies.

• Area of the country — Competition among insurance companies, state regulations, topography, and weather conditions are a few of the reasons why the cost of fire protection may be higher in one part of the country than another, even when other risk factors are the same. Building codes, for example, may provide more protection against accidental electrical fires in one city than another. Winter weather, with icy or snow-blocked streets, may increase risks — and premiums.

• Number of units in multiple-housing — If you buy a tenant's policy to protect your personal property, the premium rate is likely to be higher in a 20-apartment building than in a three-apartment

FIG. 4-1—*Homeowner Insurance Cost and Coverage Comparator (Continued)*

COVERAGE	Company A		Company B		Company C	
	Coverage Limit	Dollar Cost	Coverage Limit	Dollar Cost	Coverage Limit	Dollar Cost
Family Liability						
General						
Medical expenses (voluntary)						
TOTAL Without Deductible						
With deductible						
Extended Converage — House and Contents						
Vandalism						
Damage by vehicles (driven by members of own family)						
Water leakage						
Falling objects						
Glass breakage						
Deductible						
Collapse						
Bursting of hot-water tank or heating system						
Freezing damage to plumbing, heating system, or appliances						
Electrical damage						
Sudden smoke damage from fireplace						
Damage to contents from burglars						
Other						
Special Form — "All Risk"						
Listed exclusions						
Limits to unscheduled list						

building. Risks from water damage, smoke from a fire in any of the apartments, and the increased possibility of a fire starting in a big apartment house are reasons for the higher rate.

Policy Limitations — Insurance that provides less protection for you and your family should cost less. Sometimes it does. Sometimes, as in the case of deductible clauses, a lower price is enough less to more than compensate for the lowered protection. In other cases, you need to compare coverages provided when shopping for insurance to make sure that a lower-cost policy is not simply a lower-protection policy. Use the Homeowner Insurance Cost and Coverage Comparator (Fig. 4-1) to organize your analysis of coverages and costs. Some of the coverages to compare are:

• Deductible clauses — Most home insurance policies are or can be written with deductible clauses. When you pay the first $50 or $100 of a loss, the insurance company is relieved of the cost for processing many small claims. This saving is passed along to you as a reduced premium (See Buying Insurance for Less, page 59). A deductible may be a flat amount or a "disappearing deductible." The flat deductible, usually $50 or $100, applies regardless of the loss. However, with a disappearing deductible, you might recover the full amount of a large loss. One company writes a disappearing-deductible policy that provides coverage as follows: On losses up to $50, the company pays nothing. If a loss is more than $50 but less than $500, the company pays 111 per cent of the stated loss in excess of $50. For example, suppose fire damages to your property under this coverage amount to $350. This company would deduct the first $50 and pay 111 per cent of $300 or $333. Your actual loss not covered amounts to only $17. When a loss exceeds $500, no deductible applies. Some states make a deductible mandatory for windstorm or hail coverages.

• Exclusions — Only a careful reading of policies during comparison will disclose differences in coverage. Glass breakage, for example, may be covered up to $50 damage, but no more, under a basic policy. Extended coverage may cover any amount of glass breakage, with or without a deductible. Theft provisions tend to vary widely, particularly in relation to coverage for unscheduled property lost or stolen away from your house. Some coverages pay off under a "mysterious disappearance" clause while others require some evidence of actual theft. Most policies provide for depreciation of clothing and similar goods when figuring the dollar value of theft losses. This means that a coat taken from a restaurant will be paid for at its value when stolen. If you owned the cost for five or six years, you might recover only a small fraction of its original price.

• Special coverages — Since many items are specifically excluded from general packages, you may wish to cover items, such as jewelry, with a specified risk addition to your homeowner package policy. For example, the limit on liability coverage for most policies is $25,000. If you prefer a higher limit, you can add such coverage to the basic policy by paying a small additional premium. The cost of the added premium is considerably less than buying a separate policy that provides the same protection. Personal property coverage may be purchased separately for scheduled items, such as jewelry, camera, and sports equipment. Table 4B is a typical premium table for losses of Scheduled Personal Property. Or, you may pay considerably more for a personal property "floater" which covers many unscheduled items and names specific items excluded. These costs vary consid-

TABLE 4B — *Typical Premium Rates for Scheduled Personal Property*

RATES AND MINIMUM PREMIUMS

Class of Property	Amount of Coverage	Rates per $100
Cameras	First $5,000	$1.10
	Excess of $5,000 to $15,000	.95
	Excess of $15,000	.75
	Minimum Premium	8.50
Golfer's Equipment	Any Amount	2.60
	Minimum Premium	8.50
Fine Arts	First $10,000	.03
	Next $15,000	.02
	Next $75,000	.01
	Minimum Premium	8.50
Breakage Rates	First $50,000	.15
	Excess of $50,000	.04
Furs	Any Amount	.45
	Minimum Premium	8.50
Jewelry	First $5,000	1.10
	Excess of $5,000	1.10
	Minimum Premium	8.50
Musical Instruments		
Non-Professional	First $500	.60
	Next $1,000	.25
	Excess of $1,500	.15
	Minimum Premium	8.50
Professional	First $500	3.20
	Next $1,000	1.30
	Excess of $1,500	.45
	Minimum Premium	12.80
Silverware	Any Amount	.20
	Minimum Premium	8.50
Stamp and Coin Collections	First $5,000	1.10
	Next $10,000	.65
	Excess of $15,000	.45
	Minimum Premium	12.80

erably according to the value of the scheduled items and the protection afforded.

Tailored Coverages — Shopping for insurance that covers your needs (and those of your mortgage holder) for the least cost can involve some tailoring applicable to your own, specific house. Many companies spread the risk for certain perils over a large number of houses and families. So, if you can find the policy that provides just the right combination of coverages at the lowest price, you save money with no loss in protection. Suppose your house is modern with large areas of glass. You might pick a company that provides broad protection for glass breakage without an extra premium. Most of the houses covered will contain average-size windows or frames with many small panes that tend to limit losses. Your house, with big windows, is still covered, but you get protection at a bargain price.

Coverage against such wide-area perils as flood and earthquake is either not available or prohibitively expensive. However, you should assure yourself that policies you buy cover glass breakage whether caused by earthquake or other peril. Damage from landslide or earth movement can be costly, and some insurance companies exclude such damage from their coverage. But, if you live in a flat area, make sure your policy does not provide for coverage of landslide damage. Look for the combination of coverages that uniquely represents your house and household. Normally, such a package provides the maximum protection for the least cost.

Co-insurance — Make sure you understand the basis on which your policy covers replacement of your house in case of a total loss. You may be co-insuring or assuming part of the risk for your house without knowing it. Even if your house ends up as a pile of smoking ashes, your insurance may cover the loss only up to a proportion of the face amount of the policy. If the face amount of your policy is less than 80 per cent of the replacement cost of the building, you may be co-insuring your house. It works like this — Suppose your house burns to the ground. Replacement cost is $20,000. If your policy was written for $20,000 coverage, you would receive the full $20,000 to rebuild the building. If your policy coverage ranged from $16,000 to $20,000 you would receive the full face amount. Coverage from $16,000 to $20,000 amounts to 80 per cent or more of the current replacement cost. However, if your policy was written for $15,000, only 75 per cent of the replacement cost is covered and co-insurance provisions apply. This means that for a total loss of $20,000 you may not recover the maximum face amount of $15,000 under some policies. Most policies with a co-insurance clause will limit your recovery to 75 per cent of the depreciated value of the house in case of a total loss. Again, using the example of a $20,000 house (replacement cost) which was 10 years old. With co-insurance, the $20,000 value may be depreciated by 25 per cent to $15,000. The insurance company would then pay 75 per cent of $15,000 or $11,250. You will be stuck for the remaining $8,500 to rebuild the house.

Part losses are also affected by co-insurance clauses. Suppose your $20,000 house was damaged only to the extent of $10,000 — cash replacement cost. If you carried 80 per cent or greater coverage, the insurance company would pay the full cost of repairing the damage — $10,000. However, if you carried only $15,000, the co-insurance clause would apply (because you carried less than 80 per cent coverage), and the insurance company would pay only $7,500. Because you were a co-insurer with the company, you stand the remaining $2,500 of the loss.

Co-insurance clauses must be indicated on the declaration page of a policy in some states. A stamp that reads, "This policy includes a co-insurance clause," may be applied to comply with those states' insurance requirements. Make sure you understand the risk you are assuming if you buy less than 80 per cent coverage on the replacement cost of your home.

If you have not reviewed your insurance coverage recently, you may be co-insuring your house without knowing it. Note in the foregoing that "replacement cost" are the key words. Basically, this would be the cost to restore your house to its previous condition at current building costs. If your house cost $15,000 five or six years ago, its current replacement cost might reach $20,000. So, if you carried $12,000 insurance, your coverage would amount to only 60 per cent coverage when related to replacement cost. Review your coverage to make sure that inflation has not brought you into the co-insurance range.

When figuring replacement cost, insurance companies will normally disregard the value of grading, underground piping and wiring, drains, below-grade sewer connections, and foundations that are below the surface. You can estimate roughly the replacement cost by first figuring the livable floor area in your house, excluding garage or carport. Then multiply this total area by $14 to $16 or some other multiple representing average building costs in your area. If your house contained central air-conditioning, special design features, luxurious kitchen and bath finishing, or any other costly extras, boost your estimate of replacement cost accordingly.

Buying Insurance for Less

When you're ready to buy insurance for your home or for your property as a tenant, examine these two cost-saving possibilities:

Cost-Effectiveness of Deductibles — Normally, you can save considerable cash by assuming a small risk for deductible amounts. If you insure your property for full cost without a deductible, you end up paying an exorbitant premium for a small amount of coverage. From Table 4A you can see that for $30.10, you buy coverage for $20,000 with a $50 deductible. But, the cost for the same total amount without the deductible comes to $50.20. This means that you are paying $20.10 for $50 worth of coverage. If the deductible is the "disappearing" type, you lose nothing if the loss exceeds $500 (or whatever limit is written into the policy). You can afford to pay an occasional small loss with the savings you realize from buying coverage with a deductible.

Pay Premiums Annually or For Longer Periods — Most homeowner policies are written for three years. Some run for as long as five years. However, various easy-payment plans permit payment annually, quarterly, or monthly. If you paid the total three-year premium for the example policy detailed in Table 4A, the cost would be $101.53. When paid once a year, the total cost amounts to $106.50. Paid quarterly, the cost is $112.50. Paid monthly, total three-year cost amounts to $124.50. As you can see, considerable savings result from paying the three-year premium in one lump sum. Compared to the total of 36 monthly payments, the savings amount to $22.97. Whether you pay annually or monthly depends somewhat on how you are managing the rest of your family's budget. If you run costly revolving charge accounts in order to save the three-year premium, you would be better off to pay off the charge accounts and pay for insurance monthly. Interest on the house insurance payments amounts to only 14.7 per cent on the insurance rather than the 18 per cent on revolving charge accounts. On the other hand, paying for a homeowner policy in one lump sum will earn you moare interest than the 4 or 5 per cent paid on bank savings accounts. Although five-year policies are slightly less expensive, you might find that inflation puts you into the co-insurer classification between purchases. So, buy your homeowner policy for three-year periods and pay for it with as few payments as your finances permit.

MONEY SAVERS WHEN BUYING HOME INSURANCE

If you once believed that all home insurance is alike, costs about the same, and is scarcely worth shopping for — this chapter dispelled those old-hat ideas. Instead, you learned that —

- *Wrapping the four major coverages you need into one package saves agent fees.*
- *Shopping knowledgeably with an eye toward deductible amounts improves your insurance cost-effectiveness.*
- *Staying out of the co-insurance range can save a bundle of cash in case of a loss.*
- *Tailoring protection to suit you and your family can produce big savings despite so-called blanket coverages.*

5

Save A Bundle Of Cash
When Buying Home Equipment

Wheeling, dealing, and flamboyance by stores and salesmen plus an atmosphere reminiscent of the carnival sideshow have turned the market for home equipment into a free-for-all. Which appliance? Which brand? Which model? Pay cash — or buy on credit? Not WHETHER a discount house, but WHICH discount house. Buying home equipment is one of your best chances to practice aggressive spending, cost-effectiveness, value analysis — the whole gamut of practical money management tools. Learn how to—

- *Plan which equipment you **really** need. The equipment you could do without costs the most.*
- *Evaluate the brand, line position, gadgetry, and serviceability of equipment by studying test reports, analyzing cost vs. function, and comparing cost alternatives.*
- *Understand the value of timing purchases.*
- *Buy for cash at the big-credit dealer — and save.*
- *Check on used equipment and goods damaged in transit.*
- *Get the service and warranty protection you're entitled to.*
- *Evaluate the cost trade-off between buying and renting.*

Electric-powered and gas-burning servants are widely advertised to make life easier for the housewife. Powered lawn mowers, electric hedge clippers, and other tools likewise simplify outside maintenance chores. Manufacturers are so inventive, in fact, that the problems of storing and servicing our mechanical servants occupy an inordinate part of our time. Yet, we wouldn't do without them.

Selecting and buying appliances confront the family with a tyranny of choice — and a great opportunity to exercise aggressive spending. You must exercise at least three series of decisions if your family is to get the most benefit from its home-equipment dollar. They are, in turn:

Which Equipment? — Flip through a catalogue like Sears and you'll find page after page of different appliances, labor-saving devices, and home equipment. Even if you had the cash or credit to buy one of each, you wouldn't have room for them in your house. Counter, cabinet, or storage space limits your selection. You must decide. Do you really need a refrigerator *and* a freezer? Do you need a washing machine and a dryer plus an ironer? Can a food mixer with various attachments do the jobs around the kitchen or must you also have a portable electric beater, a blender, grinder, and food mill plus a variety of hand tools that duplicate many of these functions? Which tools really need to be powered? Persuasive advertising may have convinced you that without most of the modern appliances you're in the Dark Ages. But, check your cooking and housekeeping habits. Which appliances and which home equipment will really function? The money you save by *not* buying an appliance is a 100 per cent saving.

Which brand? — Again, persuasive advertising and promotion can influence your thinking in favor of a specific manufacturer's product. But, there are differences. Before you plunk down your hard cash or sign that credit contract, know — don't guess — which product will serve your needs best.

Where, When, and How to Buy? — Nowhere in the entire spectrum of your money-management practices do you have as many cash-saving opportunities as in the purchase of "big-ticket" items for your house. Where, when, and how you buy can mean a difference of 50 to 100 per cent in the cost of home equipment. Incredible? Not at all! Equipment merchandising practices are full of chicanery and sharp practices. Unless you are wary, you can pay many dollars more than are necessary to buy the *same* appliance.

Evaluating Home Equipment

Only you can determine which appliances you need in your home. To help you decide which appliances or home furnishings to buy, you need a plan. Buying appliances or equipment on impulse can wreck any family's spending plan. If you are contemplating moving from an apartment (where many appliances may be built in or communally available) into your own house, are already living in a house partly equipped, or are faced with replacing worn out equipment — make a plan. List the appliances and equipment you have now. Add to the list the items you believe you need. Set up a priority that includes replacement of worn equipment and furnishings (see Chapter 7) intermeshed with the purchase of new items. Use a planning form similar to the working paper in Fig. 5-1.

Which Equipment Do You Need? — When you make up your "wish list" (Fig. 5-1), you're likely to find the money needed exceeds the money you have to spend on equipment and furnishings. There's still the matter of food, rent or mortgage payments, and clothes. So, decide which items you must buy. Look at each item. First, can you do without it? Second, would a lower-cost alternative do instead for now — or for a few years? Third, could you borrow or buy used equipment instead of new?

For example, unless you like cold food, you're going to need some means for cooking food. A range? Obvious! But a range is expensive. Consider whether an electric skillet, coffeepot, toaster, and one-or two-burner hotplate would do temporarily. You will probably need a toaster and coffeepot anyway. Almost anything you can cook in a pan you can cook in an electric skillet. What do you need a range for? To roast a turkey at Thanksgiving? Instead of paying $250 for a range and sleeping on two air mattresses and a double sleeping bag on the bedroom floor — buy a good bed and cook with portable appliances for a while.

Perhaps you are considering buying a freezer either to save money or for convenience. Which reason you have becomes important when you consider the alternatives. A freezer locker for long-term storage of food is much less expensive (if reasonably close) than buying and operating your own freezer (see page 82). But, if you wish to cook meals ahead and freeze them or you need a variety of food immediately available for friends and relatives who drop in, the convenience of a freezer in the house becomes more important than the cash saving.

Which Brand and Model? — Knowledge is your key to satisfaction in service and price of appliances and home equipment. Your least effective sources of information are the colorful advertisements in magazines and other media. You need facts on which to base a decision — not manipulative generalities.

You can't expect to test and evaluate all of the many appliances on the market. But, Consumers Union and other testing laboratories completely independent of the manufacturers or government accept at least a portion of this responsibility. Consumers Union, for example, independently reports monthly on its tests in CONSUMERS RE-

ITEM	ESTIMATED CASH COST	PRIORITY RATING*	PROBABLE PURCHASE TIME
Appliances			
Toaster	$15	1	Any time
Portable dishwasher	175	3	Feb. or Aug.
Built-in oven	300	2	January
Home Equipment			
Sewing machine	275	3	Feb. or Aug.
Room heater	60	2	March
Furnishings			
Living-room draperies	150	1	July
Youth bed	60	2	Jan. or July
Bedspread	18	3	Jan. or July

*Priority classifications:	1. Urgent
	2. Necessary but postponable
	3. Wanted, when money is available

FIG. 5-1—*Appliance, Home Equipment, and Furnishings Planning Chart*

PORTS, a magazine available primarily by subscription. You can also check back issues in your library. Some newsstands carry current issues. For the measly cost of $6 a year, you have access to more information than you can usually use.

Suppose you want to buy a dishwasher. If you shopped diligently, you could find as many as 100 or more combinations of model and brand to choose from. Differences in cost, washing effectiveness, load capacity, rack design, water requirements, detergent and/or cleaning agents used, cycle variations, and potential service costs become a confusing jumble. Instead of tramping through many stores, examining many of the detailed printed specifications, or trying to separate out the facts from the chaff of salesman's patter, study the test reports in CONSUMER REPORTS. Monthly issues include reports of recent investigations. The annual buying guide is a compendium of the reports of tests over the last several years. Even a thorough investigation on your own will seldom turn up many of the facts reported. Potential safety hazards, for example, interest Consumers Union. You would also find it difficult to measure cleaning effectiveness in a dishwasher, for example. With as many facts as you can muster, choose from among the many models and brands of appliances with these ideas in mind—

• Gimmicks vs. utility — Top-of-the-line models of washing

machines, vacuum cleaners, and most of the other appliances feature a variety of gimmickry that seldom justifies their extra cost. Here your cost-effectiveness analysis technique comes to the fore. Is the extra cost of a special feature *really* worth the added price? For example, are eight drying speeds on an electric clothes dryer really necessary? Is the impressive control panel with its multiplicity of push-buttons, knobs, and dials *really* necessary to control an automatic clothes washer? Examine each feature in turn. Then, match the potential utility of the feature against the cost. Ordinarily, you will find that each manufacturer markets about three lines. Lowest in price will be a stripped-down model built primarily for competition on a price-only basis. Next higher, and there may be more than one model in the middle range, is the basic model. Highest in price is a dolled-up machine full of gimmicks and added features, probably in a choice of colors or with an expensive cabinet or shell. Your best buy is likely to be one of the middle-range models. The basic model does everything an appliance really needs to do without the costly trimmings. Also, the basic model includes working parts identical to the top-of-the-line models. Only the shell and control panel are likely to be different. But for this small difference in appearance and complexity, you pay as much as 30 to 40 per cent more. Since the store stands to earn more profit on high-priced, luxury models, these are the ones the salesmen push. Only if you are well-heeled with facts can you counter their persuasive attack and buy the exact model you need at the lowest price.

• Choosing by function — When comparing brands, the facts and test results detailed in CONSUMER REPORTS become invaluable. From these data, you can find the gallons of hot water used in a clothes washing machine, for example. Or, the square inches of cooking surface on a grill. You may also compare the suggested list price of competing brands, but such data on a national basis is seldom useful. Whether you pick the model and brand recommended by the investigators will depend on whether your needs are similar to those criteria used by the investigators.

• Private brand, mail-order brand, or major manufacturer brand? — Examine the data in CONSUMERS REPORTS. Often you'll see a remark such as "appears to be the same basic model as XXX" in the write-up for a mail-order or house brand. Most consumers realize that appliances sold by Sears, Wards, and some of the major department stores or merchandising chains are manufactured by some giant in the industry that may also sell under its own name. Whirlpool Corp., for example, makes refrigerators and washing machines and other appliances for Sears. Whirlpool also sells similar appliances under its own label. Note that the appliances are similar. They are seldom exactly the same. Perhaps only the outer shell is different. Frequently, the control panel and possibly the optional features vary slightly in detail. But the basic machinery of such operating appliances is likely to be identical because it is less expensive to manufacture one set of parts than two sets of parts. Buying a similar appliance under a house brand or from a mail-order house may cut your cost — but not always.

Shopping For Appliances And Home Equipment

Only when you know which model and brand will satisfy your needs most exactly are you ready to buy. Unless one brand and model is outstanding, consider two, or possibly, three alternatives. Then, if your shopping tactics turn up a better buy on one of the acceptable models than another, you're prepared to take advantage of it. Consider these factors when buying home equipment:

When is a Bargain a Bargain? — One definition of a bargain is "an advantageous purchase." Few buying opportunities offer you such a wide range of alternatives as buying appliances and home equipment. But, a bargain for you must combine the right price, a fair credit contract if you buy on time, a stipulated warranty and service agreement, possibly delivery, installation, and instructions. A bargain is a bargain only if the purchase satisfies your full range of requirements.

Except for the listed catalogue prices by such mail-order sellers as Sears, Wards, and others, there is no meaningful "list" or "retail" price. Car manufacturers are required by law to list all items on a ticket applied at the factory that details the suggested price for every item. No such requirement exists for the appliance and home equipment industry. You may find a "Suggested List Price" set by some manufacturers, but not all. So, beware of the "price pack." Some unscrupulous dealers inflate the total purported retail price from which enormous reductions are computed. The only real comparison is the total dollar cost to you. If you pay cash, the price you pay becomes the comparison. If you buy on credit, by all means figure your total cost in dollars. (See page 71 for data on how to compare installment credit costs.)

You can determine if a potential buy is a bargain only if you compare the cost of a total package. Use the comparative shopping guide (Fig. 5-2) to make sure you include all the elements.

Timing Your Purchase — As with most products, you can buy

appliances and home equipment for less money at certain times of the year than at other times. So, time your purchases to take advantage of seasonal and sale prices. Opportunities to look for include—

• Home furnishings sales — Most stores, including the big mail-order retail outlets, run big home furnishings sales twice a year — right after Christmas and at the end of the summer. Many stores offer across-the-board reductions on their entire line of appliances, home equipment, and furnishings during January and February to counter slumping sales volume in other lines. Even if the full line of merchandise is not discounted, there will be certain items reduced by whopping percentages. Retailers have found the big-ticket items, such as washers, dryers, etc., are usually bought on time-payment plans. Even with empty, after-Christmas pockets, people can still buy durable goods to be paid for later. Much the same happens during the late summer doldrums. The "parking-lot sale" is a regular. Big stores and mail-order outlets haul out much of the merchandise ordinarily stored in warehouses so the customers can examine many models and styles in an outdoor, holiday environment. Stores also haul out

	Store A	Mail-Order Store	Mail-Order Catalogue	Discount Store
Suggested List Price				
Cash price				
Time-payment price				
Time-payment differential				
Credit check				
Service charges				
Monthly or weekly payments				
Down payment required				
Delivery				
Installation				
Warranty coverage				
Period				
Service supplier				
Covers parts only				
Covers parts and labor				
Other features				
Sales tax				
Total Cost				

FIG. 5-2—Comparative Shopping Guide—Home Equipment

their slow-moving items, slightly damaged rejects, or last year's leftover models and promote low prices on such goods. When shopping these sales, be prepared with your shopping guide, know what you want, and refuse to be suckered into some alternative by a persuasive salesman working to make his quota of PM's (push merchandise).

• End of model sales — Appliance makers have tried, somewhat successfully in some cases, to emulate the annual model change-over so entrenched among auto makers. So, when a new line of annual models is about to be announced, the old stock is discounted for a quick sale. The model change-over timing varies among equipment lines. Television makers bring out their new lines in late summer. This timing allows them to promote new models during the fall season when new programs are aired. Television buyers develop interest in anticipation of many long winter evenings. Watch the ads at nearly any time of the year for such model change-overs in other appliances. Despite the hoopla associated with home equipment model changes, you will find few really important differences between this year's model and the outdated model. Styling changes are the most frequent changes. Or, a few gimmicks may be added to the top-of-the-line model, and these are heavily promoted. Under the skin, the basic machine is probably little changed. So, last year's model, heavily discounted, can become a "best buy."

• End-of-the-month sales — Many department stores regularly promote storewide end-of-the-month (EOM) sales. So that each department offers something and takes advantage of the store traffic generated by heavy advertising, certain appliances and home equipment may be offered at significant savings. Usually, you will find only a few models or items offered at EOM sales. But, if these fit your buying plan, be alert and ready to buy. Sometimes, the availability of a particularly good buy may affect the planned order of your purchases as defined in your planning chart (Fig. 5-1). You may also find that sales of outdated or last year's models may coincide with EOM sales.

• Special promotions — In these promotions, used mainly by mail-order houses, you may find specific appliances offered in sale catalogues mailed to regular customers. Many times these offers include merchandise sold only by mail. If so, make sure you include shipping charges into the total bill (see Fig. 5-2). Mail-order department stores may also make special mailings to catalogue customers in metropolitan areas. If you are a regular customer, you will find a pattern among the mailings — frequently coinciding with the after-Christmas and end-of-summer promotions.

Cash vs. Credit — How you buy your appliance affects your pocketbook. Most big-ticket appliances are sold on time-payment plans because most families don't have the scratch to plunk down several hundred dollars at one time. However, you can set up your own revolving family loan fund and earn the interest charges normally paid to stores or banks (see page 75). Whether called interest, time-payment differential, or simply monthly payments, any payment other than cash will cost you more than buying cash — except one. That is the "three-month, same-as-cash plan" available at many first-class department stores. Under this plan you agree to pay for the cash price of a big-ticket purchase in three monthly installments. Such an agreement amounts to an interest-free time-payment plan.

Money is a commodity with a price, like other desirable and valuable goods. So, don't figure on getting credit for nothing (except for the three-month, same-as-cash plan). Table 5A compares the cash-versus-credit cost for buying a built-in dishwasher plus installation under various plans and from different types of stores. Each purchasing plan has a gimmick of sorts. Take the first-class department store, for example (Store A in Table 5A). Its reputation is at stake, and it sells good merchandise at a fair price. Typical of this policy is the $115 installation charge, $10 under other appliance outlets. Also, Store A charges a modest 6 per cent add-on installment interest. On a 24-month contract, you could buy this dishwasher plus installation for $17.01 per month. For the privilege of buying now and paying later, your dishwasher costs an extra $43.74. But, instead of the so-called 6 per cent interest, add-on installment credit actually amounts to about 11.5 per cent annual rate. (See Fig. 5-3 for a simplified formula for figuring the annual interest rate of installment credit.)

Consider the other alternatives — Store B advertises a reduced price for the dishwasher. But, the installation charge is $10 higher, and the store adds on a $10 fee for a credit check. Store B also charges 7 per cent add-on installment interest. So, even with the $20 knocked off the price, the other elements of the contract bring the total price paid to $414.64, and the annual interest rate amounts to about 16.2 per cent.

Store C sells for full price but advertises "All the Credit You Need," "No Down Payment," and similar appeals to the buyer without cash. Also, the time-payment contract spells out the monthly payment only — $19.95, cleverly niched just under $20. Surprisingly

	CASH PRICE	MONTHLY PAYMENTS (24)	DOLLAR COST OF CREDIT	TOTAL DOLLAR COST	SIMPLE INTEREST*
Store A	$364.50	$17.01	$43.74	$408.24	11.5%
Store B	354.95	17.23	59.69	414.64	16.2%
Store C	374.50	19.95	104.30	478.80	26.7%
Store D	324.95	19.50	143.05	468.00	42.2%
Bank	324.95	15.16	38.99	363.94	11.5%

Store A — First-class department store. Nominal price $249.50 + $115.00 installation charge. Sold on 24-month contract at 6% interest (add-on installment).

Store B — Specialty appliance shop. Nominal price discounted to $229.95 + $125.00 installation charge, 24-month contract at 7% + $10.00 credit check fee.

Store C — Credit appliance outlet, $249.50 + $125.00 installation. Available on 24-month contract at $19.95/month.

Store D — Discount house, nominal price cut 20% to $199.95 + $125 installation charge. Available on 24-month contract at $19.50/month.

Bank — Borrow cash to buy from discount house. Loan at 6% add-on installment interest, 24-month contract.

*See page 76 for simple method for converting installment credit to simple annual interest rate.

TABLE 5A Comparing Credit Costs

few buyers even ask about the interest rate or the total paid over the 24-month contract. If such buyers were more conscious of the cost of credit, they would balk immediately at paying $104.30 more than the cash price and a 26.7 per cent annual interest rate for the privilege of stretching payments over 24 months.

Store D employs another stratagem. It advertises discount prices. In this case the dishwasher is cut by 20 per cent to $199.95. But the 20 per cent cut applies only to the machine; installation price remains at $125. Again, the pitch is for a low monthly payment, $19.50. Despite the lower price and the reduced monthly payment, Store D's time-payment contract exacts an annual interest rate of about 42.2 per cent from the buyer. Many discount stores use such merchandise as a medium for collecting high interest rates on loaned money.

Studying Table 5A brings into focus several factors to remember when buying big-ticket appliances or home equipment:

• Pay cash, if at all possible. Instead of depositing cash in a savings account to earn a measly 4 to 5 per cent interest while, at the same time, paying out 12 per cent or more interest on time-payment contracts, make use of your own revolving credit fund (see page 75).

• Shop the big downtown or chain department stores and compare their total price for the equipment you need. Even if the price is the same or slightly higher, you may gain from the extra services and adjustments available from a store with a community-wide reputation to protect.

• Don't compare only the cash price of an appliance. Figure out the total cost, using the Comparative Shopping Guide (Fig. 5-2). Get all the facts down and figure your own rate of installment interest.

• Your best deal may come from combining the low cash price available at a discount house with a regular consumer loan from a bank. From Table 5A, this combination costs least of all — $363.94 total cost with the dollar cost of credit only $38.99 at an annual interest rate of about 11.5 per cent.

• Consider a further alternative; that of installing the dishwasher yourself or hiring only part of the work done by a professional. Usually, a fixed installation charge is set high enough to cover unknown contingencies. Instead of buying a complete package, price out the total of paying the lowest cash price, borrowing the money from a bank, and hiring a plumber and electrician yourself to install the dishwasher. If yours is an easy installation, with easy access and a cabinet built to fit, you easily cut the installation charge in half.

Understanding Credit — When you buy goods on credit, do you know what the privilege of buying now and paying later costs you? Are you familiar with the differences between simple bank interest, discounted, and installment interest? Refer to Table 5A and the cost of a built-in dishwasher plus installation purchased from Store C.

• The dollar cost of credit — in the example, $104.30.

• Simple interest in per cent — in the example, 26.7 per cent.

Interest, as noted in Table 5B, is how much you pay to use borrowed money. But, there are different kinds of interest, and which kind you are being charged affects your dollar cost of credit.

• Simple interest (sometimes called bank interest) is the percentage of principal charged for credit over a year's time. Suppose you borrow $100 at 6 per cent interest. At the end of one year you would pay back $106. Note that you have used the full $100 for the full year and that the $6 credit charge is added on.

• Installment interest is the credit charge you pay when interest and principal are paid back on a regular basis throughout the year. For example, suppose you borrowed the same $100 and agreed to pay $6 over the year for the use of the money. Further, you agreed to pay back the total $106 owed in 12 monthly installments. For 11 months you would pay $8.83 and on the 12th month you would pay $8.87. While the dollar cost of credit is the same ($6), simple interest amounts to 11.1 per cent because you had the use of an average of about $50 for the year.

• Discount interest is subtracted from the amount of your loan at the beginning rather than being added on. For example, if you borrowed $100 and interest at the stated rate of 6 per cent is discounted, you would receive only $94. At the end of the year you would pay back $100. Note two things — 1) You pay $6 interest on $94, not $100, so your simple interest is nearly 6.4 per cent. 2) To get the full $100, you must borrow $106.36, from which $6.36 is discounted immediately.

• Discount installment interest is subtracted from the total borrowed immediately and the remaining loan is paid off in installments. If you needed $100 installment credit, you would borrow $106.36 in 12 installments. Simple interest on such a transaction amounts to 11.75 per cent.

• Monthly interest on the unpaid balance is a popular way of stating credit charges, and simply means that the percentage of the amount owed is charged each month. For example, if your unpaid balance is $100 for one month and credit charges amount to 1 per cent monthly, you will be charged $1 on the following month's bill. Since simple interest states the percentage of principal charged over a year's time, monthly interest is multiplied by 12 to get the yearly rate. In this case a 1 per cent charge amounts to 12 per cent simple interest.

TABLE 5B — Glossary of Credit Terms

Balance — the amount you still owe on an account at any given time.

Borrower — the person who buys something on time or borrows cash.

Collateral — the property put up to "secure" a loan. If the loan isn't paid, the lender may get the property.

Contract — usually a written agreement that says you will pay.

Credit — buying things and paying later, or borrowing money and paying later.

Credit Charge — mainly interest, but includes other charges such as cost of bookkeeping and investigation.

Credit Rate — the percentage that the credit charge bears to the average principal amount.

Creditor or Lender — the person, store, firm, bank, credit union, or other organizations that lend money, or sell things or services "on time."

Default — failure to pay when due. Also failure to meet any terms of the contract.

Installment — one of a series of payments to pay off a debt.

Interest — how much you pay to use borrowed money.

Principal — the amount you borrow or finance.

Repossession — the seller takes back goods when the buyer fails to meet payments.

Table 5C notes the difference in simple annual interest rates of credit or finance charges stated in various ways. When calculating the dollar cost of credit, include any extra charges, such as the cost for making a credit check, service or carrying charges or any difference in price as a result of paying over a period of time.

Usual interest stated	Dollar charges	Simple annual interest rate
4%	$4 per $100	7.4%
6%	$6 per $100	11.1%
8%	$8 per $100	14.8%
10%	$10 per $100	18.5%
1% per month	$12 per $100	22.2%

If credit charges are figured only on unpaid amount, then—

Charges	Simple annual interest rate
3/4 of 1% per month on unpaid balance	9%
1% " " " " "	12%
$1\frac{1}{4}$% " " " " "	15%
$1\frac{1}{2}$% " " " " "	18%
2% " " " " "	24%
$2\frac{1}{2}$% " " " " "	30%

TABLE 5C The Cost of Credit

How to Figure Cost of Credit — When the principal is used for the full time and either simple or discount interest is charged, you can figure both the dollar cost and interest easily. But, on installment credit, where both the principal and interest are paid back on a regular schedule, cost and interest rate are more difficult to figure. Yet, before you sign any kind of time-payment contract, you should make sure you understand both the dollar cost and the per cent of simple interest you will be paying. Fig. 5-3 charts in detail form the steps used in calculating the dollar cost and interest on an installment purchase.

Family Revolving Fund — You can reduce the cost of credit by being your own banker. When you lend yourself cash out of your own revolving fund, your savings earn 18 to 24 per cent instead of the piddling 4 to 5 per cent paid by most banks. This plan keeps you on a cash basis, makes it possible to purchase more big-ticket items in the same time, and keeps your borrowing power intact for emergencies. Here's how the family revolving fund works—

Suppose you want to buy a new clothes washer and dryer. Cash cost of a washer from a discount house amounts to $249.95. A similar washer from a department store would cost $24.69 per month for 12 months. Instead of signing up for a time-payment contract, you resolve to deposit the $24.69 in a savings account once a month. In the meantime you use the self-service laundry. A study by the United States Department of Agriculture determined that, until a family washes at least five loads per week, total costs are less in a self-service laundry. At the end of the year, you have saved $296.28. You pay the $249.95 cash price for your washer and leave the $46.33 difference in your family revolving fund. The $46.33 is the amount you earned by waiting. If you need a dryer too, continue depositing the $24.69 monthly in your revolving fund. When your fund total reaches the cash purchase price of the dryer, it's yours, free and clear. Using this system, USDA economists figure you can buy a refrigerator, washing machine, clothes dryer, and dishwasher in 107.6 months at the same monthly payment compared to 128.2 months if the items are purchased on credit. The credit savings alone would pay for another major appliance, such as a television set or room air-conditioner.

Where to Find the Best Buys — Good buys are seldom in the same place time after time. The practice of discounting has become routine for brand-name appliances and home equipment. You must shop various discount stores to find the least total cost on a big-ticket item for your home. Even discount stores run special sales to dispose of last year's model, slow-moving stock, or as a loss-leader or no-

FIG. 5-3—How to Figure Interest Rate

Rather than use a complicated formula, USDA home economists developed a short-cut method as follows: $\dfrac{\text{(Credit Charge) (Factor)}}{\text{Credit Received}} = \dfrac{\text{Annual Interest}}{\text{Rate}}$

WHERE: Credit charge is the time-payment differential.

               Credit received is the cash or cash price of the item purchased.

The factor that simplifies the computation can be found in the following table:

MONTHLY PAYMENTS		WEEKLY PAYMENTS	
No. of Payments	Factor	No. of Payments	Factor
6	343	12	800
9	240	16	612
12	185	20	495
15	150	24	416
18	126	28	359
21	109	32	315
24	96	36	281
30	77	40	254
36	65	44	231
42	56	48	212
48	49	52	196
54	44	78	132
60	39	104	99

Example:

    Dishwasher purchased from Store C (see Table 5A)

Cash price (credit received)	= $374.50
Credit charge (time-payment differential)	= 104.30
Factor for 24 months (from table above)	= 96

Annual interest rate $= \dfrac{(\$104.30)(96)}{\$374.50} = 26.7$ per cent

If the table of factors doesn't fit a specific case, use the formula:

Annual interest rate (A.I.R.) $= \dfrac{2 \times C \times M}{P \times (N + 1)}$

    where C = credit charge (time-payment differential)

            M = number of payments per year

            P = cash price (credit received)

            N = number of installment payments to be made

Example:

    Same data as above

A.I.R. $= \dfrac{2 \times \$104.30 \times 12}{\$374.50 \times (24 + 1)}$

$= \dfrac{24(104.30)}{(374.5)(25)} = 26.7$ per cent

profit item to attract customers into the store. Become alert to the market for such items as radios, TV sets, vacuum cleaners, watches, camera, hi-fi equipment, washing machines, and portable appliances. Just a few points to remember:

• Look for a full-range department store that advertises that it "won't be undersold." Market-conscious store buyers often price products at or under the lowest price in the area.

• Study Consumers Union test reports enough to recognize when a store brand is basically the same machine as a top brand. House brands are usually discounted more than nationally advertised brands.

• Watch for specials advertised by discount houses to build traffic. If you have planned your appliance and home-equipment acquisition far enough ahead, you can take advantage of a good buy when it is offered. But, make sure the special really is a special.

• Examine the "damaged in transit" outlets for big cuts in price. Despite modern packaging, TV cabinets are scratched, refrigerator doors dented, and other superficial damage incurred during shipping. A store may refuse delivery of damaged goods, and the shipper sells them to a dealer in damaged goods for whatever he can get. Stocks of appliances and home equipment are obviously limited, varied, and uncertain in such outlets. Here, above all, you need to know alternative data and market prices. While most stores seldom dicker or bargain on prices, a "damaged in transit" store operator will bargain for what the traffic will bear. Here you can dicker on price according to known prices for undamaged merchandise and the amount of damage. Since you buy damaged goods "as is" without a warranty, consider such protection in the total price package. Locate these "damaged in transit" stores in classified ad section of your telephone directory or by examining the various columns of classified ads in a Sunday newspaper.

• A thrift basement or corner in a major mail-order house operates much like a "damaged in transit" store. Here, however, the store accepts delivery of an item damaged in shipping (with a damage adjustment from the carrier) and offers the item at a discounted price. Normally, such thrift basements are not advertised. Ferret them out by asking an employee or calling customer service. When such a store sells its own damaged goods, the items will usually carry a warranty.

How to Buy Used Equipment — Whether you can benefit from buying used appliances depends on how much time you can spend searching out good buys, whether you can make repairs yourself, and your know-how. Used home equipment sells at ridiculously low prices.

If you qualify on all counts, use these ideas for buying the equipment you need used — at big savings:

• Buy a completely overhauled machine from a reputable dealer. Some dealers take outdated machines in trade on a new item. Rather than junk them, the dealer keeps his own service crew busy between calls overhauling the better trade-ins. The dealer buys parts at wholesale, and fill-in labor is available. Such overhauled units will frequently carry a warranty from several months up to a year. Prices may be slightly higher than you would pay for the same machine without a warranty, but such protection indicates the dealer's confidence that the overhaul will provide trouble-free service.

• Don't buy used equipment from second-hand stores, organizations which pick up discarded items, or indiscriminately through classified newspaper ads. Such units are likely to be old, worn out, and barely workable.

• Consider buying an appliance through the classified ads if the owner is selling his entire household goods. Many times a family will sell everything but personal items if they are moving overseas, across the country, or into a small apartment. Goods sold in such a sale vary widely in age and condition. If you know what you need and can spend the time attending such sales or auctions, you can pick up equipment for as little as 10 cents on the dollar. Be prepared to pay cash and to haul your purchase home.

• Buy inoperable equipment and repair or recondition the unit yourself. Surprisingly good buys are available for repair if you can diagnose the trouble and fix it yourself. Parts are readily available in nearly every community. Mail-order houses maintain parts service for everything they sell, and parts can be ordered through the mail.

Warranties And Service — How to Get What You're Entitled to

Before discounting and price-cutting affected selling practices, stores and dealers provided their own service and covered warranties for manufacturers. But discounters cut costs by eliminating service. Manufacturers were forced into the service business to protect their widely advertised name. Now, in most communities, warranty complaints and service for appliances are handled by factory branches or authorized service shops.

Read the warranty tag closely. It spells out in exact detail the protection you are entitled to. If it's not in the warranty, you probably won't get it. We say, probably, because circumstances sometimes encourage a manufacturer to make good on some defect outside the warranty protection.

Warranty Coverage — Most written warranties specify the time over which the warranty applies and limit liability to the correction of faults in materials or manufacture. Such redress will be accomplished only if the item is brought or mailed to a factory service branch or authorized service shop. Labor spent in correcting a fault may or may not be included. Sometimes a warranty provides more protection on some parts than others. For example, a television set may include a manufacturer's warranty for 90 days on the entire set and one full year on the picture tube. A dealer may add a clause on his own to provide free service during the first 90 days. If a tube or some other part of the set turned out to be faulty, the dealer's serviceman could obtain a replacement at no cost. If the terms of the warranty require you to return a warranty registration card, be sure to comply. Otherwise, if you complain later, the manufacturer will have no record of your ownership.

Service Coverage — When you need service for an appliance still covered by warranty, you must usually take it to a specified shop — either one operated by the manufacturer for exclusive service or to an authorized shop. Sometimes these authorized shops represent several noncompeting manufacturers. The warranty usually reserves the right to either repair the item or replace it with a new one of the same type.

But what recourse do you have if the service is unsatisfactory? Suppose you keep returning an appliance to an authorized shop and the problem is not corrected. Don't give up! You still have several avenues to explore before throwing the unit in the rubbish and buying another, competitive brand—

• Write to the manufacturer's service manager. Suppose you had a fault with a toaster. After several tries, the authorized service shop has not corrected the trouble and now the warranty period has expired. A factual letter addressed to the factory explaining the symptoms of the trouble and your actions to have it corrected in chronological order will usually bring results. A local dealer may be instructed to replace the unit and return your unsatisfactory toaster to the factory laboratory for testing. The factory service manager will probably check your story with the authorized service shop manager. Your complaint may lead to a change in the manufacturer's service shop for your community.

• Complain to the store where you bought the appliance. A major department store's customer service representative may take your case to the manufacturer if you have a justified case.

• Write to one of the magazines that advertise appliances. The terms, "Guaranteed by GOOD HOUSEKEEPING," "Use-Tested by McCALLS," and "Commended by the Consumer Service Bureau of PARENTS MAGAZINE," mean that readers are assured of the satisfactory performance of articles advertised on their pages. If your complaint is legitimate and the steps you have taken to get service are well documented, the service editor of one of these magazines will take your case to the manufacturer.

Buy or Rent Home Equipment?

Service centers in most communities offer a wide variety of equipment for rent at reasonable prices per hour or per day. When studying the alternatives of buying vs. renting, consider several factors:

• Is the article expensive? Rental rates tend to be expensive on low-value items. A rototiller may rent for $5 per day and cost $200. A lawn roller, on the other hand, may rent for $1 per day but cost only $20 new. The fee for renting the rototiller represents only 1/40 of the cost, but the fee for renting the roller represents 1/20 of the cost.

• How often are you likely to use the item? If you use an electric buffer-polisher on tile floors once a month, you might consider buying it to save money and for the convenience. But, if you need a lawn roller only once when you are putting in a new lawn, It makes sense to rent it.

• Do you have the storage space? Sometimes renting bulky items when you need them makes sense because storage space is limited. Suppose you use a boat trailer to haul a boat from one body of water to another several times a year. Even if it would cost you less to own one, you may have no place to store it between moves.

• Can you borrow or use equipment when buying materials? Many stores will lend you a spreader when you buy several sacks of lawn fertilizer. Even if there's no sign or the salesman doesn't offer, try asking. If you are a regular customer and the store keeps spreaders for customer use, you can usually borrow a spreader for no cost. A carpet shampoo machine can usually be borrowed at no cost when you buy the cleaning materials.

Figure the alternative costs of renting vs. buying on an earned-money basis. For example, suppose you rent a roll-away bed every time your in-laws visit. If the bed sells for $50 and you rent it once a year for $5, the money you spend buying the bed rather than renting earns 10 per cent per year. If you rented the bed twice a year, you could earn 20 per cent by buying. You could afford to pay a hefty credit charge and buy the bed on a time-payment plan and still come out ahead if you rented the bed more than twice a year. But, if you rented a vacation trailer for $50 per week and the trailer cost $2,000, your money would be earning only 2½ per cent if you bought the trailer for cash. And, if you bought the trailer on credit, the interest alone would be greater than the rental charge.

Should You Buy a Freezer? Will it Pay?

In a survey of families with freezers, a research team from the United States Department of Agriculture (USDA) discovered that 40 per cent of the urban families and 52 per cent of the farm families had bought freezers to save money. However, a previous study by the USDA indicated that few freezer owners earned the savings they cited as reasons for buying. When all freezer operating costs are totaled, you really have to work at using a freezer's full effectiveness to make one pay off in dollars and cents only.

The second most popular reason for buying a freezer was for convenience. The third reason cited was to store fresh fruits and vegetables in season. Table 5D* details an analysis of the costs for using a 15-cubic-foot freezer. A difference in the purchase price and, particularly, a lower rate for electricity than the 2 cents/KWHR would affect the cost per pound of food stored. But, the key to making a freezer pay off is to use it — that is, keep it full and use the food out of it regularly. Merely using the freezer as a long-term repository for food is least economical. If long-term storage of seasonal food is your aim, a commercial freezer locker would probably cost less. In many communities, locker plants lease below-zero storage space at a cost less than the electricity to operate the freezer. For example, a 15-cubic-foot locker rents for $15.60 per year in one area. For Table 5D, the electricity for maintaining the freezer alone amounts to $25.51. The cost of electricity for freezing food initially adds to the cost according to the amount of food frozen. So, use a small freezer or the freezer portion of a refrigerator-freezer combination along with a rented frozen-food locker. A trip to the locker every two to three weeks enables you to transfer food to the home freezer. Or, when freezing fresh or cooked foods, use the home freezer to prepare the

*Merle E. Dowd, *How to Live Better and Spend 20% Less,* (West Nyack, N.Y.: Parker Publishing Co., Inc.)

foods while flavors are at their peak and transfer a bunch at a time to the locker when convenient.

Cost Item	400 lbs.	800 lbs.	1200 lbs.	1600 lbs.
Depreciation cost[1]	$18.33	$18.33	$18.33	$ 18.33
Interest on investment (average) @ $4\frac{1}{2}\%$	4.95	4.95	4.95	4.95
Repairs	6.60	6.60	6.60	6.60
Electricity[2]				
Freezing cost[3]	9.32	18.64	27.96	37.28
Maintaining 0°F[4]	25.51	25.51	25.51	25.51
Packaging[5]	4.00	8.00	12.00	16.00
Total cost	$68.71	$82.03	$96.35	$108.67
Cost per pound (cents)	17.18	10.25	8.00	6.79

1. Straight-line basis, 12 years, 0 residual.
2. Kilowatt-hour (Kw-Hr.) @ 2.33 cents—national average.
3. 0.1 Kw-Hr. per lb.
4. 0.2 Kw-Hr. per cu. ft. per 24 hr. @ 2.33 cents.
5. @ 2 cents per lb. (half to be wrapped).

TABLE 5D Home Freezer Costs

If you own a freezer or are contemplating buying one, use these ideas to make your freezer pay its way—*

• Buy sale-priced steaks at the opening of a new supermarket. Typically you're likely to find extra low prices and, even more important, better steaks. Practice the same economy of buying stocks of frozen food on extra-special sales of frozen orange juice, lemonade, chickens, or convenience foods.

• Stock up on frozen fruits and vegetables just before a new season hits. Strawberries, for example, are often priced far below special sale price to unload any remaining stock in warehouses to make space for a new crop.

• Day-old bread is not always available when you need it. So, buy plenty and freeze it when you have the opportunity. If you are driving near one of the "thrift" stores for outdated bakery goods, stock up

*Ibid.

with 20 or 30 loaves of bread, rolls, doughnuts or other pastries. Freeze them immediately upon getting home.

• Jams, fresh fruit, applesauce, and fruit juices can be processed for storage much more easily by freezing that ny old-fashioned canning methods — and freezing preserves the fresh taste. Store berry juice in large containers during the season. Later, thaw the juice and make smaller batches of fresh-tasting jams or jellies with a minimum of cooking. Or freeze berries, such as blueberries, whole for later use in pies.

• Buy half a steer, a whole salmon, halibut, hog, or lamb and store it at a lower price per pound than the individual pieces. Here again, though, use this bulk food regularly rather than keeping it stored. Keep the food moving in and out of your freezer.

• Cook several meals at a time, particularly spaghetti sauce, stews, and other meals that normally require a long cooking time. You not only save on time, but you save on cooking fuel and reduce the total number of dirtied pans. Later, just warm up the meals when time is short. Take turkey, for example. Since big birds are less expensive than small ones, cook a really big bird (20 pounds or more), serve it right out of the oven at the Thanksgiving feast, then make up a half-dozen or so batches of turkey a-la-king for the freezer, or freeze slices in broth to keep them from drying out.

• Coffee is often a good buy in 3-pound cans — too much to use ordinarily before it gets stale. But with a freezer, immediately after opening the can, repackage the ground coffee in half-pound containers and stash it in the freezer — the flavor stays fresh for months at 0° F.

MONEY SAVERS WHEN BUYING HOME EQUIPMENT

Watch the big bucks! A big-business maxim that pays off in managing your home costs — "Big savings are possibly only on big expenditures." When buying big-ticket items — washing machine, refrigerator, room air-conditioner, etc. — you can afford to spend extra time to plan what you need, then buy each item for less cash. That's what this chapter was all about. Some of the highlights were —

- *Writing out your **wish list** for equipment and furnishings — develop a plan for what you need — when you need it — how you can buy it for less. Impulse buying is out — that is, OUT!*
- *How and where to find the factual data you need to decide which brand, line, model, gadgets, and gimmickry suit you best.*
- *Where to buy — discount house, bargain basement, mail-order house, damaged-goods dealer?*
- *How to avoid or minimize the high cost of credit.*
- *How to use a Comparative Shopping Guide for objective buying.*
- *When to buy to get the same equipment (and furnishings) for less.*
- *Whether used equipment could satisfy your needs — temporarily or for good, and how to find the best buy in used equipment.*
- *Learning how to decide whether to rent or buy equipment.*

6

Be Your Own Decorator— And Save Cash

Decorating is personal! Whether you hire a decorator to learn about the inner YOU — and the personal whims, likes, and hates of each of your family — or you take the time to learn how decorating can reflect you own charm and warmth — personally — depends on you and your pocketbook. Here's one place you can save cash — and decorate your home so that it shouts — ME — This is MY HOUSE. Here's how —

- *Learn from colorful examples in the popular magazines, library books on decorating, and sample rooms in stores.*
- *Enroll in an adult evening class at your local high school or college.*
- *Take a university correspondence course — one designed for the individual, not one aimed at making you a professional.*
- *Examine the many manufacturers' booklets and pamphlets.*
- *Study the hand-outs from your state's extension service.*
- *Practice the "no-cost," indispensable ingredient in all good decorating — imagination.*
- *Develop a decorating plan starting from objectives, work through timing, budgeting, buying, and doing-it-yourself.*

Interior decoration is a profession and an art akin to architecture. Professional decorating advice is readily available, but at a price. Decorators help you plan your furnishings, coordinate room color schemes, design window treatments, and select floor materials. But somewhere along the line you must step in, you must decide whether to keep the comfortable wing-back chair or replace it with a short-back, modern rimmed stool that feels like a stadium seat when your team is three touchdowns behind. You decide whether to pay $15 per square yard — or go the limit at $25 per yard. So, if you must still make the decisions — and pay the bills — why not decide from the start? And pay less.

If you do go the decorator route, make sure you communicate. Maybe you've heard — "Decorators choose the thing for *your* house that they like themselves." If this happens to you, the fault is at least 50 per cent yours. Or, "But everything looks so formal. The house looks like a show window. I want a place to *live* in." Such results happen because — 1) Decorators fuss with many details families don't think of or ignore. 2) Decorators show their wares better when asked to decorate formal or high-style houses. 3) Decorators tend to be less sympathetic, even impatient, with informal plans where children and the disorders they create are part of the scene.

Time is a valuable commodity for decorators — and other professional people. To please you, a decorator may have to spend many hours learning your likes and dislikes, your philosophy of living, and house-related values. If you can't afford the cost of a decorator's time, you may end up with a plan that fits you and your family's needs like a hand-tailored suit would fit if the tailor took only half as many measurements as he needed and guessed at the rest. So, if your budget for furnishings is strictly limited, ask yourself — "Is it easier to educate a decorator to what I like — or to learn about decorating myself?" You may not learn all the theory, but you have one great advantage. You know what you like. You also must live every day with what you select. Knowing the essentials, you can decorate your own home and pocket the savings.

How and Where to Learn Decorating — For Your Home

Few subjects are as well covered for the do-it-yourself practitioner as decorating. There is no shortage of information. You simply help yourself to as much as you need or have time for from these sources:

Home-Oriented Magazines — Different groups of magazines use color lavishly in their treatment of ideas and plans for home decorating:

• AMERICAN HOME and BETTER HOMES AND GARDENS are keyed to practical advice with many, many ideas for home-crafting certain ideas. You can buy detail plans to build specific projects. From the pictured example you learn about the coordinated use of colors, carpeting, draperies, wallpaper or wall paint, and furniture. These magazines base decorating examples on elementary theory. Don't attempt to copy one or more of the example plans. Your best bet is to review a number of back copies and assimilate the theory and reasoning that led to the selections. Ask yourself — "Why did the decorator select these specific colors and items? What were the decorator's and owner's objectives? How did they get what they wanted?" When you read enough of these articles, you begin to understand some of the principles and basics of decorator planning. Then, use the same fundamental approach in decorating your own house. Look at it like this — You can cook a variety of dishes by following step-by-step directions explicitly. Or, you can, with experience and an understanding of why things happen with food, concoct your own recipes or vary others with confidence that the results will be tasty. Applying the same principles to decorating will give you confidence in your planning and selection.

• HOUSE & GARDEN and HOUSE BEAUTIFUL are big, expensive magazines tuned to buyers of expensive houses. Articles on decorating tend toward the lavish and exotic. Example homes are mainly architect-designed custom houses. Landscaping and interior decorating are likewise professionally done. You can use these magazines as sources of ideas to be adapted with variations for smaller houses and thinner pocketbooks.

• WOMAN'S DAY and FAMILY CIRCLE are widely distributed through supermarkets and are keyed to a wide spectrum of home owners. Advice tends to be quite practical. Selections of furniture, fabrics, and notions tend toward the less expensive end of the price scale. Many of the articles include do-it-yourself instructions that enable the reader-craftsman to build, sew, or paint the items featured in the articles.

• POPULAR HOME and other specialty publications feature considerable decorating advice with colorful illustrations of example rooms and houses. POPULAR HOME is distributed free through many local lumberyards as a publication of the U.S. Gypsum Company. Check with your local lumberyards to see if they participate in this program and, if so, to get on their mailing list.

• McCALLS, LADIES' HOME JOURNAL, and GOOD HOUSEKEEPING are multipurpose women's magazines that include well-done articles on decorating, accompanied by beautiful, full-color illustrations of outstanding examples. They devote only a few pages to decorating. From time to time these and other magazines offer columns of advice on decorating in the format of questions from readers with answers by a professional interior decorator on the magazine's staff.

• Many other magazines offer advice on decorating but on an irregular schedule. Browse among the current magazines displayed at your library for clues to specific articles of interest. If you have a special problem, consult the READER'S GUIDE for leads to articles on the subject of concern.

Public Library — Find the shelf where books on interior decorating are racked in your library by asking the librarian or by looking under *Interior Decorating* in the subject card catalog. Many of the books are reprints of articles from magazines with the same color plates. In a book you're likely to find a full treatment of the basic or theoretical aspects of decorating. Use these books in combination with the articles on specific examples from magazines to formulate plans for your own home.

Adult Education Classes — One of the most popular subjects offered in evening classes is interior decoration. Usually, these courses are taught by a practicing professional decorator. Inquire at your high school about courses offered. Or, if there is a university or junior college in your area, ask the office of information about their evening classes. Vocational high schools and colleges also offer daytime courses in interior decorating.

Attending a class offers two distinct advantages over trying to dig out information on decoration from books and magazines on your own — 1) You have the person-to-person communication between yourself and the instructor. You can ask questions on points you don't fully understand. Also, questions by other students bring answers to points you may not have thought about. 2) You can frequently bring a decorating problem of your own to class for counseling with the instructor. Or, you may work on your problem as a homework assignment and get a professional opinion on your solution. Registration fees for adult education classes are slight, because most of the cost is paid for by the school district or your state.

Correspondence and Extension Courses — Further adult education classes are offered by mail through the extension service of many universities. Correspondence courses lack the personal student-instructor interplay. However, in working out assignments, you can pose questions and problems related to your own house and get a professional evaluation of your ideas.

Avoid the advertised home-study courses in interior decoration. Instead, check with the state college or university of your state for a catalogue of extension courses offered. If your state university's offerings do not include courses in interior decoration, write to the director for a lead to another school. However, as a resident of a state, you pay less tuition than if you apply to another state and pay nonresident fees. So, check with your own schools first.

Extension Service Pamphlets — Home economists and decorators at the United States Department of Agriculture and many cooperating extension services at universities in each state publish a variety of practical, down-to-earth booklets and pamphlets on subjects related to decorating. One pamphlet may be on selection of carpeting, for example. Others may cover furniture. Single copies are usually free to residents of the state. Check with the extension service at your own state's university. If you can't find where to write, ask your librarian or call the local county agent.

Manufacturers' and Association Literature — Makers of furniture, lighting fixtures, carpeting, and the myriad of other products you're likely to buy for your house publish a veritable storm of colorful pamphlets and brochures. They follow the proved "cookbook" approach. That is, if they persuade you to bake a cake, you might buy their flour. A manufacturer of Early American furniture may send you a free pamphlet on arrangement ideas for the use of Early American-style chairs, table, and sideboard in your dining room. If the message is persuasive enough, you may end up buying a dining room set — probably from a dealer who sells that particular manufacturer's product. Window curtaining and drapery ideas are plentiful and cover a wide variety of problem windows in a beautiful brochure published by a drapery rod manufacturer. The list is almost endless. Look for invitations to write for such pamphlets and brochures in the "Books and Booklets" column of AMERICAN HOME, for example. Other magazines either list new offerings as a reader's service or advertisements will include an offer to write for a booklet. Many pamphlets are free. Or, there might be a charge of 10 cents to keep the school children and paper collectors from wasting the supply.

Imagination — The "No-Cost" Ingredient of Decorating

Professional decorators are truly creative people. Their stock in trade is their store of ideas — ones they may have used before or ones they originate to solve a peculiar problem. You can develop your own imagination to achieve unique, highly individual, professional results at a fraction of professional costs. Some of the proved ideas for developing your imagination and using ideas for your own house are:

Brainstorm the Problem — Books have been written about the techniques of idea generation loosely called brainstorming. This system works best if two or more exchange ideas in a group. But, you can brainstorm on your own. Briefly, it works by zeroing in on a problem. You, and possibly others, think of as many ideas as possible for the solution. Write all of them down without trying to determine whether they are practical or too costly. Later, when the idea wells have run dry, examine each idea for practicality. Estimate the cost and compare the end results for several of the better ideas. You'll be surprised at how the brainstorming technique releases your imagination.

Suppose you are brainstorming possible solutions to a knotty window treatment problem. The shape and size of the windows make draping or curtaining expensive and difficult to coordinate with other room furnishings. Ideas you dream up during brainstorming might range from completely rebuilding the windows to some method of hiding them with built-ins or converting the windows to a doorway. During a hot brainstorming session, you might come up with 20 to 40 ideas. Some of the ideas will be too wild to use. But, as often as not, the wild idea thrown into the discussion leads to a related, practical idea that would not have been considered otherwise. The inviting thing about imagination is that the price is right — nothing, or possibly a pot of coffee to stimulate discussion.

Borrowing and Adapting — Editors of magazines featuring articles on interior decorating recognize that few, if any, readers will copy the example rooms exactly. They expect the articles, color photographs, and imaginative ideas to spark your own thinking — to generate ideas of your own. You may find the ideal solution to your window problem from a treatment that was only in the background of a room photograph. Once you have identified your objectives, look for the variety of ways other decorators have treated the same objective from books or magazines. Then, apply your own twist in adapting the idea to your own home.

Build Your Own Plan From Pieces — Suppose you are planning to refurbish your living room. Over several months you can clip photographs and ideas from magazines that show how professional decorators have refurbished similar rooms. Then, by taking an idea from one photograph for lamps, an idea from another for furniture arrangement, and selection of furniture from still another, you can build your own integrated plan that fits your home exactly. But, make sure you understand some of the philosophy back of the original selections. Otherwise, the pieces may not fit into an integrated whole.

Here's where an understanding of decorating fundamentals becomes useful.

Building Around Things You Have — Your imagination can be most useful in developing a plan around your antiques or in refurbishing existing furniture and furnishings. For example, how can you refinish an authentic antique table to become a focal point for a dining room? Or, how can you adapt some old cabinet, discarded slab of marble, or other oddment as a coffee table-conversation piece in a newly decorated room? Okay! But, maybe you don't own any antiques or something old that can be redone for a fraction of the cost of something new. Once you fire up your imagination and get it hitting on all eight cylinders, visit the local Goodwill discard shop, the Salvation Army surplus store, or other outlet for discarded furniture. There, your imagination refurbishes, recovers, and refinishes in your mind's eye, the old, the beat-up, and the thrown-away piece. New materials now make refinishing and antiquing simpler and less time consuming than a few years ago. So, unleash your imagination; let it run rampant — it costs nothing to dream and plan. And the results can be inspired, inexpensive decorating ideas that achieve outstanding results for *your home alone.*

Getting Started at Decoration

Basic to any program you may have for redoing your home is a plan. Don't lift a paintbrush or buy a thing until you have a plan.

HERE'S HOW: *Start With Objectives* — What are you really trying to do? Are you trying to develop furnishings that complement your entertaining? Or, are you trying to achieve a homey, informal atmosphere that, at the same time, resists wear and clutter of several young children? Whatever your aims — write them down. Until you define your objectives, your planning will vacillate. Some of the factors to consider are:

• What is your living plan? Do you entertain formally or in small informal groups? Are your home activities sometimes related to business? Answers to this line of questioning will influence your thinking about how you furnish dining and living rooms. If your entertaining is likely to be formal, you will want to separate kitchen from dining room, concentrate on a fine china service, commodious dining room furniture, a large coffee table for drinks, and the like. On the other hand, if you entertain in small groups, informally, consider your kitchen and family room as part of the living portion of your house — all good parties end up in the kitchen anyway. If you entertain seldom, you may be more interested in planning your home mainly for family use with emphasis on records, readily available bookshelves, television, and space or provisions for creative hobbies. But, whatever your living plan, determine what it is and how it affects your decorating objectives.

• What is your position in life? Mainly this question involves children. If your children are small, you can figure that walls, floors, tables, and anything within their reach will take a beating. You may decide on either of two approaches here — 1) Declare living areas "off limits" to small children. Expensive carpeting and good furniture in a living room, for example, are too costly to permit their exposure to children. So ban the little house wreckers. 2) Plan furniture, walls, and carpeting or tile floors on an interim basis. That is, consider furnishings expendable. Sure, you'll regularly wipe dirty finger marks off the walls and clean spills from the carpets. But, plan to replace everything when the children reach a responsible age. During the interim, inexpensive, easy-to-maintain furnishings are the rule. At the other end are the teen-age children who need a place to entertain their friends. Further along, children are away to college, and even later, they bring grandchildren to visit. Each stage demands your best thinking and planning.

• What are your home interests? Closely related to your living plan and to your "housepower" are your family's basic interests. Do you and your family prefer to spend time around the home — gardening, entertaining, or simply reading and watching TV? Or, when time and money are available, do you head outside the home for sports, vacations, food, and other away-from-home activities? Your frank answers to such questions help you to decide whether to spend money on home furnishings at all — or use the money saved for the out-of-home activities.

Consider Your Budget — Basically, how does your plan match the money available. Should you, for example, go all out, buy a house full of furniture and furnishings, and pay for them in installments over the next umpty-ump years? Or, would you get more for your money by decorating in steps as cash becomes available? These are two of the extremes. In the middle is the plan that makes do with some items, borrows others, uses second-hand pieces where practicable, and allows the do-it-yourselfer to contribute in refinishing furniture, repainting or papering walls, and building bookshelves. As you see from Chapter 5, a plan, patience, and cash provide more furnishings for the same number of bucks than heavy reliance on credit. Sometimes, no matter how you plan, how long you wait, or your shopping ingenuity, there simply are not enough dollars to provide the furnishings you want. Here is where a detailed plan with realistic costs helps you to sort out what is most important, what is next most important, and so on. Use the technique most big corporations use by first totaling your home equipment and furnishings "wish list" (see Fig. 5-1). Compare the total dollar figure with the money available now and projected for the future. Finally, compare trade-offs in cost and utility for the various pieces or items on your wish list to find the combination that best suits your needs within the budget you have available. Such an analytical look prevents you from acting on impulse, from buying something expensive you need "right now," or from impatiently ordering too much on credit and running dangerously low on money for other purposes.

WHAT TO DO: *Lay Out Your Plan on Paper* — Just as in remodeling, the mistakes you make on paper cost less than the mistakes you make with furniture, rugs and accessories. Begin your planning for a specific room, or the whole house, with a scale drawing. Use paper ruled in squares with lines ¼ inch apart. This convenient scale is the one most used by architects and planners and equates to ¼ inch equals one foot. Trace and cut out scale manikins of your furniture (Fig. 6-1) and place them around the scale drawing. This way you can move furniture about as often as you want without straining your back — or temper. Manikins in Fig. 6-1 do not allow space for use, so allow space to pull out drawers, open doors, shift chairs away from tables, and to work around beds, buffets, and server. Only when you see the total esfect can you evaluate and choose among alternatives. Again, depending on your objectives and your budget, develop the final "grand plan" and implement it in stages. Such a "grand plan" opens up alternative avenues for accomplishment —

• Hold and advance on selected fronts — Rather than attempt to furnish every room a piece at a time until the whole house is furnished, consider shutting off one room, a lower level, or second-floor living space. This way, you pour all your resources into one or more areas. Later, you switch the stream of resources toward the bypassed areas. Try variations on this theme by using interim furniture. For example, instead of buying an integrated bedroom suite, buy only a mattress and bed frame, use inexpensive, unfinished chests of drawers, a cheap mirror on the wall, and do without carpeting. Later, move the unfinished chests to the attic for out-of-season storage and replace

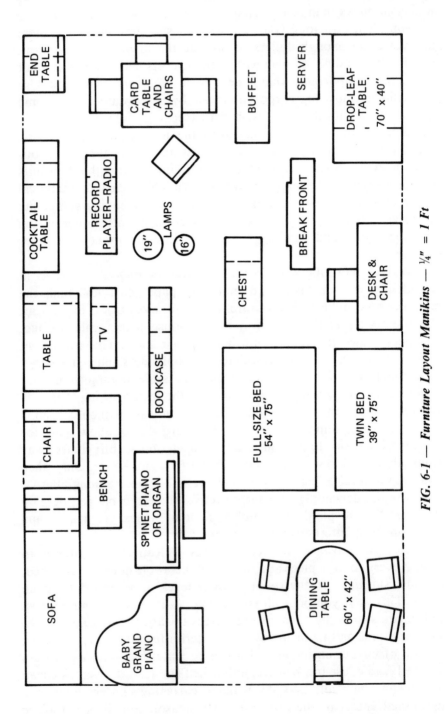

FIG. 6-1 — Furniture Layout Manikins — ¼″ = 1 Ft

them with fine furniture units. Later, add a matching bed, carpeting, draperies, and accessories to complete the room. But, during the wait, your living room took shape rapidly according to plan.

• Furnish with interim pieces and replace piece by piece — Closely related to the "hold and advance" plan is the selection of used or borrowed furniture throughout the house. Such a procedure makes sense if your children are small and your over-all plan calls for complete replacement several years in the future. You can pick up good-quality, used furniture at peanut prices through newspaper classified ads — if you know what you want (see Chapter 7). When you start buying replacements, concentrate first on rooms least likely to be impacted by small children. In your master bedroom, for example, replace the interim, used furniture with pieces to fit your final plan.

• Buy used pieces and build for the future — Instead of planning to replace interim furniture and furnishings, select pieces from the beginning that can be upgraded to fit your final plan. For example, as noted in Chapter 7, upholstered furniture consists basically of two parts — frame and an outer covering. You can find bargains in well-constructed upholstered furniture with badly worn or damaged coverings. Later, you reupholster it yourself or have it done at a fraction of the cost of a completely new piece. Apply the same philosophy to walls and floor coverings. For example, your final plan for a study-den-guest room combination may call for wood paneling. But paneling is easily postponable. So, you fit out the study-den-guest room and paint the walls yourself. Later, you add the wood paneling to finish the room.

• Buy what you really need on credit but pay off quickly — Sometimes, you have no choice but to order furnishings on credit — you have no close relatives to help furnish part of your house in the style of "old attic" or "old relative." Or, you may have been living in a tiny apartment and, when you move into a house, you need many things all at once. If you decide to buy furniture on credit, consider the added costs as detailed in Chapter 5. Furniture (or anything else) costs you more if you buy on credit than if you pay cash. Try one of the 90-day-same-as-cash deals available from many department stores. If this doesn't work, figure where you can obtain what you need at the lowest cost for credit; then, pay it off as quickly as possible. Rather than continue credit purchases, buy only what you absolutely have to have and pay for it quickly. Put money away for the next purchase in your plan, and keep on a cash basis. If you follow this hard line — and it isn't easy — you'll end up with much more furniture and furnishings for the same number of bucks than if you go the credit route. Establish your own "home credit fund," as detailed in Chapter 5, as a substitute for credit.

MONEY SAVERS WHEN DOING YOUR OWN DECORATING

Tackling anything new can be a challenge — and scary! We're all afraid of the unknown. But, doing your own decorating not only offers you a gold-plated chance to save money; it gives you a chance to express your own personality. To pull this one off successfully, you learned —

- *How to develop confidence by learning the basics of decorating from the flood of free information available.*
- *How to benefit from expert consultation through adult evening classes or correspondence courses in decorating.*
- *How to turn your own imagination loose through the planned use of "brainstorming."*
- *How to build your decorating plan around your own family and how you live in your own house.*
- *How to fit your decorating to your budget — and make it stick.*

7

How To Save Money When
Buying Home Furnishings

You're batting in a tough league when you buy furniture, carpets, and accessories. You're on your own much more when buying furnishings than when buying equipment or appliances. So, don't get caught with your "buymanship" down. Only you can sort through the misleading advertising, learn to recognize the quality you want, and discover the out-of-the-way place where you buy what you want for a third — or more — off. Here's where you put the plan you developed as your own, do-it-yourself decorator into action. You want to complete your plan with the fewest number of bucks. Here's how—

- *Recognize the makers of quality in wood and upholstered furniture. There are differences — and you can search them out.*
- *Plan your buying to take advantage of timing, of the back-alley shop that sells for less, or of doing part of the work yourself.*
- *Consider the cost-effectiveness of rebuilding upholstered pieces to your own specifications.*
- *Select the right carpeting — fiber, construction, and quality to match your needs — then pay less for the complete job.*
- *Pick the fabric, color, and cost-effectiveness of draperies that fit your decorating plan.*
- *Shop for towels, sheets, and other linens with an eye to quality and wear.*

Buying home furnishings offers you two great opportunities—
- To buy the furniture, carpets, and accessories that will turn your house into a "home" that suits you and your family.
- To practice your aggressive spending techniques. Here's where your "buymanship" makes a big difference in how many bucks you spend for the quality and satisfaction you get.

But, take care! The home-furnishings market is packed with high-pressure pushers, "schlock" merchants, the dealer who operates just within the law — and the outright crook. Not all dealers are out to fleece you — the lamb. But, it's up to you to know what you're buying and the "right" price. Develop the "wolf" side of your buying personality. The home-furnishings market has all the attributes favorable to the fast-buck dealer, namely—

- A large markup on goods sold.
- Big-ticket sales largely dependent on credit.
- Products that are difficult to judge for quality.
- Limited nationally advertised brand names.
- Little or no warranty coverage.

Your defense is know-how — learning to recognize quality, a healthy suspicion of "bargains," a willingness to shop around, and a revolving credit fund to eliminate buying on time. From the planning you did in Chapter 6, you know what you want to buy and the order of priority. Now, you're ready to put your plan into action.

Where And When To Save On Furniture

Except for wall-to-wall carpeting, your big buys in home furnishings are likely to be pieces of furniture. Maybe you've already sat in a few showroom chairs, peeked under the skirts of a sofa or two, or pulled open a few bureau drawers. Now, you're ready to shop in earnest. But, remember — low price without quality is no bargain. And only you will judge quality. Asking the salesman about quality is like the lamb asking the wolf for directions back to the flock.

How to Judge Wood Furniture — Often called "case goods," wood furniture varies widely in quality. Obviously, you can expect to pay more for good quality wood and construction than for lesser quality, but price alone is not a reliable guide. Check these construction details, finishing, and materials when judging:

- Solid wood or plywood? — It used to be that the best wood furniture was made from *solid* walnut, birch, mahogany, or other fine furniture wood. Today, the best furniture is largely plywood with veneered layers of expensive woods for appearance. Plywood construction offers greater strength, resistance to cracking and shrinkage, and lower costs than comparable solid-wood construction. So, don't shy away from veneered plywood in furniture. More important than whether solid wood or plywood is used are construction details.
- Joints — Craftsmanship shows up readily in well-fitted joints

with mechanical features, such as dadoes, rabbets, dovetails, mortise-and-tenons, and dowels, to improve joint strength. Look also for corner-blocks to reinforce the corners of tables and chairs, for glue blocks to reinforce panels, and cleats for extra reinforcement where they are not visible.

• Drawer construction — If the furniture includes drawers, they will likely indicate the quality level of the whole piece. Look for dovetailed joints where drawer sides engage the front. In good-quality drawers you'll find straight-grain wood, not scraps with many knots, warped grain, or solid wood with splits. Bottoms should be plywood or hardboard dadoed into the sides, front, and back, with many small triangular glue blocks underneath the bottom. Drawers should slide easily in and out with a center guide.

• General construction — Backs should be fitted into rabbets all around and screwed into place. Dust panels of thin plywood or hardboard should be well fitted between drawers. All wood should be finished, though hidden pieces may have only a sealer. Hardware, if any, should be heavy duty, attractive, and matched to the piece. Plastic guides, cushioned rubber stops, and other niceties indicate a consideration for quality.

• Finish — Hand-rubbed, stain, and oil finishes are the most expensive because they show everything underneath. Look for matched grain patterns in the veneer from surface to surface. A maker can paint over his mistakes, so, an oil finish indicates quality — and is easier to maintain. Least quality is the sprayed lacquer finish or solid enamel. Any opaque, cover-up coating will show chips and nicks quickly. A "distressed" finish is an attempt to make reproductions of antiques look old and used. There's a fine line between the authentic look of a blunted corner, fly-specked paint, and nicked or gouged surfaces — and cheap copies. If you're a bug on antiques, you'll know when a copy looks like a copy — and when it passes for the real thing.

No amount of armchair reading will make you an expert. Practice a little in judging quality. Visit a decorator showroom and examine the case goods. Pull open the drawers. Look for the glue blocks, the dovetail joints, the dadoed fitting of drawer bottoms, and the reinforced joints at corners of top quality furniture. Then, visit one of the schlock merchants. Wow! What a difference. Once you see the difference in quality, you'll feel more confident about picking furniture that will last — furniture you can be proud to own.

How to Judge Upholstered Furniture — Except for the outer fabric, you're in trouble right from the start in judging upholstered furniture — most of what you need to see is covered. But you can check these features by tipping the divan or chair over so you can see the bottom. Inspect the bottom wood frame — it should be built from kiln-dried hardwood with reinforcing corner blocks glued into corners, doweled or rabbeted joints, and enough structure for good support.

• Look at the springs and how they are tied. If necessary, borrow a flashlight and look through the gauzy dust cover on the bottom. Deep coil springs should rest on steel or heavy wood cross braces. At the top, heavy, wide webbing should crisscross the springs and each spring should be tied both directions to keep it from shifting. Look for padding on top of the springs — curled horsehair is best. Rubberized hair may lose its resilience and is normal for low-cost pieces. Foam (either rubber or urethane) runs from low-to high-quality pieces and forms a smooth base for cushions. Count the springs. There should be at least 12. More springs provide a more even surface but limit depth. Fewer springs may leave a lumpy feel. Zigzag ("no-sag") springs are good and reduce bulk. But zigzag springs are less springy and provide less deep-seated comfort.

• Cushions — Here you'll find a wide range of stuffing materials. Zip off a part of the cushion cover and look for the tag (required by law) that identifies the material used. Foam is one of the best. Quality makers use down for chair pillows to give and settle with your every turn and to provide a "crushed" look. Dacron is a less-crushable (and less-expensive) substitute for soft pillows. Seat cushions should be full and the covering stretched tight. If the cushions or pillows are tufted, look for extra fabric reinforcing where each button is attached.

• Covering — Here's where differences really show up, both in the fabric and the craftsmanship. Look at differences in fabrics first—

1. Nylon tends to wear like a pig's nose, is really resistant to the scrunching, sliding, and fidgeting of children. Recent weaves and surface texture minimize the "pilling" that characterized early nylon fabrics.
2. Cotton is less resilient than wool or nylon and may wrinkle unless stretched tightly over a resilient padding like foam. But, cotton wears well when woven tightly in heavy weights.
3. Wool, when woven tightly is another good fabric, although it tends to be itchy, possibly abrasive.
4. Rayon is seldom found alone; usually it is blended with cotton to add sheen, lustre, and variety of texture.

Whatever the fabric fiber content, look for material that is tightly and sturdily woven and a material that doesn't pull or stretch out of shape easily. Look also at the weave for the kind of service you want—

1. Flat-weave fabrics, brocade, jacquard satin, damask, or cretonne, wear well but show spots easily, may pull out at seams unless firmly sewed. Shiny, satiny surfaces show any caught thread and quickly develop a dull, worn look. Use flat weaves mainly on odd chairs or more decorative elements that will get less wear.
2. Pile fabrics, velvet, plush, frieze, and boucle, absorb wear and can be used on divans or sofas that get a lot of traffic.
3. Heavily textured or tweedy weaves tend to hide spots, wear well, and give a three-dimensional look to coverings.
4. Nonwoven materials, vinyl and leather, are long-wearing but tend to look cold (vinyl) or to cost like the devil (leather). Make sure that any vinyl covering material used includes a heavy cloth backing bonded to the plastic surface.
5. Mixed primary colors, like turquoise, green-blues, orangy reds, and purples, fade more easily than primary reds, blues, and yellows. But, any deep-colored fabric will fade if exposed to bright sunlight. Where will your furniture sit? If it's close to south and west windows, pick colors that are less likely to fade and make sure the color is vat-dyed or solution-dyed.
6. Patterns fit best when scaled to furniture — big patterns for big pieces like a sofa, small patterns for chairs or seat cushions. You're likely to tire quickly of elaborate patterns that contrast strongly with backgrounds. Instead, pick a diffused pattern that works with surface texture.

Check all fabrics for factory-applied surface finishes, such as *Scotchgard, Zepel, Syl-mer,* and *Zelan,* that help the upholstery covering resist soil. Examine the tag — it tells of any surface treatment and how to clean the covering without negating the protection.

• Covering construction — Look to see that upholstery fabric runs from front to back on cushions and from top to bottom on back cushions. The fabric pattern may be run from end to end across the back of sofas. Look for welts that are sewn tightly with matching material cut on a bias for stretchability. Check the skirts around sofas and chairs — is the extra material neatly gathered and fastened to hang neatly, or is it bunched and uneven along the bottom?

• How's the feel? — There's no test like sitting for judging how a sofa or upholstered chair fits you. Are the cushions long enough to support your full length if you are tall? Or do the ends of the cushions hit the backs of your legs if you are short? How about the angle? Seat wide enough? Is there head support in case you doze off while reading? One industrial designer commented after looking at some far-out chairs — "You can sit on anything" — Maybe so, but you and I know there's a difference between just sitting and sitting comfortably. All the other jazz about fabrics and construction are unimportant if a chair isn't comfortable. Fortunately, good quality chairs tend to be more comfortable than cheapies because springs are better and there are more of them, cushions are softer, and more design thought went into size and shape. So, comfort — your comfort — is a further clue to quality.

Buy Furniture for Less Cash — Now, you're ready to sally forth and buy. You've planned what you want. You know how to recognize the quality you can afford. Here are the keys to buying that furniture for less—

• Time your buying for one of the twice-a-year home furnishing sales — even the big department stores and the quality decorator or specialty furniture stores sell for less twice a year. So, save your money and be prepared to take advantage of the reduced prices in February and August or September. Slow-moving items, floor samples, slightly scratched or nicked pieces, and obsolete or after-trend items are cut drastically, up to 50 — even 60 per cent. But don't deviate from your plan just because a $200 chair is marked down to $99.95. Stores also mark down good-quality floor samples so they can change their store's look. These are good buys. Dark-covered pieces that fit winter may be marked down in a February sale so the store can substitute brighter spring or summer colors. If the piece fits your plan, snap it up — but only if it fits. Better still are the store-wide reductions, usually about 20 per cent, that apply even on special-order items — the chair you order with your choice of covering, for example.

Why do stores offer such bargains twice a year? Because they like to sell things. Following the after-Christmas sales of clothing and other expendable goodies, most buyers exhibit pocketbook-fatigue. In this condition your usually thin wallet is thinner still. In August, either you have taken your vacation and are broke or you're about to sweep up the family and head for the mountains or shore, so you hang onto every nickel. Where does this leave the home-furnishings salesmen? Talking to each other! So, stores devise sales to bring in customers. Since big-ticket items like sofas, dining room sets, etc., are usually sold on credit, buyers don't need cash. When a store brings these factors together, they generate business during usually dull selling seasons. But, you, the smart buyer, benefit by waiting. After all, you're going to be sitting on your sofe for five, ten, maybe fifteen years, right? What's another three or four months to wait, particularly if you buy for 20, 30, or 50 per cent less. That's enough on a big-ticket item to buy another chair, coffee table, or pair of lamps.

• Look for the back-alley or basement catalogue outlet for brand merchandise — You'll find these "stores" in low-rent districts. Here's how they work — Suppose you want to buy a "Slumber Sweet" mattress and spring set. The "Slumber Sweet" brand is nationally advertised. You have seen the mattress-spring set in Gallump's Department Store priced at $89.50 each — total $179. But the "Little Olde Upholstery Shoppe — No Job Too Small" will sell you the identical mattress-spring set for 30 per cent less — for $125.30 instead of $179. Not a bad saving for a walk two blocks north, half a block west, and down the stairs. The "Little Olde Upholstery Shoppe" really works at reupholstering furniture, but it also maintains a five-foot shelf of furniture manufacturers' catalogues. The owner may talk to you with upholstery tacks in his mouth, but he takes your order. The freight forwarder delivers the mattress and springs directly to your house. You can buy anything from a catalogue you can identify by brand, color, model, style, and manufacturer. The "Little Olde Upholstery Shoppe" maintains no stock, sells only for cash, has little capital invested, operates in a low-cost workroom, delivers nothing — and cuts the cost to you by 30 per cent or more. Bigger price reductions are available during nation-wide special promotions sponsored by the manufacturer. Suppose the "Slumber Sweet" mattress-spring set is advertised in a women's magazine at $10 off — each. Gallump's now features the pair at $159 instead of the usual $179. But the "Little Olde Upholstery Shoppe" counters by offering 35 per cent off normal price or $116.35. The catalogue store also buys the mattress-spring set for less because the manufacturer promotes the sale.

Locate one of these catalogue-outlets by asking among your friends. Look particularly at shops that advertise upholstery or custom furniture building. Search through the classified listing in your telephone directory for leads. An anonymous phone call to several of the businesses listed may turn up a lead to a wholesaler who sells through catalogues only. These outlets keep their overhead low by not advertising. So, you must exercise initiative to find them. But, they do exist in every town and city of any size.

• Stay away from the dealers who advertise "Going Out of Business," "Lost Our Warehouse Lease," "Everything Must Go," "No Money Down — 24 Months to Pay," "Factory-to-You Prices," and the like. Such gimmicks are bait to get you into the store. There, you're likely to fall under the miasmic spell of a salesman who dulls your usual skeptical reserve, and palms off a schlock piece of junk furniture on you and your family. Stores that run special sales throughout the year seldom sell for lower prices. When generous credit is available, look out — you're about to be taken. One of the profitable gambits furniture salesmen have borrowed from the used-car salesmen is the "bait and switch" tactic. Here's how that one works — AAA Furniture advertises "Three rooms of furniture for $115 — 60 items in all." Sound unbelievable? It is unbelievable. When you ask to buy the 60 pieces, you find the offer includes nine pieces of furniture, 50 towels, doilies, and knickknacks, and one lamp. One look and you can see the stuff is junk. So, the salesmen picks you up on the rebound and steers you to "something better — something a person of your taste can really appreciate." The "something better" is likely to be more costly than similar quality merchandise in a reputable department store.

Some of the other promotion schemes to steer clear of include—

1. Discount cards, admission cards, or introduction cards passed out around your plant or office. These cards are little more than advertising, but they imply that you will get a better deal on price than someone else. These "special" cards appeal to your sense of larceny. But, you end up paying retail prices just like everyone else.

2. Big discounts from preticketed prices. Here, the shady manufacturer may conspire with the retailer. You can easily see that the price label stitched on at the factory reads $89.95 for a mattress. But you pay only $39.95. Wow — what a discount! The mattress is $39.95 quality that the manufacturer preticketed with an inflated price so the dealer could mark it down drastically.

3. Credit padding. If you buy on credit, make sure you understand what the time-payment differential includes. Use the formula in Chapter Five to figure true dollar and interest costs. Don't sign any contract that adds delivery, installation, warehouse handling, credit check, or other charges. In fact, don't sign any conditional sales contract until you fully understand what you're buying, your "take-back" privileges, the cash price, and the time-payment differential, if any.

• Buy furniture by mail — You can benefit from the large-volume operations of Sears, Roebuck and Montgomery Ward to cut your cost of furniture. Examine the pieces you may want in a retail store with an eye to their quality. You won't find at Sears or Wards the fine, hand-crafted quality you saw in decorator outlets. But do you need top quality for children's rooms, family rooms, the kitchen, or rec room? Furniture from big mail-order houses has a mass-produced look and is usually sturdy. The mass-produced look is designed for appeal to a wide range of buyers rather than to your distinctive taste. If you find what you want in a catalogue, order it during one of their twice-a-year sales for a big saving.

• Buy knocked-down or finish-it-yourself furniture — Usually these lines of furniture feature low-cost and low quality. But, don't discard the idea. If you need interim furniture while you're still living in a small apartment or if you want to save on children's furniture, turn part of your spare time to profit by assembling and/or finishing pieces. But, before rushing into such a deal, compare the cost of knocked-down or unfinished furniture to higher-quality furniture you can buy through a catalogue outlet or to good-quality used furniture that could be refinished. You'll usually find a better grade of used furniture available for the same price as new unfinished pieces.

• Buy used furniture at bargain prices — Don't buy used furniture at second-hand stores; the price is likely to be too high for what you get. Instead, search the want-ads in your Sunday paper for families that are selling out a whole houseful of furniture in preparation for moving to a foreign country, to a retirement home, to an apartment, or to settle an estate. Prices are likely to be from 25 to 60 per cent less than the pieces sold for new. Some "used" pieces look as if they were just moved in from the decorator's showroom. Other pieces may be rickety and worn, so learn to be picky. Look first for items that are near the top of your priority list. Look also beyond the piece as it sits — What would it look like if it were refinished or recovered? Could you convert a chair from one use to another? Let your imagination loose! Rebuilding and recovering offer you a really cost-effective purchase whether you do it yourself or hire it done!

Here's How Rebuilding Works — Suppose your decorating plan calls for a new sofa or divan. You've priced out what you want at $575. But, your cash on hand or in your revolving credit fund won't handle that price. Consider the alternatives—

1. You could wait for a store-wide sale. A 20-per cent reduction would bring the price down to $460. Still too much.

2. You could pay $300 cash during the sale and finance the rest at

1-1/2 per cent per month for a year. Your total cost would be $488.80. Still too much because payments would delay building up revolving credit fund again.

3. Consider buying an old frame and having it reupholstered. A well-used divan in the style and size you want might cost you $50. You sand and refinish the legs that will show. The rest of the frame is sturdy and joints are tight. Only the badly worn fabric and lumpy cushions caused the former owners to throw it out. But, for another $200 you can have the piece completely reupholstered — in your choice of fabric, with retied springs, and new cushion material. Total cost — $250 and two trips in your station wagon. Your cash fund still has $50 left as a nest egg. If you are a do-it-yourselfer, you reupholster the divan yourself and save another $100 — or more. You can learn these skills — and many others — through your high school adult education classes. If you were to rebuild and refinish all the furniture for your house, you could save about two-thirds the cost of professionally built furniture. Also, the furniture would be completely your own — in your choice of finishes and coverings.

How To Save On Carpeting

Your next biggest cost in home furnishings is for carpeting. You may want carpeting only in your living room and hall. Or, you may want it throughout your home — including the bathrooms. If you build your own home, plan ahead — don't build an expensive hardwood floor and then cover it with a carpet. If you plan for carpeting in living areas, install only a plywood floor and save the cost of expensive hardwood.

Select the Right Carpet — As in judging quality furniture, only you can decide the kind of carpet — fiber, construction, color, and surface texture — that's best for you. Price is important too, but before talking price and how you can buy carpeting for less, let's look at what you need to know to choose intelligently—

• Fiber content — wool is the traditional standard that you measure all other carpet fibers by. Table 7A compares ten different carpet fibers and is adapted from a publication issued by the Cooperative Extension Service of Washington State University. How can you use these data? Well, for a hall or stairway, you might select nylon because of its wear resistance. If you select a carpet for a bedroom where a sleeper may be subject to allergy, pick an olefin carpet instead of wool, because olefin is practically inert. For extra luxury and pile depth, wool is hard to beat for your well-decorated living rooms. Cotton or rayon are easily washed, so you may use them in a bathroom. Look at your needs — then pick the carpet fiber that fits.

• Quality — Price may be a fair criterion of quality, but don't depend on it. You *can* tell the difference in carpet quality yourself. Notice the depth of pile, back construction, and general weight of a sample. Density is the key to quality — the deeper, the denser, the better! Pile density refers to the closeness of surface yarns as they are packed together. The difference between a $6.95 per square yard and a $9.95 per square yard nylon carpet usually results from the difference in number of ounces of nylon per square yard in the pile. Read the labels — all carpets for sale have them. The label tells you what kind of fiber is in the carpet — but not how much. If the fiber is a blend, wear and other characteristics will reflect the characteristics of the fiber making up most of the blend. One clue — stay away from carpets that bear labels with high percentages of "other fibers." Construction also affects wear and service. Carpets may be woven on a huge loom in one operation or they may be tufted with yarns which poke through a backing. Both types may be coated with a latex backing to hold fibers tightly. Either construction permits a cut or looped pile. Loop piles tend to wear better than cut piles, but women may catch their spike heels in loop piles. Twisted fibers tend to wear longer than straight fibers. As you shop, study samples, listen to salesmen, become knowledgeable about fiber density, fiber differences, and construction — then make up your own mind.

• Analyze the trade-offs that affect your choice of carpeting — Are you likely to move within a few years? Will you be redecorating within the next three to six years? Are you buying an interim carpet? Remember, you seldom take carpeting with you when you move. If you're one of today's gypsies, ever on the move, buying a carpet that will last 20 years doesn't make sense. Also, buying a long-life carpet may inhibit your plans if you redecorate every few years. On the other hand, labor to install a $5.95 carpet costs just as much as labor to install a $13.95 carpet — prices are per square yard. So, if you plan to keep a carpet for many years or you are buying a carpet for a heavy-traffic area, install a durable carpet — and save.

• Padding or underlayment — Don't forget the pad; it's almost as important as the type of carpet you choose. Padding gives your carpet that extra feeling of depth and luxury, adds quiet, acts as a shock absorber, and extends your carpet's life. You'll find two types — felted hair and rubber. Felted pads tend to mat down and become

Carpet Fibers	Wool	Nylon	Acrylic	Modacrylic	Rayon	Cotton	Polypropylene (Olefin)	Polyester	Saran
Wear Life	G	E	G	G	F	E	G to E	G	E
Crush Resistance	E	VG	G to VG	F	F	P	G to F	G	G
Soil Resistance	VG	G	G	G	F	F	G	P	VG
Cleanability	E	VG	VG	VG	G	F	VG	F	VG
Price Range of "Good" Carpets	$10-20	$8-12	$10-14	Med to High	$6-9	$6-13	$8-10	Med to High	--
Trade Names		Celanese Nylon 66 Caprolan Cumuloft DuPont 501 Enkaloft Nyloft Tycora Antron	Acrilan Creslan Orlon-33 Zefran Zefkrome	Dynel Verel	Avicolor Avisco Avicron Coloray Kolorbon Skyloft Corval Fibro Skybloom Super-L Rayon		Herculon Marvess Polycrest Vectra	Dacron Fortrel Kodel Vycron 55	Rovana
Comments	(1)	(2)	(3)	(4)	(5)	(6)	(7)	(8)	(9)

(1) Many grades. Avoid "bargains" below $10. Burns slowly. Extinguishes slowly without smoldering.
(2) "First-grade carpet nylon" is manufacturer's specification on the label for top-grade nylon.
(3) Often used in high pile rugs. Closely-packed, tightly-twisted pile wears better than shaggy sparse pile.
(4) Often used in high pile rugs and often used in blends. Fire resistant. Pills easily.
(5) Tweeds and patterns disguise soiling and crushing. Key to rayon carpeting is in the construction, (character- istics improve with density). Super-L Rayon, specially designed carpet rayon, crushes less, has good soil resistance.
(6) Look for shrink-resistant and colorfast labels.
(7) Solution-dyed for excellent colorfastness. Sheds water. Similar to continuous filament nylon in performance characteristics.
(8) New type polyesters are on the market that should offer much better wearability than shown above. However, period of use of the new polyesters has not been long enough to evaluate sufficiently at this time.
(9) For outdoor use primarily. Sheds water.

Key: E = Excellent, VG = Very Good, G = Good, F = Fair, P = Poor

TABLE 7A Characteristics of Carpet Fibers

Carpet Fibers	Desirable Characteristics	Limitations
Wool	Very good durability. Springy and crush resistant. Soil resistant. Warm to touch. Flame resistant. Adaptable to styling.	Must be mothproofed. Damaged by alkaline detergents. Waste or reprocessed wool can be poor choice.
Cotton	Soft. Cleans easily. Excellent durability. Economical. Wide color range. Not attacked by moths, mildew.	Poor flame resistance. Crushes easily. Soils fairly easily. Fiber and color destroyed by lye and bleach.
Nylon	Exceptional durability. Springy and crush resistant. Cleans fairly easily. Nonallergenic. Not affected by mildew.	Soils fairly easily in bright fibers; pilling in staple loop pile; some static electricity; all less so in never type fibers. Cool to touch. Therm melts. (Buy virgin, not waste nylon.)
Rayon	Takes color well. Soft. Moderately priced. Adaptable to styling. Good chemical resistance. Not affected by moths.	In less dense pile has poor flame resistance; crushes; poor durability. Poor soil resistance. May be subject to silverfish damage.
Acrylic	Takes color well. Springy and crush resistant. Cleans easily. Good soil resistance.	Not very good flame resistance. Medium-high price range.
Modacrylic	Flame resistant. Very good durability. Good soil resistance. Cleans easily. Usable in high pile rugs.	Lacks good resilience. Pills easily. Medium-high price range.
Olefin	Exceptional durability. Good soil resistance. Cleans easily. Moderately priced. Nonallergenic. Lightweight.	Therm melts. In some lower grades crushes.

TABLE 7A (Continued) Rug Fiber Characteristics —
Medium to High Quality Grades

firmer or more compact with use. Unless laid expertly, rubber pads may "creep" or move with use. Rubber pads come as a smooth sponge type or in a waffle, textured pattern. Your carpet may be damaged if women's sharp heels force a piece of carpet into deep holes or voids in a waffle-pattern pad. Felted paddings come in various weights and are noted as so many ounces per square yard. A 40-ounce pad is a good weight for home use. Rubber cushions are usually measured by thickness. They range from 1/8 to 1/2 inch thick. Select your sponge rubber pad in the 1/4 or 3/8-inch thickness. One caution — if your floors are radiantly heated, don't use a rubber pad.

Buying Your Carpet for Less — It's "no holds barred" when it comes to actually buying carpeting. Prices for exactly the same carpet vary all over the scale, and discounts up to 25, even 30, per cent are common. Make sure you get what you want at the best price by —

• Shopping the stores rather than asking a carpet salesman to haul bundles of carpet samples to your home. Remember, these salesmen don't work for nothing, despite their claims of "no obligation to buy." The commission they charge buyers must also cover their time spent with the "looker" who didn't buy.

• Examining the label carefully. Note if the carpet is "irregular" or a "second." You may get a good buy this way, but learn what the flaw is and whether it will affect appearance or wearing qualities. If you find an irregular carpet with flaws that do not affect either appearance or wear, you can usually negotiate a big discount.

• Shopping and negotiating for a price. Few carpet companies or department stores charge the same price for the same carpet. Most carpeting is purchased from a manufacturer's warehouse for a specific job. Whoever sells you the job pays basically the same wholesale price for exactly enough carpet to fit your rooms. Price differences evolve from the markup one salesman or store will accept, installation labor, and variations in carpet padding.

• Not falling for the old trick of switching you from a good carpet manufactured by a national, reputable company to one "just as good" at a slightly lower price. The basic price for the unknown carpet is likely to be much less — so the salesman pockets a higher profit.

• Bargaining for a total job. Tie everything into a package — specific carpet, specific pad, and installation. Stores that are big enough to hire their own installation crews can usually cut installation price a bit. Also, such stores buy padding in bulk quantities, so that price can be less. Don't be shy about asking for a discount — as often as not, you'll get it.

• Paying cash. Carpeting is costly, and carpeting salesmen like to push low monthly payments, particularly those salesmen who bring bundles of samples to your home. If you can't pay cash, borrow the money from a bank and pay cash to the carpet house. Follow the same route for buying carpeting that you do for appliances (see Chapter 5); that is, buy for cash at the store or carpet company that sells mainly on credit. These outfits often price their total installed price close to cost and make their profit from a fat financing contract.

• Searching out the small carpet outlet. Like the catalogue store in the low-rent district where you can buy quality furniture for less, look for the one- or two-man shop. The owner buys directly from a wholesaler and installs the carpeting himself. In fact, the main business of the small carpet outlet may be installation. He sells the carpet only to get the job of installing it. Ask among your friends for a lead to one of these installer-salesmen. You can negotiate a big discount from the price you would otherwise pay in a high-overhead, prestige-location store.

Check Installation — Don't settle for a "quick and dirty" installation. Examine the fitting around doorways, registers, and corners. Make certain there are no wrinkles in the padding or carpeting. Examine any sewed seams. They should be practically invisible without raised edges and with a continuous pile surface across the seam. Unless a job is installed to your complete satisfaction — don't accept it. Get a guarantee that covers any callback for loose edges, puckered seams, or shifted padding. Tacks around the edges show and leave an uneven edge. The best carpet installers use the "no-tack" system where a plywood strip with many slanted metal points holds the stretched carpet around the edge.

Draperies And Curtains For Less

Examine the factors in cost-effectiveness for window drapes or curtains and you'll find three items — durability, cleaning cost, and initial price. Miss one, and your cost goes up. So, let's look at each in turn.

Durability — That "ole debbil sun" is the culprit here. Not only will the sun fade colored draperies, but it actually causes them to deteriorate. Smog, dirt, and handling also raise cain with draperies. Fiber content is one key to long life in the sun. Fiber glass resists the sun best but may have other problems, such as color fastness and resistance to handling. Polyester fibers are next best for hanging in bright, sunny windows. Least sun-resistant fibers are linen, rayon, cotton, and acetate. Don't use silk in sunny windows; it deteriorates rapidly. Remember these other points on durability too—

• Shiny finish fabrics resist the sun better than dull or satin finishes.

• Loose weaves, particularly those made of fine threads, resist sun damage less than tight weaves of heavier threads.

• Dark colors, particularly those of color mixes, such as blue-greens, yellow-reds, and others, tend to fade more than light, primary colors. But, any color will fade in time if exposed to strong sunlight.

• Lined draperies combine the appearance you want with resistance to sunlight when you pick the right fabrics. Use a sun-resistant polyester fiber for a lining to protect a rayon or cotton decorative pattern. Linings also aid in draping and keep window areas warmer (see Chapter 2).

• How you clean, dust, and shift curtains affects their durability. Dust, acid from smog, and dampness gang up to shorten the life of even the best drapes. See Chapter 8 for money-saving hints on maintaining draperies and curtains.

Initial Cost — The price you pay for draperies depends on your shopping know-how; that is, how aggressively you spend cash or credit. Let's look at the alternatives—

• Make them yourself? If you have a sewing machine and a big space to work, you save money by providing the labor. You save a bundle, particularly if you buy the fabric on sale or from a fabric discount house — or both. Look for do-it-yourself instructions in one of the booklets offered by drapery-rod manufacturers. Or, ask your extension service for a pamphlet of directions.

• Adapt standard sizes. All stores and the big mail-order houses sell drapes that fit stock-size windows. If you can use these stock sizes, you can save because they are made to conserve fabric and on an assembly line to cut labor costs. Even if the sizes available don't match your windows exactly, consider trimming one edge to narrow the width or cutting the bottom and rehemming to a new height. You'll find it easier to adapt a stock size than building the full drapes from scratch.

• Measure your own windows, order custom sizes, and hang drapes yourself. A big part of the cost of custom-made draperies is the time spent to measure and hang custom draperies. When you handle this job, you cut your costs by as much as a third. Allow from 2-1/4 to 2-1/2 times the width of windows for ample draping. If drapes run to the floor, size them to clear the floor by one-half inch and allow for a four-inch hem. Curtain rods slip in and out to fit a range of window sizes. But, for a smooth, custom job, measure the exact width, and have a rod cut in one piece to fit the window.

• Buy your drapes and curtains at home-furnishings sales. Here's your best chance to save. If you don't have the time, talent, or patience to make your own draperies, look for the special promotion that charges only for the material you pick. The store tosses in the labor free — or charges only a nominal $1 per window. Whether you buy the material at a big reduction and pay regular prices for custom fabrication and hanging or buy a package that includes fabric and labor depends on your shopping ability. Check special promotions by Sears, Wards, and Penneys. For the package prices available to you at home furnishing events, you can hardly afford to make your own.

• Don't buy from the salesman who comes to your home with handfuls of fabrics and claims to include labor and hanging free. Watch out for his credit package or the cost per yard. Before spending a cent on draperies, compare total price for fabric, installation, and credit — wherever you buy.

Buying Linens, Bedding, And Acessories

"A well-stocked trousseau should last a girl for at least 10 years," or so you've heard. Maybe so. But neatly monogrammed towels and percale sheets do wear out. And, as the family grows, so does your need for sheets, pillows, towels, blankets — *ad infinitum*. You can really practice your aggressive spending techniques in this area.

Shopping for Sheets, Towels, etc. — Two factors affect the cost-effectiveness equation for bedding — durability and price. Combine good buying in both and save up to 50 per cent.

• Quality and durability — Measure quality of sheets and pillow-cases by thread count — 112 threads to the inch up to 180 for muslin and 180 to 200 for percale. For durability and long wear, select the 140-count muslin sheets. For smooth, luxurious feel, pick the percales. To achieve the high thread count for smooth percales, thread size must be small — and durability falls. Tests and performance both point to the middle range — high thread count muslin in the 140-160 range.

• Buying quality for less — Not only do high-count muslin sheets last longer than percale, but they cost less. Save more by buying them on sale. No traditional sale is more firmly established than the January white sale. August white sales came along later. But they happen as regularly as Christmas, so schedule your buying to take advantage of these sales. Not so regular are the linen sales that are part of special home-furnishing events. Here you're likely to find "selected irregulars" or "seconds" as bait. Irregulars can be a good buy — even better when on sale. You're likely to find irregulars and seconds in a bargain basement. But, look for the flaw before you buy. Irregulars are likely to be higher quality; that is, fewer and less noticeable flaws, than seconds.

• Limit your buying of nonstandard sizes. Quantity and competition keep prices down on the most-used sizes. You may find that it is not the first price of a queen- or king-size bed that breaks you; it's the upkeep. For example, for the same quality percale, you might pay $5.95 for a king-size (100 x 120) while an 81 x 108 regular size costs only $2.35.

• Don't use fitted sheets if long wear is your goal. Changing sheets from top to bottom and from side to side extends life by spreading the wear pattern.

• Consider blends of polyester or rayon fibers with cotton for long life. Polyester fibers add a no-press feature as well as increasing durability

Shopping for Pillows — Even more varied than bed linen are your choices for pillows — from goose down for unbelievable softness to foam for support and nonallergenic properties. A good pillow will spring back to shape after you press down with fingers extended — and then let go. Heaviness indicates poor quality. In descending order of quality, pillow fillings rank thus — Down, either white or gray, is tops. Goose feathers are next, followed by duck feathers. Far down the list are turkey feathers and, even lower, chicken feathers. Synthetic filling materials include polyester and acrylic fibers. Both are good — less soft than down, softer than turkey or chicken feathers and nonallergenic, washable, mothproof, and unaffected by mildew. Foam fillings may be from latex or urethane; but select one molded to shape rather than a sack of cut-up pieces. Buy pillows the way you buy bedding — on sale, as irregulars when available, and in a standard size if possible.

Shopping for Accessories — Here's where you can really let yourself go! Let your imagination run rampant! Express your individuality! Whether you select a chunk of driftwood bored and fitted as a lamp base, or hang a simple lampshade from a ceiling hook over a corner table, your conversation-piece "finds" are likely to fit better and cost less than expensive lamps from a decorator shop. From knickknacks to antimacassars — bring yourself into the act. Coffee tables fit into this category too — from a glass-covered wagon wheel you resurrected from a dump to a beautiful chunk of marble salvaged for a pittance from a rococo 1890 theater — you often gain more by spending time, imagination, and thought than by spending money.

Antiques? Sure! Here is where you mix a bit of the past with modern technology. Antique items that seldom saw daily use — like a coffee grinder or finely wrought, hand-blown glass — tend to last longer, and so are in better condition today. See if you can beat the professional to the punch in converting old or discarded items to a new use — like the cobbler's bench to a coffee table.

Search through the import stores with a second eye — the one that sees beyond what may be on the floor to a final use for an entirely different purpose in your home. How about converting a huge brass gong to a throw-in magazine table — or a pair of hammered copper pitchers to matching end-table lamps. One of the most imaginative conversions was to use wallpaper printing rollers as lamp bases. You know, of course, that the fittings for converting almost anything from an ancient whiskey bottle to a modern sculpture into a lamp cost about $1.50. Add a simple shade, and you've saved yourself $48.45 — or more.

Convert your hobby into home accessories—Like gardening? Then dress your home in living plants that add a feeling of life and variety. Every kind of plant from dwarf lemon trees to African violets adds a distinctive touch to living and dining room. Are you a collector? Then display your finest specimens in a series of window shelves, on a fireplace mantle, or in a special case. Only the limits of your own imagination can put a stop to adding interest through accessories and conversation-starters.

MONEY SAVERS WHEN BUYING HOME FURNISHINGS

Quality and the price vary more widely for home furnishings than just about any other home expense. Here's where effective "buymanship" pays big dividends. But, the schlock merchants, the "ready credit" pushers, the shady operators, and the real lack of quality guides and warranty coverage can be major stumbling blocks in buying home furnishings. To avoid buying junk at high prices on credit, you learned about—

- Judging the quality of furniture, both wood and upholstered types, from the clues you can see.
- Avoiding the phony sales and credit come-on tactics of dealers who operate within a footfall of the law.
- Recognizing the real cost of paying too little — and how to avoid paying too much for every kind of furnishing and accessory in your house.
- Analyzing the cost and value trade-offs from finishing furniture yourself, rebuilding used pieces, assembling knocked-down items, and buying used, quality pieces that fit your plan.
- Extending your aggressive spending techniques to the "soft" furnishings — draperies and linens.

8

Simple Methods For Maintaining Home Equipment And Furnishings

Do you know what bothers homeowners more than any one thing today? SERVICE — how to get it and how much it costs. Trying to get reliable, low-cost service to keep your carpets, furniture, and draperies showroom fresh and your electrical-mechanical servants working effectively can be frustrating. But, you can do something about it — and save cash at the same time. Here's how —

- *Avoid the service call you really don't need — for some fault you could easily fix yourself or because you didn't read the instruction book.*
- *Keep from overloading your appliances and help them run longer between service calls — and pocket the cash saving.*
- *Locate the many legitimate sources of free service.*
- *Avoid the "free service" or "no-cash, lots-of-credit" bait advertising.*
- *Repair or refurbish your own furniture, carpets, and draperies.*

Do you suffer that pocketbook-sinking feeling when the panel truck with SERVICE on the side drives into your driveway? The serviceman seems to come so often these days! Well, take a stand — you CAN cut the high cost of equipment service. A little know-how each day keeps the serviceman away.

Maybe you haven't been giving your faithful (?) mechanical servants enough TLC — tender loving care. You know, of course, that appliance makers build home equipment, including TV, with the premise that owners provide almost no care. So, a little attention, following instructions, and preventive maintenance really pay off.

Keep Your Appliances And Home Equipment Working — For Less Cash

By actual count, 43 out of every hundred service calls are pure waste. Instead of a real problem, servicemen find an appliance isn't plugged in. A fuse is blown. A circuit breaker tripped. Maybe the water faucet isn't turned on. Or, there may be a loose wire in a plug — usually loosened by jerking it from a socket. Spending $7.50 for a serviceman to plug your clothes dryer into a socket is a waste you can do without.

Ignorance and lack of interest are the next biggest reasons for service calls, according to manufacturers' service departments. Users simply don't learn how to operate their appliances. Just think of the poor manufacturers. They spend thousands of dollars on clearly written, lavishly illustrated instruction books. And what happens? Nobody appears to read them. Housewives (and husbands) regularly toss the books aside and start pushing buttons. Result — unneeded, costly service calls that waste a serviceman's time. Paying ten bucks to learn that a misset timer prevents an oven from heating is pretty expensive instruction.

Maybe you can't do without your electrical servants — but you can keep them operating for a lot less cash if you pay attention.

HOW TO DO IT: *Give Your Equipment a Break* — The clothes dryer that runs longer and hotter because the lint trap is full will break down sooner. Think of it like this — You could probably walk two miles, but if you had to run, you'd probably give up and quit after half a mile — a mile? A block? So, help your dryer help you — clean out the lint regularly. Anything you can do to keep an appliance working without extra load will prolong its life — and cost you less. A few ideas—

• Dust the condenser coils of your refrigerator or freezer. You'll find them at the back or underneath the mechanism. A refrigerator cools the inside by transferring heat to room air through the condenser coils or finned radiator panel. Dust and/or lint insulates the coils, slows heat transfer, and causes your cooling mechanism to run longer. Give your refrigerator a break by keeping the coils clean.

• Dump the dust bag on your vacuum cleaner. Suction is less if the air must force dirt through a collection of lint and dust in a bag — so your cleaner is inefficient, picks up only the easy, surface dirt, and/or you spend longer at it. So, dump that dust bag often and keep your vacuum operating at peak efficiency.

• Keep door seals tight around refrigerator and freezer compartment doors. As cold air leaks out, warm, moisture-laden air flows in. Your unit runs longer to freeze out the moisture as frost and to cool the warm air that leaks in. The thicker the frost layer, the harder your unit works. Make sure the door seal fits tightly, is flexible, and that the door remains closed.

• Check water strainers and valves in an automatic washer to make sure they are clean and fully open. Otherwise, the machine must work harder — or clothes aren't fully cleaned.

• Don't overload your dishwasher, clothes washer, and dryer. When you put too many dishes or clothes in a load, two things happen — the machine must work harder and your dishes or clothes may not get clean or dry. Too many clothes in a dryer force every part of the machine to strain — and lead to early breakdown. Also, effective drying action depends on the clothes tumbling freely. Much the same goes for the clothes washer. If the clothes are jammed in, the hot soapy water can't reach all the fibers. In a dishwasher, the spray pattern may be blocked and some dishes will not be cleaned during the cycle. If your clothes or dishes are not coming out clean, check the load before calling a serviceman.

• Lubricate any bearings, transmissions, gears, or other mechanical units that are not fully sealed at the factory. Check the maintenance instructions in your owners handbook for directions.

Any appliance that must overcome obstacles, such as partly closed valves, dry bearings, etc., will break down sooner than a clean, well-maintained machine. When you give your electrical-mechanical servants a break, you pocket the savings.

Make Sure You Really Need Service — When an appliance won't operate, get in the habit or checking a few simple items before calling the serviceman.

• Read your instruction book — We'll say it again — and again — and again! No single bit of advice will pay off more handsomely than — FOLLOW DIRECTIONS! Know where to set the control dial on your refrigerator when you're defrosting or cleaning — and how to turn it back on again. Is the dial set for 40-42 ° in the box? Check the cycle dial on a dishwasher to make sure it is ready for a new cycle. Children sometimes move it to a dry cycle. Naturally the water won't flow in. If there's a safety door switch on your clothes washer, don't try to start it operating without closing the door. Any number of things might give you the impression that your favorite appliance is on the blink. You feel mighty silly — and a little broke — if all the serviceman does is change a dial setting or close a door to return your appliance to operation.

• Check fuses or circuit breakers — Your home's electrical system includes either fuses or circuit breakers to guard against wiring overloads. Round, screw-in fuses usually protect lighting circuits. You may find cartridge fuses in appliance or heating circuits, certainly in 220-volt circuits. If an appliance won't work and is plugged into a socket, look for a blown fuse. But, before replacing the fuse, disconnect all appliances from that circuit. Screw a light bulb into the fuse holder. If the bulb lights, you've got circuit problems; don't replace the fuse until you find the short in the system. If the bulb doesn't light, the problem is in your appliance or its cord. When replacing fuses, first open the main switch, stand on a dry board or floor, and screw in the right replacement fuse. If a 220-volt cartridge fuse blows, better call for professional help. Circuit breakers take the place of fuses and a switch. To reset a circuit breaker, first move the handle to OFF, then return handle to ON.

• Test cords and plugs — If you suspect trouble in a cord or plug, test the electrical socket by inserting the bared ends of a trouble lamp into the two holes. The lamp should light if the socket is "hot". Plug a suspected cord into the socket and insert the ends of the trouble lamp into the plug end. Flex the cord if the lamp does not light. If the lamp flickers as you bend a part of the cord, replace the cord. If flexing causes no change, the trouble is probably in the plug or socket. Check each for loose or broken wires by unscrewing the outlet or removing the insulating cap at the plug end. Tighten any loose wires. If a wire is broken, strip back more insulation and reattach the wires.

• Check out possible faults yourself — look in the back of the owners manual or instruction book that came with your appliance. Frequently, you'll find service hints, a diagram of the parts and functions, and an illustrated diagram of parts. Possibly you'll find a "fault tree," a planned sequence of "try this — if you get results, try —," to isolate the fault. If you are mechanically minded, you can find the fault from this trouble-shooting guide. Then, you decide whether you can fix it yourself or if you should call for service.

There's a real dollar-saving incentive to fix things yourself, because the big element of service bills is the labor charge. Look at a typical bill sometime. It may read — "New frammis-fuget — 59 cents — service call — $12 — total $12.59 plus tax." If you can replace the frammis-fuget yourself, you save the $12 for labor. But, unless you *are* the handy-with-tools type and know what you're doing, don't tear the innards out of a machine and then call a serviceman to put them together again. If the instruction or operating manual you receive doesn't include an illustrated parts list and service instruction, write to the manufacturer for service information. Include the exact model type and serial number from the nameplate on your specific appliance. Many manufacturers publish service manuals to aid shops. If you are the handyman type, this added information may be all you need to fix 90 per cent of the faults. Sears and Wards include easy-to-read part number diagrams with their equipment, and you can order parts by number through the mails.

Simple Fixes You Do Yourself — Appliances do break down, even if you baby them with care. Some of these failures are simple to fix, even if you are all thumbs. Before checking the yellow pages of your telephone directory for a service shop, see if you can fix one of your electrical or mechanical servants with one of these simple fixes:

• Electrical cords and plugs take a beating around most homes. Learn how to take plugs and sockets apart, strip back the insulation from new ends of wire, and refasten the new cords. For step-by-step photographs and diagrams, check your state's Agricultural Extension Service for a guidebook on servicing home equipment. The University of Tennessee published one real dandy of a book in cooperation with the Tennessee Valley Authority. Other states have revised the book and reissued it for their own residents.

• Check the contacts of on-off switches in automatic cycling dishwashers, clothes dryers, refrigerators, pop-up toasters, fry-pans — almost any portable or major appliance that operates automatically. Make-break contacts are the key element in the on-off cycling for changes in operation or temperature control. Contacts are rounded or flat-surfaced pieces of metal about half the size of a lead pencil at the end of flat springs. The contacts make or break the circuit by springing together or apart at the right time or at a preset temperature. After many make or break contacts, the tips may be burned by the heavy surges of current. Rough surfaces may interfere with current flow to cause erratic operation, or chunks may burn away to interrupt the circuit. Simply cleaning and brightening the contacts with an emery board is enough to return many units to reliable operation. If points are burned so badly they no longer touch, you'll need new ones. Most thermostats or timers cannot be repaired. Replace the entire contact or timer assembly if cleaning or tightening spring tension doesn't correct the problem.

• Broken heating wires may be the cause of a malfunctioning

toaster, surface cooking element, oven element, or any of the other heating or cooking appliances. Heating wire is brittle and breaks easily. Check a toaster that won't heat by removing the outer shell (after disconnecting it from the socket, of course). The most frequent break occurs right at the attachment screw. If you find such a break, remove the broken loop from under the attachment point, bend a new loop and reattach. If the wire is broken away from the terminal, buy a completely new heating element and install it. Look for the same kind of a break near the attachment screw for counter cooking elements or a hotplate.

• Write to the manufacturer for help in replacing burned handles, worn can-opener drive wheels, or other small parts. A manufacturer is not likely to establish a local source for parts to fix a $3.95 manually-operated can opener. But, when the cutting wheel and notched drive wheels become worn, don't throw away the whole unit and buy another. Instead, write to the manufacturer for a new set of wheels. Address your inquiry to the Customer Service Department and include the exact model number. Too often you may decide it's too much trouble trying to get a new handle for a coffeepot or a new set of mixer blades for a portable mixer. Don't toss the item into the rubbish before writing to see if you can get the parts to make the item as good as new. It works — I've used this system for years. You can too.

• Proctor-Silex recently took a major step forward in the servicing of portable appliances, such as toasters, pressing irons, and automatic coffeemakers. Their *Lifelong* appliances are assembled with take-apart components. When one component fails, you simply snap in a new component yourself. For example, there's no need to take a steam iron into a shop for service, and pay a $5 or greater tab — the new Proctor iron includes modules that are "easier to replace than a light bulb." The steam iron's heat-control or "fabric selector" switch costs only $1.50 — and you put it in yourself.

• Don't hesitate to troubleshoot your ailing appliances. Once you remove the chrome-plated outer shell, most toasters, coffeepots, and the like are surprisingly simple. A quick examination may show up a loose connection, broken wire loop at an attachment screw, or a jammed mechanism.

How to Pay Less for Service When You Need It — Okay, you've tried everything and still your dishwasher, toaster, TV, or what-have-you won't work. Or, you've found the trouble, but you can't fix it yourself. You need help — dependable service that costs you the least cash.

Here's What To Do—

• Check the warranty — If your equipment is covered by a warranty or service policy, find out who's responsible and call for help.

• Call on your electric power or natural gas company — A cooking range, oven, or electric clothes dryer uses lots of electricity and many power companies offer free service to keep these heavy power-using appliances working. You pay only for the parts replaced. Some electric power companies extend this no-cost service (except for parts) to portable appliances brought to the company's service shop. Gas companies are conscious of possible explosion hazards and may offer service to assure safe operation of a furnace, stove, and dryer. Most power companies don't advertise this service widely, but a phone call may save you a bundle.

• Look for a factory service branch — Two kinds of service shops operate under the "factory" label. 1) True service branches operated directly by the manufacturer. 2) Independent shops authorized by a manufacturer to handle warranty claims. Both maintain a stock of approved replacement parts. The manufacturer, conscious of his image, is likely to maintain some control over the "Authorized Service" shop. Avoid service organizations with AAA in their name (to get a preferred alphabetical listing in the classified section), who offer "free diagnosis," "no charge for service," or some similar bait gimmick. No outfit can afford to offer free house calls. Your bill will include a pad somewhere to cover the "free service."

• Haul your troubled equipment to the service shop — With portable appliances, this is easy. When you save the serviceman's time by taking a toaster or television set into the service shop, you save an expensive part of your bill. If you can't haul the whole unit to a shop, try removing the mechanism or faulty part.

• Wait while the serviceman checks your appliance — The shop that is too busy to find the trouble while you wait is the shop likely to bill you for unneeded service. This is particularly true of television service. Most shops can quickly spot the trouble. You may have to leave the faulty appliance to be fixed later, but insist on an analysis while you wait. If you don't get one, haul your troubled set somewhere else.

• Get a second or third estimate if repairs are high — Here's where waiting for an analysis pays off. Don't pay $30 to $50 for repairs on one shop's say-so. Get a corroborating analysis. Simply take your machine or TV to another shop and request an estimate of the cost to fix it. You'll be surprised at the differences!

• Call a member of some organization of service shops — Legitimate service shops in metropolitan areas have banded together for protection against the fast-buck artists. Just being a member of some local technicians' association doesn't guarantee a low-cost, completely satisfactory fix. But, your chances are better. And, if the repair isn't satisfactory and your complaints to the shopowner go unheeded, complain to the association.

• Insist on a return of replaced parts and an itemized bill — These actions won't insure honest service, but they put the serviceman on notice that he might be asked to justify replacement of each item and each charge. The honest shop makes its money from service — not by selling shoddy parts or by charging you for parts not replaced.

• If all else fails, write to the manufacturer — Suppose you continue to have problems with an appliance. You pay for several service calls and the fault remains. Either the authorized service shop can't fix the fault, doesn't know what the real fault is, keeps making repairs in the blind hope that something will work, or is "taking you". The manufacturer would like to know the facts. Simply address a letter to the Customer Service Department at the manufacturer's main office. Itemize the symptoms of your problem with the appliance, the service shop reports, the bills you have paid, and the present status. A reputable manufacturer will respond to an objective letter.

Avoid Service Contracts — Increasingly popular are the service contracts offered by factory service branches to cover service problems after the expiration of a warranty. Regardless of what may go wrong with your appliance or TV, you're covered for a fixed price per year. Parts and labor are included. Sounds great! Like Santa Claus comes all year! But, look closer! Service contracts will cost you more than they are worth if you are a prudent homeowner with a house full of appliances. Human nature being what it is, the owner of an appliance covered by a service contract is likely to call for more service than is really needed. We've already noted that many house calls result from a plug pulled out or a water faucet turned off. Or, a befuddled housewife doesn't understand or hasn't read the operating instructions. Since service shops are in business to make money, they set the service contract fee high enough to cover such nuisance calls. The chances are that if your appliance is working well at the expiration of the warranty period, it will continue to operate for many years with a minimum of service. You won't pay for a service call to plug in a cord, or overload the dishwasher, and you understand all the controls. Why pay part of the service costs of those owners who are not so knowledgeable? Instead of buying a service contract, bank the yearly fee and use the accumulation to buy service when it is really needed. Over the years you can spend what you save on new clothes — even a new appliance. If you should own an appliance that breaks down regularly, you may have a legitimate complaint against the manufacturer. If you buy a service contract, you may pay for correcting the manufacturer's mistake.

Keep Your Television Functioning For Less Cash

You don't have to be an Edison or keep a cabinet full of electronic test gear to fix many of the troubles that plague both black and white and color television receivers. All kinds of poor pictures can result from simple-to-fix problems. Here are just a few—

• Check your antenna — Ghosts, snow, and poor picture definition result mainly from a poor signal to your set. Picking up the signal is the job for your antenna. Is it a modern, high-performance, multielement antenna that matches the performance capability of your new set? Antennas have been improved, too. If yours is a color set, you need a complex antenna to bring in crisp, natural colors. If you see ghosts on one channel but not on others, bouncing signals from one station may be delivering more than one set of instructions to your set. If transmitting stations are widely separated, you may need more than one antenna to bring each channel in clearly. Check your lead-in for cracks, the commections at an outside antenna for corrosion, or loose wires that interfere with signal strength. Check the antenna itself for dirt and corrosion at electrical joints. Many, many TV problems go away when the antenna is brought up to full strength.

• Look for tube problems — Failures in tubes cause about 90 per cent of the problems in television circuits. You can check your own tubes by pulling off the back (after disconnecting the set) and gently removing the tubes. Check the circuit diagram for the location of tubes by number. Test tubes in a parts store (usually at no cost) or one of the supermarket tube-checkers. Order replacement tubes from a mail-order source or buy them in a discount outlet to cut the cost of new tubes in half. But, don't buy off-brand tubes; they are likely to be as bad as the ones you pull out.

• Buy one of the TV DIY guides — If you are mechanically inclined, one of the television service booklets will help you diagnose faults from picture or sound symptoms. Many of the fixes require soldering and circuit changes for correction. Other fixes zero in on the specific type of tube that may be faulty. However, many of the problems described can be traced to a poor antenna.

Maintaining Your Fine Furniture

Valued antiques, brand-new pieces, slate or marble tops — all take a beating from daily use and contact in a family. Nicks, scratches, alcohol spills, candle wax drippings, heat marks, ink stains, dents, burns, spots of all kinds, in addition to normal wear can quickly reduce your furniture to a shambles. But, prompt attention, the right fix for minor problems, and TLC for the finish rise to the rescue.

Regular TLC for Antiques and New Furniture Alike — Like so many things around your house, routine preventive maintenance pays off in long-lasting appearance and fewer repairs. Furniture, particularly, responds to tender loving care (TLC) — the soft polish and regular waxing for gloss finishes, regular wiping with oil or creamy wax for satiny good looks on sophisticated oil finishes, and the cleaning that produces unspotted, deep-looking finishes on marble or slate. Coasters under drinks, whether alcohol or not, keep rings off stone or marble and save much rubbing on wood finishes. Don't use the new cleaning waxes when caring for antiques. You're likely to remove the scratch-covering patina of age or the old wax coats that provide the antique glow of age you prize so much. Instead, use paste wax designed for floor or car; then polish with a soft-as-baby's-skin cloth.

Quick Fixes for Furniture Problems — Quick is the key word here. Promptness pays off in less damage and simpler fixes for spots and blemishes.

• Minor scratches and blemishes — Apply one of the scratch-hiding polishes. Use a light-pigmented polish for birch, oak, and maple. Use one of the dark shades for walnut, cherry, or other dark wood. For some special color, try a sharp-tipped children's crayon that matches, then cover with a paste wax — not a cleaner that may remove the color. Or, try a shoe polish or iodine on reddish mahogany. Specialty stores now offer touch-up sticks for hiding scratches and blemishes in furniture. Rub the repaired area with rottenstone and oil, then finish with an all-over waxing.

• Medium to severe scratches and blemishes — If one of the already-mentioned quick fixes won't do, work on the wood from the bottom up. First, remove any wax by wiping with a cloth dipped in naphtha or other cleaning fluid. Second, stain the wood in the deep scratch or gouge with a matching wood stain. Depending on the size of the blemish, you might want to use a cotton-tipped toothpick or tiny artist's brush. Third, for a dent blemish, fill the area with stick shellac. Select a matching color and apply with a spatula heated over an electric burner — not a gas flame or candle, because the soot will dirty the finish. When all is dry, apply white or orange shellac. You may need several coats to build the finish even with surrounding areas. Sand with very fine (8/0) sandpaper, rub with a paste or rottenstone and oil, then polish with wax.

• Deep burns — Two factors complicate these repairs; the surface is charred and, when all damaged finish and wood is removed, you've got a hole to fill. First, clean away dirt and charred wood or finish with a sharp razor blade and fine sandpaper. Then proceed with stain, shellac stick, and final finish as for deep blemishes above.

• White spots, possibly from water, possibly from causes unknown — Rub the spots with a cloth dampened with light sewing machine oil on which you shake cigarette or cigar ashes. Wipe off immediately. If this doesn't work, try rubbing with rottenstone or salt and oil on a cloth. Another aid may be to heat the area with a pressing iron over a dampened ink-type blotter. Rub the spots between the moist-heat treatments with rottenstone and liquid wax. If the basic finish is varnish or shellac — not lacquer — dab the area with spirits of camphor or peppermint, followed by a rubdown with rottenstone in oil.

• Alcohol stains — Wipe up drink spills as quickly as possible to prevent alcohol from etching the finish. Coasters catch many spills. However, if a stain develops, rub the area with a cloth dampened in ammonia or one of the special finish-restoring products like *Blem.* Silver polish sometimes removes alcohol stains. For deep stains, rub first with rottenstone and oil, then finish with paste wax.

• Heat-caused blemishes — Really deep rings or spots burned into the surface may require completely refinishing the surface. Try removing lighter blemishes by lightly dabbing with a cloth dampened with camphorated oil. Wipe up immediately with a lintless, clean cloth. If this treatment doesn't work, rub the area gently with a rottenstone-in-oil mix on a soft cloth. On a nonlacquer finish, try daubing the blemished area with spirits of camphor or peppermint. When all signs of damage are gone, finish with rubbed wax.

• Ink or paint stains — Colored stains from ink, paint, or stain on bare wood or spots laid bare by wear are practically impossible to remove, particularly from light-colored woods. If you are around when ink spills, blot it up immediately to keep it from penetrating into the wood fibers. For ink marks, clean with a creamy surface cleaner. Try blotting some of the ink stain out of the wood by daubing with a continually rotated clean cloth. Light surface staining can sometimes be removed by rubbing with rottenstone in oil. Paint stains also wipe up more easily if you get to them before the paint dries. Soak old paint stains with linseed oil until they soften, then remove the spots with rottenstone in oil. Nail-polish stains are similar to paint, and if some shellac, varnish, or wax finish keeps the nail polish from penetrating the wood, you can wipe up the stains by using cream cleaning wax or by rubbing with a liquid wax and fine steel wool.

• Candle wax — Keep from removing spots of finish along with candle wax by cooling the wax with an ice cube. Try pulling up the hardened bits with a fingernail or the dull edge of a table knife. Wipe up any melted ice water immediately to keep from water-spotting the surface. Rub the spots where wax was removed with liquid furniture wax.

Keeping Upholstery Looking Fresh — Many of the same cleaning directions for carpets (see page 129) are applicable to the coverings on upholstered furniture. Factory-applied surface treatments help fabrics resist oily and water-mix stains. Spray cans of stain-resistant fabric finish you apply yourself help some. Remove spots and stains quickly before they dry or set for two reasons — they come up easier and they are less likely to leave a permanent stain if treated promptly. Use the detergent-vinegar-water solution described later for food and similar stains, and dry-cleaning solvent for greasy or oily spots.

Special upholstery foams are best for all-over cleaning or to freshen colors. Foams are available in spray cans or you can whip up your own with a tablespoon of mild detergent in a cup of water. Mix with a food mixer until the foam is stiff, almost dry. If you buy a special foam upholstery cleaner, follow directions according to the type you buy. If you use your own whipped suds, scrub into the surface with a circular motion, using a sponge. Immediately, wipe clean with another sponge dampened in clear water but squeezed dry. Too much liquid in either the foam cleaner or in the wiping sponge will soak into the upholstery and be forever drying. You might also consider one of the rental upholstery shampoo machines.

Keep Your Carpets Looking New-Laid Fresh

Three types of cleaning and attention you can do in your home will keep your carpeting looking fresh and clean.

Regular Vacuuming and Brushing — A heavy-duty vacuum cleaner is your best all-purpose tool for cleaning wall-to-wall carpets and room-size rugs. Small throw rugs or accent carpets can be picked up and shaken or vacuumed in place. For carpets, a plain suction machine isn't enough. You need three-way cleaning action — thumping or beating, brushing, and vacuuming. The beating brings imbedded dirt to the surface where it can be sucked up into the cleaner bag. The rotating brush loosens sticky soil or lint enough so the vacuum pulls it up. A common fault is to allow a heavy-duty cleaner to deteriorate. Maybe the belt no longer turns the beater with enough speed to give the carpet a vigorous thump every time it rotates. Or, the fibers on the brush become worn and no longer whisk soil and lint off the surface. Unless you empty the cleaner bag regularly, suction gets weak, and cleaning efficiency drops off. So, keep your cleaner operating effectively and replace the belt and brush at least once a year. Vacuum heavily traveled areas daily or at least three times a week. Work over the other surfaces thoroughly at least once a week — possibly more often, depending on traffic and exposure.

Surface Brightening — Light-colored carpets develop a surface dullness from soil that won't vacuum-clean after weeks and months of wear. When this happens, try one of two methods to restore a clean, bright look to the surface.

• Dry method — Several powder-type cleaners contain solvent or detergent soaked into a filler, usually sawdust. After a thorough vacuuming, sprinkle the powder on the carpet and brush it over the surface. Be sure to follow package directions. The treated particles rub soil from the fibers of the carpet. Allow the carpet to dry, then vacuum up the powder. Dump the cleaner bag several times to assure thorough suction.

• Wet method — Hand methods are okay for shampooing small, heavy-traffic areas. For all-over use, you're better off to rent one of the special carpet-shampoo machines. For cleaning by hand, use only a light, neutral detergent sold for light home laundering — the kind for hand-washing undies. Do not use soap, ammonia, strong detergents or washing soda. Make a light suds of the neutral detergent and apply it sparingly to the carpet surface with a sponge or cloth. Wipe the surface with a gentle motion that doesn't distort the surface pile. Do not use enough suds to wet through to the back of the carpet. Wipe the surface with a clean, damp — not wet — sponge and dry the area quickly. Pick a hot dry day, if possible, or use a fan to speed drying. Remove any furniture or put plastic film under legs to prevent rust stains at the spots.

If you rent a carpet-shampoo machine, use the special cleaner recommended and follow directions carefully. These shampoo machines include a fresh suds container, cleaning brushes, and a vacuum device for slurping up the wet suds.

Spot and Stain Removal — Quick action is again your best answer for spots. Wipe up food and drink spills before they dry. Immediately sop up ink, paint, urine, or vomit to keep these materials from soaking into the fibers. Some nonabsorbent carpet fibers, like nylon or olefin, resist staining more than wool, rayon, or cotton. Basically, you need two kinds of cleaner—

• Detergent-vinegar-water solution for removing food and nonoily stuff. Make your own solution by adding one teaspoonful of a neutral detergent and one teaspoonful of white vinegar to one quart of water. Keep this solution on hand, ready for instant use.

• Dry-cleaning solvent that you buy. This is the same kind of dry-cleaning fluid you use for removing spots from clothing.

For any stain, remove as much of the material as possible with a dull table knife, dry absorbent cloth or white paper towel, or with a brush. Treat the stain according to the kind of material spilled —

• Oily materials — grease, road tar off shoes, butter, hand cream, ballpoint pen ink, bicycle grease, etc. Wipe up as much of the oily spot as possible with a white paper towel, then wipe the stain with a soft cloth dampened in dry-cleaning solvent. Use a clean spot on the cloth with each pass to absorb more of the stain. Repeat until the stain is gone. After the pile dries, brush it to restore the texture.

• Oily-base mixtures of food — coffee, salad dressing, ice cream, milk, cooked sauces or gravy, chocolate, egg, vomit, etc. Scrape and absorb as much of the spill as possible, then gently pick up the remainder with a cloth dampened in the detergent-vinegar solution. When the spot is dry, remove any oily residue with the dry-cleaning solvent. Brush the pile to restore texture when dry.

• Nonoily foods — alcoholic drinks, candy, pop, etc. Soak up as much of the liquid as possible immediately; DO NOT allow drinks to dry on the carpet. Apply the detergent-vinegar-water solution with the mopping action necessary to remove the stain. Reapply as many times as necessary, but prevent soaking the base of the carpet. Brush when dry.

• Tough stuff — paint, gum, lipstick, crayon, heavy grease. Give these stains both barrels. After removing as much of the stuff mechanically as possible, alternate dry-cleaning solvent with detergent-vinegar treatments until the stain disappears. Really bad stains require much patience — and an occasional swat at the culprit to restore your motivation.

• Nail polish — probably the toughest stain of all to remove, nail polish will actually eat up acetate fibers. Also, nail polish remover, mainly an acetate liquid itself, is about the only solvent that will touch the colored stuff. Dyes may not be fast to the remover, so try a bit at some location that won't show to see what the reaction will be. Fast action to blot up as much of the polish as possible is absolutely essential. Use an eye dropper to apply the polish remover, allow it to soften the polish, then scrape as much of the stain as possible. Repeat with a few drops at a time.

• Cigarette burns are not true stains. The burns are charred ends of carpet fibers. Really bad burns can only be fixed by reweaving or by cutting a patch into the carpet — both jobs for professionals. For small burns, try clipping off the charred ends with nail scissors; then treat the area with detergent-vinegar solution to remove residue.

• Other stains or spots — Rust stains require special treatment if they are old and heavy. Light stains may come up with a detergent-vinegar solution treatment. If this doesn't work and the stain is noticeable, call a professional. Permanent ink that has dried also requires special solvents best handled by a pro.

Rather than use homemade spotting materials, you may prefer to invest in one of the several carpet-care kits that contain a variety of solvents and explicit directions for removing stains. One of the best includes a circular stain-guide that automatically describes what to do when the arrow points to a specific stain.

Protect Your Carpets from Moths and Beetles — When wool carpets were the only ones used, moths and carpet beetles grew fat and sassy from the regular diet most homes provided. Not so today. First, wool carpets are usually mothproofed for life at the factory. You don't have to do a thing. Also, nylon, olefin, and other man-made fibers are immune to insects. Insecticides are better than ever, so, if your carpet is not permanently mothproofed, you can easily control moths and beetles by spraying edges with a water-soluble moth and beetle insecticide.

Regardless of how well you vacuum, remove spots quickly, and brighten the surface occasionally, an expensive carpet needs professional cleaning once every year or two. If you can possibly take up room-size carpets, haul them to the rug cleaner's plant yourself — and save about 30 per cent. Plant equipment can clean carpets much better than any treatment in your home. With wall-to-wall carpeting, of course, you're stuck with in-home treatment.

Get Longer Wear from Draperies

You might not think of draperies "wearing", but they do deteriorate from the sun and are damaged from dust and air pollutants unless cleaned. You can extend the life of your draperies by regular attention —

• Dust, soot, and lint should be vacuumed from drapes every four to six weeks — possibly more often in summer when windows are left open.

• Where windows are the same size, rotate the various parts of drapes to different windows for varied exposure to sunlight and heat.

• In air pollution areas, smoke and fumes combine with moisture from the air to form a weak acid that actually weakens drapery fibers. Draperies exposed to direct sunlight show weaknesses more readily than draperies hung on shaded windows. Agitation during dry cleaning may break the fume-weakened fibers and the draperies come back to you with holes. You can retard, if not completely stop, such damage by selecting fiber glass or polyester fiber curtains. Protect drapes further by lining. Cotton, linen, and rayon fibers are most easily damaged.

• Once a year, send draperies to a cleaner for renovation and to remove the buildup of soil and air pollutants. In between times, shake the dust out occasionally.

MONEY SAVERS WHEN MAINTAINING FURNISHINGS AND HOME EQUIPMENT

Budget-bending service calls never seem to happen when you've got an extra $15 you don't know what to do with. That washing machine, dryer, or oven goes on the blink at the worst possible time — and the serviceman usually insists on cash — or you pay plenty extra for credit. A hard look at service for home equipment and the maintenance of furnishings indicates these costs are climbing higher and faster than nearly any other item in your spending plans. Also, planning for service is either ineffective or costly. These are the troubles we faced up to in this chaper, and you learned that —

- *The service call you avoid is the lowest cost call of all — and a little know-how on your part can help you avoid one call out of three.*
- *Service contracts can be a comfort to the mind but a real leak in the pocketbook.*
- *Many equipment faults are repaired free or for only the cost of replacement parts, by utility companies.*
- *Little troubles are frequently easy to repair youself — and much less expensive.*
- *Carpets can be kept looking their best with regular and prompt attention to spots and stains.*
- *Repairing furniture yourself is easier than you think.*
- *Getting longer wear from carpets, draperies, and upholstery is a major key to cutting maintenance expenses for furnishings.*

9

Learn To Know How And Where To Save Cash On Home Maintenance

*Scrimp on maintenance and it shows — by a ragged-edge lawn, peeling paint, cracks in the wallboard, worn patterns on the floor — dozens of places. Price — **housepower** — home management — are all wrapped up in maintenance. If you don't do it yourself or forget to pay for effective maintenance, you can't escape the effects. A rundown house is a drag on the market at selling time. Repairs usually cost more than preventive maintenance. Use, wear, and weather — all take their toll. The facts you need to keep home-maintenace costs low include—*

- *Learning the skills and sources of information you need to handle much of the routine maintenance around your home.*
- *Understanding the cost-effectiveness and income-tax effects of DIY maintenance.*
- *Recognizing the need for preventive maintenance — fixing leaks, examining the reasons for cracks, preventing condensation troubles, and keeping moving parts and equipment well lubricated.*
- *Knowing the differences between preventive and corrective maintenance — and how a fix in time saves cash in the end.*
- *Protecting your house against insects.*
- *Avoiding the home-improvement frauds and quick-buck artists.*
- *Knowing where and how to hire the maintenance help you need for the best job and lowest over-all cost.*

Is "a penny saved — a penny earned?" Not today. This old maxim, originally credited to Ben Franklin, is obsolete, outdated by our income tax laws. Instead of pennies, let's use dollars, and paraphrase the old saying to read — "A dollar saved is a dollar and 16 cents earned." The 16 cents represents income tax — and may easily be more. If you pay higher rates (and most families do), read 18, 20, 24, or 30 cents saved in addition to the dollar not spent. Here's how you figure it—

Suppose you plan to pay a professional $400 to paint the outside of your house. If you are in the 16-per cent income tax bracket, you must earn about 19 per cent more than $400 in order to pay the 16 per cent tax. The mathematics work out like this:

$$x = \frac{\$400}{.84} = \$476$$

$$\frac{76}{400} \times 100 = 19 \text{ per cent}$$

As an alternative, consider that *you* buy the paint, a couple of new brushes, thinner for cleaning brushes, possibly a roller and a ladder. Total cost of the expendable supplies plus the ladder, brushes, and roller comes to $60. Since you pay 16 per cent income tax on the out-of-pocket costs, you must earn about $71 to pay for the paint and equipment. Your labor makes up the difference of $405 ($476 −$71 = $405). So, instead of paying out $400 to the painter plus $76 to Uncle Sam, you pay out $60 for materials plus $11 to Uncle Sam and earn $405 for your labor. And, you pay no income tax on the earned $405. Not bad for about four weekends' work. Also, you still own the brushes, roller, and ladder free and clear for the next job.

Where Do-It-Yourself (DIY) Home Maintenance Pays Off

Not all home-maintenance tasks pay off so handsomely. Painting is a natural for two reasons: 1) Materials are readily available and make up a small portion of the total cost. 2) Skills required are easily learned; patience and time are big factors in the total cost. Paint manufacturers have helped by developing water-mixed paints for both inside and outside — including enamel that cleans up in water only. Wallpaper manufacturers are in the DIY act too. Prepasted and pretrimmed papers make it easy for you to trade a few hours' labor for a completely redecorated room at minimum cost.

Other DIY activities you might consider, even if you are an amateur or inexperienced, include laying floor tile and ceiling tile, installing insulation (see Chapter 2), building in shelves, and simple remodeling. Outdoor tasks range from lawn-building and landscape-planting (see Chapter 11) to building patios, flagstone walkways, and outdoor barbecue ovens. Only your available time and skills limit the jobs you might tackle.

But steer clear of plumbing and electrical work unless you are highly skilled and local regulations permit. Threading and fitting pipes and valves require many special tools. You probably wouldn't use these tools often enough to pay for them. Of course, fixing dripping faucets, running toilets, or plugged drains require only simple tools and a minimum of know-how. Local codes and possibly your fire insurance limit electrical repairs to professionals licensed in the community. Heating system repairs, particularly any adjustments that affect the safety or fire hazards of the heating system, are frequently restricted to licensed mechanics.

Don't be a tool collector. Consider renting special tools needed for a one-time job. But, an investment in tools that will be used again and again, such as basic carpentry tools, good brushes, ladders, etc., usually pays off. When you buy tools, get good ones. Cheap tools that complicate your jobs, use up extra hours of your time, or result in poor quality are a poor investment.

Where to Find Do-It-Yourself Information

You are a new homeowner about to take on the job of keeping your home in good shape. Or, you are a long-suffering homeowner tired of shelling out hard cash for maintenance you believe you might do yourself. In either case, you need specific information and training to develop your skills.

Where to Find Information on Maintaining Your House and Yard — Most of the information you need is free. Or, if there is a cost, it's nominal. Don't be tricked into buying a whole shelf of books. Instead, look at each of the following information sources in turn:

• Free guides and do-it-yourself pamphlets for specific tasks — Paint manufacturers publish an almost inexhaustible array of guides to advise you on home painting problems inside and outside. Check these booklets for information on surface preparation, which paint to use, labor-saving tips, brush or roller choice, and safety. Other company literature covers everything from specialized coatings for leaky basement walls to guides for doing you own plumbing. You'll find pamphlets on pruning shrubs and trees, laying tile, hanging draperies, refinishing furniture, building storage cabinets, installing paneling, and on and on *ad infinitum.* Look for new booklets offered by manufacturers in regular columns of nationally circulated magazines. Product advertisements often include a coupon for a do-it-yourself guide.

• Library books and back issues of magazines — Library shelves abound with home-maintenance books. So, check with your librarian for advice on where to find specialized information. Or, check the READER'S GUIDE for clues to recent magazine articles dealing with a specific subject, such as "How to Lay Floor Tile."

• Government pamphlets and booklets — Either free or at a cost so low as to be practically free are a wide array of pamphlets flooding from the United States government and state agencies. Almost any subject you can name is covered. Your best bet is to look up the subject in one of the indexes, such as:

1. "A Consumer's Guide to USDA Services," Miscellaneous Publication No. 959, issued by the Department of Agriculture. The "Guide" is free, but you must pay for many of the pamphlets and booklets indexed or referenced if you order from the Superintendent of Documents. Instead, try asking your county agent for single copies free. Or, write directly to the specific branch of the USDA or to your congressman or senator for a free single copy.

2. "Consumer Information," also issued as Price List 86 (PL 86) by the Superintendent of Documents, PL 86 lists publications generally relating to consumer interests, with a short summary of the contents of each. Copies of the listed publications are sold by the Superintendent of Documents, but again, you may obtain single copies free.

3. "Selected United States Government Publications," issued every two weeks at no cost. Write to the Superintendent of Documents, U.S. Government Printing Office, Washington, D. C. 20402 and request that your name be added to their mailing list. This listing covers a variety of subjects on which publications have been issued or revised recently by government agencies.

• State-issued publications — Each state also issues booklets and information aids for maintaining your home. State-issued publications are often more useful than the U. S. publications because they reference product trade names rather than generic terms or generalities. Also, state publications are keyed to problems unique to your locality. To locate state publications, address a request for aid to your state's agricultural university or to a university that offers home economics programs. If you are still baffled, ask your county agent or county extension representative where to write for a catalogue of state-issued publications. Single copies are free or sold at nominal cost to residents of the state. This is one of the services your taxes support.

• Magazines offering DIY and how-to information — The mechanical magazines, POPULAR MECHANICS, POPULAR SCIENCE,

SCIENCE AND MECHANICS, and MECHANIX ILLUS-TRATED, offer practical, illustrated information on practically every home maintenance problem you are likely to encounter. Articles are keyed to the season, and over a year, you can accumulate a clipping library of valuable information that will save many times the subscription price of the magazines. FAMILY HANDYMAN also carries home-maintenance articles. AMERICAN HOME regularly publishes specialized articles on home maintenance along with information on new products that may simplify home-maintenance tasks.

Where to Learn Home Maintenance Skills — Information alone is sometimes not enough for you to work on home-maintenance jobs. In past years, such skills were passed along from father to son. Today, such training may be a case of the "blind leading the blind." If your training bypassed the skills of carpentry, painting, plumbing, and electrical repairing, you can build your capabilities by one or more of the following:

• Follow printed instructions and practice — The DIY articles in such magazines as POPULAR MECHANICS are designed for both the experienced craftsman and the novice. Many unskilled home-owners simply lack confidence. But, if you screw up your courage to start and follow the detailed instructions available, you're not likely to run into trouble. Suppose you tackle the job of painting your house. You may make mistakes, and you'll find that practice with brush and/or roller makes the job easier. But, if you follow instructions, you learn as you go. Most first-time painters run into trouble because they don't read the label on the paint can, fail to understand the need for properly preparing the surfaces to be painted, or impatiently skip some important step, such as failing to provide adequate dropcloths to catch drips and splatters.

• Attend adult education classes — If your high school schedules didn't include basic shop or manual training courses when you went to school, investigate the adult education programs offered in your community. High schools often offer courses in basic shop, plumbing, appliances repair, welding, and many other skills. Vocational high schools regularly offer day and night classes in a wide variety of subjects. These courses, again, are partly paid for by your taxes and cost only nominal fees. In shop or carpentry courses, you learn how to finish a basement or attic, install cabinets, or even build an extension to your house.

• Learn from a journeyman or other expert — Follow the apprentice path to some of the skills you need. Plan to help a carpenter build some major project, such as finishing a basement. As you work with him, learn how to handle saws, how to lay out walls and square corners, how to build in space for heating or electrical elements and the like. From this basic training, you can progress on your own by following illustrated instructions in books or magazines.

Preventive Maintenance

Look at your house as one big machine — of sorts. It needs regular care to keep it functioning, operating at peak efficiency, or to prevent it from deteriorating to the point where major corrective maintenance is required. The old saying, "A stitch in time saves nine," while mainly applicable to the care of clothing, also applies in spades to your house. There's a big difference between your home and your car. If you neglect your car, you can trade it in on a new one when things begin to go wrong. Not so with your house. If you neglect your home, then try to sell it later in a rundown condition, you'll lose heavily because the sale price will be discounted from its true or inherent value. A house's appearance implies care and attention — to your loss if the appearance bespeaks neglect. Preventive maintenance not only keeps your house looking "young," but the time, skill, and money you spend pays dividends in satisfaction and in cash when you sell (see Chapter 15). The important places where preventive maintenance pays off are:

Surface Maintenance — "Save the surface and you save all!" — from roof to foundation — inside and outside your house.

• Wall surfaces — Outside walls need regular attention because weather gradually takes its toll. If your house is painted, recover the surfaces at four to eight-year intervals depending on your climate and the kind of paint you use. Stained exterior surfaces usually require more frequent attention. Regular painting or staining not only protects the materials from the onslaught of rain, temperature changes, and deteriorating influences of polluted air, but freshens appearance. Paints, calks, and other materials that protect your home from the weather are constantly being improved. Water-mix paints not only simplify cleanup but tend to last longer than older, traditional coatings. Most painting problems develop if you postpone repainting too long. Then, instead of simple recoating, you may have to scrape, burn, or sand the surface before painting is possible.

You're likely to repaint interior walls mainly to restore appearances. Here, again, paint manufacturers' new products simplify your job. Paints roll or brush on easily, and self-leveling additives tend to eradicate uneven application, brush marks, and roller overlaps. Even a duffer can do a creditable job of repainting.

• Smooth-finish floors — Adopting the Japanese idea of removing our shoes at the door would solve most floor maintenance problems. However, few families could practice such a work-saving plan. There's no reason, though, why children can't shuck their outdoor shoes in a "mud room" or on a rack inside the back entrance. A factory worker may also change his shoes with grease and abrasives particles imbedded in the soles at the entry door. Such tactics save untold cleaning in many households. If changing shoes isn't practical, at least use thick mats to remove as much grime as possible. Then, shake or vacuum the mats regularly, because they fill up quickly.

Regular maintenance is the key to good-looking and long-wearing floors. Wax applied to wood and tile floors prevents wear and provides an easy-to-clean finish. But make sure you use the right wax.

Solvent-base wax requires buffing or polishing whether you apply it in liquid or paste form. The solvent blends new and old waxes so traffic areas can be rewaxed without showing. Liquid forms may contain a cleaner that removes dirt while leaving a thin coating of wax. Use the solvent-base waxes only on wood and cork floors. You can also use these waxes on furniture.

Water-base waxes are known as self-polishing waxes. A few of the self-polishing waxes are designed for machine buffing and do not dry to a high gloss unless buffed. Use only water-base waxes on asphalt tile or rubber tile. Use either the solvent- or water-base waxes on linoleum, vinyl, ceramic tile, concrete, brick, slate, terazzo, or flagstone.

• Carpets and rugs — Whether laid wall to wall or loosely over another floor, soft-finish floors require regular attention. See Chapter 8 for specific maintenance directions.

• Roofs — Nowhere does regular preventive maintenance pay more dividends than in keeping your roof watertight. Regardless of whether your roof is slate or hand-split shakes, find the cause of every tiny leak when you first notice it — and fix it pronto. Leaks can cause ceiling stains at best; at worst, they can rot the wall and ceiling structure of your house and lead to major rebuilding. Roof leaks are most likely to develop around openings or at changes in the roof contour. Look particularly for leaks around chimneys, along the edges of built-up roofs with gravel stops, and along gutters or valleys. Sometimes you'll have to turn "private-eye" to trace leaks to their source because water may travel for several feet or yards before it drops onto a ceiling and spots the surface.

Water-Leak Fixes — Roof leaks are only one of the many sources of water damage to a house. Check up on these other locations around your house:

• Seepage leaks — Openings around windows, doors, at corners, around dormers, or at any other surface change or joint may allow water to enter. Surprising quantities of water run into the open joint where siding abuts window and door frames. Open joints at corners also allow water to run in. Tightly fitted window and screen frames admit water through capillary action. Houses in southern states from Louisiana east to the Atlantic are most likely to be damaged by seepage water because the humid, warm air slows drying and encourages decay and fungus. But houses in most of the other states except those in the arid Southwest can also be damaged from seepage water. Protect your house from seepage-water damage by calking the butt-joints between siding and window or door frames with a permanent, synthetic rubber calk. Water tends to collect in rivulets and run by gravity into joints where the surface is interrupted, as around windows and doors. Also, water runs into cracks or breaks in boards. Examine the roof edge boards, fascia, or gutter supports for evidence of seepage water and correct the fault with calking or roof cement.

• Condensation water — Your house may be suffering from condensation without your knowing it. An effective vapor barrier prevents water vapor from permeating walls toward the outside from warm house interiors. Without this barrier, water vapor condenses inside the wall or on the back side of siding. Too much water in the walls causes rotting and soaks insulation. Examine your house on the outside, particularly outside of bath and kitchen areas. Paint peeling and blistering over large areas signals condensation water back of the surface. (If you see paint peeling around joints, water seepage from the outside through joints is the likely cause.) You may also notice damp, even dripping roof rafters inside an attic where a vapor seal is no longer effective. Vapor barriers are easiest to install before the final wall surface is nailed on during original construction. However, if your house is suffering from condensation inside walls, apply two coats of aluminum paint in a varnish-type base to the inside surface of exterior walls. Then, apply your regular decorative finish over the aluminum paint. The overlapping action of the aluminum flake pigment effectively seals the surface and prevents water vapor from permeating the wall.

• Leaky joints — Joints between tub and wall tile crack open because lumber shrinks as a house dries out. The grout used to seal ceramic tile is about as flexible as glass. So, any shifting or shrinkage quickly breaks the seal. Instead of replacing the hard cement, chip out the grout or cement and seal the joint between tub and tile with a silicone rubber sealant that will remain flexible and keep the joint leak tight for the life of your house. Check similar joints between tiles in a shower, particularly at corners. Look also for leaks around kitchen sinks, wash basins built into counters, and around all plumbing. Finding and stopping leaks when they start is the key to keeping the bill for water damage to a minumun.

Lubricants Keep House Systems Operating — A touch of oil or grease at the right time is a cost-saving action that prevents breakdowns in everything from the furnace blower to casement windows. Drop light machine oil on the hinge pins at doors, particularly those holding outside doors, at least once a year. Coat sliding windows and the operating arms of window opening hardware once or twice a year with a grease or spray silicone lubricant. Keep bearing oil reservoirs full in blower fans and pump motors. Make a list of the items that operate in your house. Anything that is motor driven may require lubrication. But, manufacturers years ago despaired of asking forgetful homeowners to lubricate their equipment. Now most motors and mechanical equipment from lawn mowers to air conditioners are built with sealed, nonfriction bearings that last through the useful life of the item. So, if your house is old, many of the fans, motors, hand-operated equipment may still require regular lubrication. Just a few drops of oil regularly may be all that's necessary to prevent a costly breakdown. Include everything on your list that moves, from garage doors to hand-cranked windows. If you find that an item needs oil or grease, add it to your list. If the item is lubricated for life, forget it. Check your instruction books (if you still have them) or look for instruction plates riveted to the equipment for lubrication directions; then follow them.

Look For Signs of Trouble

Corrective home maintenance differs from routine preventive maintenance. That is, when you find something haywire, you fix it. Cracks, breaks, leaks, and malfunctioning mechanical equipment usually require some form of corrective maintenance rather than regular attention. Some faults are not serious; others may require immediate action. Learn to know which are which—

Cracks — Damage or unsightly appearance from cracking affects just about every house ever built. To learn how to live with cracks, become familiar with the story cracks tell you about your home's construction and the clues they provide for corrective action.

• Tiny wall cracks usually result from wood shrinkage. Most houses are built with green lumber, and a 2x12 floor joist can shrink as much as 3/4 inch as it dries. Something has to give, and the least flexible part of the wall is the plaster or wallboard. Cracks show up around door and window openings or between interior and exterior walls. Such cracks are common, so don't despair. After about a year, fill the cracks with spackle, sand smooth and repaint.

• Large diagonal wall cracks usually result when one corner of your house settles more than the rest of the house. Crack size tells you how much of a problem you have. Such differential settling usually results from building on filled dirt. A very large crack may require foundation work. If cracking stops after a full warm-cold, wet-dry cycle, the settling has probably stopped. Repair the damage and paint over the area. If cracking continues, call in a builder to correct the fault.

• Large ceiling cracks running parallel with floor joists plus diagonal wall cracks usually indicate some fault in the framing that supports interior walls. You're most likely to notice such cracks on a bearing wall that supports the ridge line of a roof. Such cracks may call for additional bracing or structure under the bearing wall.

• Concrete floor cracks may result from shrinkage of the slurpy concrete mix that is easy to push from the truck to far corners of a floor. When the excess water evaporates, the concrete shrinks — and you have cracks. Such cracks are likely to be fairly thin and cause few problems. They should be filled before applying tile or roll goods to the floor. Wide, gaping cracks with noticeable differences in slope result from a failure of the subgrade. Either the sand and gravel under the floor is washing away or the builder poured the floor over loosely packed clay or dirt. In either case, cracking may indicate a need to repair the subgrade or to determine what is washing away the fill under the floor. Simply filling the crack with a slurry of cement and fine sand will not do; the crack will continue to open until the basic fault is corrected. You may notice three other types of concrete cracks:

1. Floor cracks from six to ten inches away from and parallel to outside walls indicate that fill under the floor has settled. Concrete close to the wall is being supported by the extension of the footing. Unless the settling continues, repairing the crack and covering it with

flooring is usually sufficient.

2. Radiating cracks around posts or supports indicate they are supporting excessive weight. Steel pipe lally columns, for example, may be resting only on the floor rather than on a footing under the floor. Possibly, additional weight has been added to the column, as happens when a major addition is built topside without considering the strength of the foundation or supporting structure. If cracks radiate out from a steel column used to jack up a low spot in the floor above, the floor is overloaded. Planks, several patio blocks or a poured footing may be necessary to spread the weight over a greater area.

3. Cracks spreading outward from a chimney also result from excessive weight. Normally, a special footing cast under the floor supports the heavy masonry chimney. If the cracks radiate at angles from the chimney, you can blame an inadequate footing. If cracks parallel the face or ends of the chimney, the weight of the chimney is causing it and the footing below to settle at a slower or faster rate than the floor itself. Note particularly if there appears to be more settling along one side or end than the other. Such differential settling can tip the chimney. Repair tipping immediately.

Leaks — In addition to the leaks already mentioned in the house itself, you may find leaky basement walls or floors.

• Basement wall leaks usually result from a crack or break in the wall. Water may actually run from the crack and across the floor to a drain. For such bad leaks consider several causes:

1. Where does the water come from? You may have diverted surface drainage from its natural course to your basement wall by grading or foundation dams. Unless the ground water can be diverted away from your house, leaks will continue to develop. Extensive grading may be necessary. Another solution may be to install an automatic sump pump in a well outside the wall to remove the water. And, don't overwater shrubs planted around the house. Some of this water may be finding its way into your basement.

2. If the natural terrain does not appear to be the cause and water leakage is barely noticeable, you might try chipping out the crack and refilling it with an expanding concrete patching compound, like *Kay-Tite*. For small cracks that drip only occasionally, wait until the crack is dry, brush out all loose material, and calk with one of the polysulfide rubber calks, such as PRC 5000 (Products Research Company).

3. Leaks too large to seal with patching cement or calking may require a footing drain. To install one after a house is built, dig around

the outside of the basement wall to the level of the footing under foundation or basement walls. Install drain tile, cover with gravel, and connect the tile to a storm sewer or to a sump well. An automatic-operation pump lifts collected water to the surface where it can drain away from the house. Well-built houses include such drains when they are built. If your house had one, check to make sure it is not plugged. You can open it with a powered router or possibly a hose. Ground water soaks into the drain tile and drains away without developing the hydrostatic pressure that causes basement wall leaks.

Rust — Reddish ferrous oxide, commonly called rust, is a harbinger of trouble. Galvanized steel gutters, flashing, downspouts, heating ducts, and piping will rust in time. The zinc galvanizing merely holds off corrosion of the iron by sacrificing itself to the corrosive effects of oxygen and water. You can hold off rust and save the cost of expensive repairs by keeping the zinc coating intact. Several of the cost-saving preventive actions in this category are —

• Gutters — Weak acids form in gutters when standing water leaches chemicals from collected leaves or sun-deteriorated roofing tar. At least twice a year, remove any collected leaves, twigs, and dirt from gutters. If water stands regularly in part of a gutter, correct the slope. At least 1/16 inch drop per foot óf gutter is necessary to assure drainage. Stick a 1/16-inch filler block under one end of a foot-long level. When the bubble centers, slope is correct. House settling or bending of gutter hangers can easily change slope. Finally, coat the inside of gutters at least once every two years with a plastic asphalt roof coating that contains asbestos fibers and aluminum flakes.

• Flashing — Around chimneys and over windows, doors and changes in walls, metal flashing helps to keep water from seeping into your house. Protect existing flashings, because they are expensive to replace. Paint galvanized metal flashings with a zinc-bonding primer and finish with a paint designed for metal. Undersides of flashings may be coated with an asphalt roof coating if you can reach them.

• Heating ducts — Galvanized steel ducts may rust when exposed to high humidities, such as in a crawl space. Or, if your house is airconditioned, condensate may set up a corrosive action inside ducts. High humidity usually attacks only the outside. Protect these surfaces with prime and finish coats of paint designed for application to metal. A better way is to cover the ducts with insulating material (see Chapter 2). Condensation inside ducts can be difficult to control. Here, again, some coating is necessary to keep water and air from the surface. One of the synthetic rubber coatings will do, but a better long-term solution is to cover the inside of ducts with insulation sealed at the joints. The insulation can be bedded in mastic cements that also protect the metal surface.

• Piping — Galvanized pipe seldom rusts through from the outside. However, rust spots from inside may break through to cause leaks. There is little you can do to prevent such rusting. High-quality houses today are built with copper or plastic piping that resists corrosion.

Prevent Insect Attacks

Insects of all kinds can be a nuisance or deadly destructive, such as termites and carpenter ants. About the only state not affected by termites is Alaska. These insects live in the ground but feed on dampish lumber in a house, chewing away at the insides, with little surface indication of their presence. Because they flourish in warm, damp climates, states with wet, warm weather are most likely to support termites. If your house is infested with termites (and you may have to call for professional help to find out), don't try to handle them yourself. Call an exterminator. However, your best offense here is a good defense — keep all kinds of ants, termites, and other insects out of your house. Practice these preventive measures against insect infestations in your home —

• Keep all wood away from the ground. Not only does wood rot quickly when in contact with earth, but termites, ants, and other crawling insects use this shortcut into your house.

• Treat the soil around foundation walls with chlordane.

• Fill spaces between bottom of wallboard and the floor with calking to close off inviting runs for insects, particularly ants and roaches.

• Use the right chemical and control measure for various insects. The lowest-cost sources of definitive information of insect control are government pamphlets published to help you — the individual homeowner. Some of the ones you'll find most useful are:

Subterranean Termites, their Prevention and Control in Buildings (G-64) 15c.
Soil Treatment — An Aid in Termite Control (L-324) 5c.
Ants in the Home and Garden: How to Control Them (G-28) 10c.
Cockroaches: How to Control Them (L-430) 5c.
Controlling Household Pests (G-96) 15c.
Silverfish and Firebrats: How to Control them (L-412) 5c.

Order these pamphlets from the Superintendent of Documents, U. S. Government Printing Office, Washington, D. C. 20402.

Save Money When Buying Maintenance

Despite all the potential savings from DIY maintenance, you will need help for some jobs. How and where you buy professional maintenance greatly affects your dollar cost.

HOW TO DO IT: *Avoid Frauds and Quick-Buck Contractors* — Home maintenace and improvement work continues to attract the professional crook. Some of the tried-and-proved-wrong frauds you can easily avoid include—

• Door-to-door salesmen for everything from a custom-installed water softener to new siding for your old house. Categorically — avoid any door-to-door salesman who tries to sell you storm windows, new siding, a new roof, a fire- or burglar-alarm system, or any of the other products or services you might conceivably need. Door-to-door salesmen represent do-it-quick, scoot-off-with-your-money outfits that will not be around to make good on the guarantee they talk about so blithely. Remember, if a builder, painting contractor, or general fix-up man is any good at all, he can get all the work he can possibly handle through word-of-mouth referrals. A legitimate outfit doesn't need to sell door to door.

• Avoid maintenance or home-improvement companies that advertise in the television section of your Sunday or daily newspaper. For some reason not fully understood, persons who read the ads along with program listing from TV schedules are suckers for the glowing promises of good work at give-away prices — and lots of credit.

• Avoid any attempt to use the old referral fraud where you " — get your new siding installed for practically no cost by earning rebates from friends who buy on your referral." This scheme has two pitfalls — 1) You may get a call that mentions one of your friends' names — so the call slips by one of your defenses. 2) The idea appeals to that "somethingfornothing" weakness in most of us. The idea, as presented is, " — we'll do the job. When it's finished, you can show your friends what a wonderful improvement it is and you can supply us with names of prospects. We do the selling, but every prospect name you supply, we will rebate part of the cost." Sounds great! But, it doesn't work. Save your money — and your friends' names. Any job such an outfit can do, you can hire done better for less by a local, legitimate outfit.

• Avoid the sales gimmick of "practically no cost to you because we have picked your house to be a showcase, a sample installation that we can use for pictures and advertising." Flatterly frequently gets these birds somewhere. But, don't you fall for this rotten-apple idea that never seems to go away. The usual gimmick is to quote a big reduction in price from an obviously inflated price — so you think you are getting a bargain — for "using your house as an advertisement."

• Examine carefully the credentials of any person who arrives unannounced at your door proclaiming to be a "fire inspector," "surveyor of insect infestations," or any one of many other seemingly official titles. One nationwide company used the "furnace inspector" gambit to gain entrance for the supposed purpose of examining a home's heating system. Most of the time these "inspectors" found a major fault in the furnace, alarmed the owner over safety, and recommended immediate repairs that the phony inspector's company could make quickly and with no money down. Most of the recommended repairs were unneeded and the homeowner paid as much as 100 per cent more than a legitimate shop would have charged. So, beware of phony inspectors. If you have any doubt, call the fire department, Better Business Bureau, or police to check on credentials.

Find Local Tradesmen for Your Home Maintenance — Old Charlie, who could fix anything with little more than a screwdriver and paintbrush, has disappeared. But, there are many hard-working journeymen painters, plumbers, carpenters, concrete finishers, brick masons, and gardeners who depend on repeat business with their customers for their living. Nearly every community has these home maintenance specialists; your problem — find them! They don't advertise. They are like good dentists or doctors; they already have so much business their problem is finding time to handle all the jobs offered by satisfied customers. They may not be taking on any new clients. The reason they are so busy is because they work hard, know their business, make good on any unsatisfactory work, use good materials they know will stand up, and charge a fair price — not a low price, but a fair price. And, you'll probably pay them in cash. How do you find these paragons of home maintenance service? Try one or all of these ideas—

• Ask a long-time resident of your community. The man you're looking for has probably been around for years, so a native, or long-time resident is likely to know him by name.

• Ask a friend, neighbor, or business associate for leads. Maybe they have already been the route of looking for help and you can short-circuit the process. Also, you can check on the man's or company's record. If the man did a good job for your friend, he is likely to do a good job for you.

• Ask another tradesman you respect for a reference. If you have located a good car mechanic or gardener, ask him for a lead to a good plumber or painter. Tradesmen get to know other professionals — and also how to avoid the fast-buck charlies.

• Join one of the local Home Owners Associations. These locally organized associations act as your agents when you have an emergency or a maintenance problem. They check out tradesmen, journeymen, and home-maintenance companies for their skill, fair dealing, and prices. Your membership fee covers a number of services, but the one important to you is referral to a reputable professional for doing your home repair and maintenance. You're not likely to get any price bargains working through a Home Owners Association, but you are likely to get good work at a fair price. If you don't, you have a place to bring your compaint — someone on your side who understands your problems.

Hire Part-Time or Student Help — Many of your maintenance tasks may not need the practiced hand of a pro. If not, consider hiring willing hands you find through a variety of sources:

• High school and college-bound students vary widely in skills and attitude, but if you find a good one, you can get your house painted, lawn and garden cared for, and much of the heavy work associated with your own do-it-yourself activities for less cash than you would spend hiring a professional. Students have little overhead and seldom earn enough to pay income taxes, so they work for less cash per hour. However, they may be worth less per hour unless they have learned basic skills and know how to work. Before hiring students, check their references by calling others they have worked for. If you find a student through some agency, such as a Kiwanis Student Job Service project or some other plan for helping students find work, check for comments from others who have hired a particular boy. Then, observe and rate a boy's performance during the first few hours or days he may be working. You can tell, for example, after watching a boy handle paint brushes, ladders, and drop cloths whether he will do the kind of a paint job you require. You're likely to get more work for your money if you hire a student to work along with you on a project than if you turn him loose by himself.

• Moonlighters may help you when specific skills are needed, such as plumbing, laying tile, painting, or carpentry. These skilled mechanics work at their regular job during the day, but they also work for themselves during the evening or on week ends. Union regulations vary in different communities, and enforcement is not uniform. Usually, union members are forbidden to work at their own skill, but they may work at some other related skill — or they simply disregard union rules. You can locate moonlighters through stores that sell supplies — paint stores, lumber yards, floor covering stores, etc. Or, you can ask among your friends or associates for a lead to a skilled mechanic who is looking for extra money.

• Part-timers may be looking for extra work outside of their own skills. Teachers, firemen, or factory workers may work part time to earn extra money. These part-timers, like students, may not be so skilled as full-time professionals, so check references and watch their progress at the beginning. Some part-timers may be persons who are selling skills learned in their own **DIY** activities. Locate these part-timers through ads in the classified section of local, weekly newspapers, through signs posted on community bulletin boards, through local employment agencies, or by word of mouth from friends.

MONEY SAVERS WHEN MAINTAINING YOUR HOME

You can't avoid spending money on home maintenance — some time. If you put off those maintenance chores too long, you pay more for repairs or your home loses value when you sell. Your best, most cost-effective approach is to keep your home young as it lives — to keep problems from piling up — to spend a penny preventing troubles to keep from spending dollars to fix them later. Knowing what to do and when to do it can be your best long-term money savers for home maintenance. Some of the cash-saving maintenance practices you learned —

* *How labor — yours or the type you hire — accounts for most of the cost of home maintenance. Here's where doing-it-yourself really pays off.*
* *How keeping the surface of your home in good shape saves the whole structure.*
* *How spending a little to prevent problems keeps repair costs to a minimum.*
* *How to pick up the know-how and skills you need to keep your house living young at the lowest cost.*
* *How door-to-door salesmen and bait advertising prey on unsuspecting homeowners — and how you can avoid these expensive pitfalls.*
* *How you can find the true craftsman to correct faults when they develop.*
* *How you can spend less muscle-money by hiring part-time and student help for some home maintenance jobs.*

10

Prevent Costly Damage Or Losses
By Being Prepared For Emergencies

Floods, earthquakes, tornadoes, hurricanes, and other wide-area disasters are almost impossible to defend yourself and your home against. But you CAN do something about fires, some effects of floods, and burglaries. Here's how —

- *Prevent careless fires by keeping your home fire-safe.*
- *Be prepared in case a fire does strike by an early warning and by having the tools you need handy.*
- *Develop your house defenses against surface water and backed-up sewers.*
- *Make your house as burglar-proof as possible.*
- *Be prepared for electrical power outages.*

"It won't happen to us!" you say. "Fires, floods, and burglaries only happen to the other guy!" Nonsense! Only the eternal optimism of the human race keeps families from planning for trouble. You hope it won't happen to you. But if an emergency strikes, you can save your family from catastrophic loss, injury — possibly death — if you are prepared. So, borrow the motto of the Boy Scouts — BE PREPARED.

Fire

In an average year, 550,000 fires strike homes in the United States, causing 6,300 deaths, injuring 250,000 other persons, and damaging property to the tune of about $330 million. Where do these fires occur? In the living room 37 per cent, kitchen 22 per cent, bedrooms 13 per cent, and the rest in attic and basements. You can reduce the chances of a fire starting in your home by regular inspections. Use the checklist in Fig. 10-1. You can reduce the probability of damage, injury, and cost from a fire by installing an alarm, having the right kind of fire extinguisher quickly available, or other precaution, such as fire-resistant paint.

	Yes	No
Household — Do you —		
Keep oily or paint rags in airtight cans or dispose of them immediately after use?		
Throw out trash, papers, rags, and old clothing?		
Keep dust mop in well-ventilated space?		
Store paint, thinner, and other combustible liquids in tight metal cans — away from heat?		
Prohibit use of gasoline, benzine, or flammable cleaning fluids in the house?		
Forbid use of fire-starter fluids in fireplace or barbecue grill?		
Keep kitchen stove, oven, and rotisserie free of grease?		
Keep matches away from children in secure place?		
Clean up scrap and sawdust from shop?		
Keep plenty of ash trays around?		
Make it a rule never to smoke in bed?		
Heating System — Do you —		
Service and inspect central heating system once a year?		
Make sure flues and chimney do not contact combustible materials?		
Inspect room or wall heaters regularly?		
Turn off oil and gas room heaters when sleeping?		
Make sure heaters, stoves, and cooking appliances are separated from drapes, curtains, and clothing?		
Electrical — Do you —		
Repair frayed electrical cords promptly?		
Limit fuses to no more than 15 amps?		
Use extension cords only when in good condition and not under rugs, in contact with metal hangers, or through doors?		
Use cooking appliances and pressing iron with heat-limit controls?		
Buy only those electrical goods approved by the UL?		
General — Do you —		
Keep yard free of dry leaves and burnable trash?		
Keep fuel for lawn mowers and boats in safe, metal cans?		
Forbid use of matches or candles for light in attic, closets, or basement?		

Figure 10-1. Fire Prevention Checklist

Fire Extinguishers — You can choose from at least seven types of fire extinguishers for use around your home. A fire isn't just any kind of blaze — nothing's that simple any more. If you use the wrong type of extinguisher on the wrong class of fire, you could be in trouble — so, learn the differences. The fire you extinguish could be in your home!

• Class A fires — Most common are the fires where wood, paper, cloth, or "trash" burns. Water, mixed with some foaming agent or forced from a container by chemical or gaseous action, is your most effective way to fight Class A fires. Extinguishers adapted for these fires include:

1. Plain water in a tank with a hand pump.
2. Water solution of bicarbonate of soda, with a separate container of sulfuric acid. When these tanks are turned upside down, the acid mixes with the soda solution and the liquid spews out from the hose under pressure generated by the chemical reaction.
3. Plain water with a carbon dioxide cartridge. When you turn the tank over and bump it, the carbon dioxide cartridge breaks open and the gas propels the water from the tank.

• Class B fires — Hot and likely to spread fast are fires that burn flammable liquids, such as gasoline, oil, and kerosene, and oil-base chemicals, such as tar, paint, and kitchen greases. Extinguishers adapted for fighting Class B fires include:

4. Foam formed when a solution of aluminum sulfate and bicarbonate of soda are mixed by turning the tank upside down. The foam spews from the tank under chemically generated gas pressure. Foam can also be used on Class A fires. DO NOT — repeat — DO NOT use water extinguishers against flammable liquid fires, because burning gasoline and other liquids float on water. As the burning liquids float, they spread the fire and are not extinguished.
5. Carbon tetrachloride liquid must be pumped out of the extinguisher by hand. In the presence of heat it evaporates to smother the fire. Carbon-tet is effective against Class B fires only. Be careful to avoid breathing the vapors, particularly in a small space.

• Class C fires — Electrical in origin, Class C fires usually burn something close by. Never use a water-type extinguisher on Class C fires because of the electrical shock hazard. Extinguishers adapted for fighting Class C fires include:

6. Carbon dioxide from pressure tanks is released by pulling a pin or a trigger mechanism. The CO_2 smothers a fire by displacing the oxygen necessary to keep a fire burning. Carbon dioxide extinguishers are effective against Class B and C fires but are not effective against Class A fires.

7. Dry chemicals include bicarbonate of soda mixed with other chemicals in a pressure tank. A trigger releases CO_2 gas that propels the dry chemical mix onto the fire. There the chemicals develop a smothering gas. The dry chemical extinguisher is the only one that is effective against all classes of fires. These extinguishers also provide more pounds of effective chemical per pound of total extinguisher than other types, so they are particularly adaptable for home use.

One of the best fire extinguishers, one that won't run dry, is a hose attached to your water system and mounted, ready for instant use in a kitchen cabinet or on the wall of a furnace room or shop. Just remember not to use water to extinguish electrical or flammable liquid fires.

Remember these several points about fire extinguishers: 1) You need them when and where you are likely to find a fire. Keep an extinguisher handy in the kitchen, preferably near the living room. Keep another one handy in the garage and another in the basement near shop and furnace room. 2) Make sure the extinguisher is approved by the Underwriters Laboratories. This independent testing organization determines the effectiveness of an extinguisher before awarding its UL seal. If the extinguisher doesn't carry the UL seal, don't buy it. 3) Maintain your extinguishers in full operating condition. Instructions for checking and refilling are noted directly on the unit or in an accompanying booklet.

Fire Alarms — Early and definite notice that a fire has started in your house gives you a chance to get your family out to safety. Also, an early alarm gives you the jump on a fire just starting and possibly a chance to extinguish it before it spreads. Two kinds of alarms are marketed for home use — the single-station, self-contained alarm, and the central, multistation alarm. An alarm must detect a fire and then activate some bell, horn, or other device to waken sleepers. Single-station alarms usually include a heat-sensitive metal that melts to release a gas propellant which, in turn, blows a loud horn. Multistation alarm systems are electrical and detect a fire by some heat-sensitive device. When the detector activates the system, the electrical system rings a bell, horn, or other loud device. With a multistation system, you can locate the noise device near sleeping quarters and spot detectors around the house at a number of fire-sensitive locations.

Check these features to make sure you have a reliable, effective fire-alarm system: 1) A loud alarm, loud enough to wake the soundest sleeper. 2) Approval by Underwriters Laboratories (UL). 3) A back-up electrical power system that will sound the alarm even if the house electrical system fails. 4) A means for testing or checking the system.

Do not buy a fire-alarm system from a door-to-door salesman. If you do, you are likely to pay as much as $600 for a system. Beware of salesmen posing as fire inspectors, counselors, or researchers. Instead, buy your system from a reputable local firm or from a mail-order house.

Fire Retardants — Two types of flame or fire retardants can slow the spread of fire in your home. Fire retardants buy you time to get your family out of the house to safety and may keep a fire small enough to extinguish quickly — by yourself or the fire department.

• Special fire-retardant paints have reached such a state of development that the Underwriters Laboratories have approved a number for home application. Fire-retardant paints work either of two ways: One type releases nontoxic vapors that help to smother the fire and prevent it from spreading. A second type swells and puffs up to many times its original thickness to act as an insulator. The thick layers of chemical and air keep underlying wood relatively cool for many minutes. Remember, paints are not fireproof. Use them in furnace rooms, garages, shops, attics, closets, and storage areas where a fire may start without being noticed. Apply the paints with a brush or roller like other paints. Although many of the fire-retardant paints are colored and can be used in place of normal paints, they cost up to double the price of normal paints. Also, for best protection, fire-retardant paints should be applied in three coats.

• Fabrics of all kinds can be treated chemically for fire resistance. Drapes and curtains aid the rapid spread of fire unless treated. Specific directions are contained in a government pamphlet, *Making Household Fabrics Flame Resistant,* Catalogue No. A 1.35:454/3, from Superintendent of Documents, U.S. Government Printing Office, Washington, D.C. 20402 — cost five cents.

Prevent Burglaries

Two preventive measures help you reduce the hazard of burglars breaking in and looting:

• Improved locks — Ordinary key locks open easily in the fingers of professional burglars. Many key-in-knob locks open easily for nearly anyone who tries. Protect your home by one or all of these special locks that make entry into your home difficult:

1. Door chains that cannot be opened from the outside.
2. Dead-bolts that also cannot be opened from the outside. Either of these means can secure all doors but the one used to exit when no one is home.
3. Secure key locks that defy most burglars. Contact your lock-and-key specialist or ask your local police for clues to these secure locks.
4. Combination locks that secure without keys. As many as five buttons or plungers must be operated in the correct sequence before these locks will release.
5. Window locks that prevent entry through windows, unless they are broken. Some window locks prevent a window from being opened wide from a partly-open position.

• Burglar alarms — You can protect your home from burglars with an inexpensive alarm system keyed to windows and doors. Home systems usually include detection through wires, infrared sensitive elements, or electric-eye units. When something trips one of these detection units, the alarm system rings a loud bell, preferably inside and outside. The outside bell may bring help even if you are away from the house. More expensive systems signal an entry at a remote station, either the police or a private protection agency. Burglar booby-trap systems cost more than fire-alarm systems and may run from $75 to as much as $500. Here, too, the fask-buck artists operate door-to-door. Check with your local police or Better Business Bureau for a reliable, local installer. Set up your system to protect all basement and ground-floor points of entry — doors and windows.

Floods and Backed-Up Sewers

Flood waters that cover hundreds of square miles are true disasters. There is little you can do in such area-wide disasters except to prepare for the worst. Keep alert, listen to news of water crests, and, if the flood does threaten your house, remove your portable furnishings and belongings early. However, you can protect your house from lesser floods by one of the following:

Flooded Storm Sewers — Even though flood waters may not lap around your house, they can shut off normal rain and storm sewers. If your foundation drain tile system is hooked into such a storm sewer, you may find water seeping or flooding into your basement through the joint between walls and floor. Reduce such damage by installing a sump pump that collects any basement water and pumps it to the outside. Collection pipes may be under the floor and around the full perimeter inside the foundation. An automatic float-actuated switch will turn on the pump as soon as water begins collecting in the sump. Be prepared with a hand-operated pump in case floods or storms knock out electrical power.

Sewer Back-Ups — Related to the flooded storm sewers is the more frequent case of sanitary sewers backing up and flooding a basement. A flood, pump failure, or blockage may cause a sewer to back up. Since the basement floor drain is the lowest outlet, the back-up appears there first. To prevent damage in such cases, install a basement drain with a threaded connection under the floor plate. Then, when flood or back-up threatens, screw a standpipe into the threads. The standpipe can be as high as the basement ceiling. Any back-up will rise in the pipe and not flood a basement unless the level rises above the top of the pipe. Since water seeks its own level, the small amount of water in the standpipe counts for as much hydrostatic pressure on the sewer system as a whole basement full. If your laundry tubs are in the basement, install a large gate valve in the sewer line or use a screw connection with a standpipe similar to the one for the floor drain.

What To Do When Your Freezer Stops

Home freezers may store several hundred dollars worth of food. If the freezer stops, you run a chance of this much food spoiling. Freezers can protect food for as long as five days if the freezer is big, full of food, and not opened. So, if the power fails, determine whether there is much chance of it being off for longer than a day or two. On islands and in remote areas, neighbors sometimes band together to purchase a gasoline-powered generator. They take turns using the generator to take the temperature of the freezer down to below zero once every two days.

If the power is on and your freezer unit fails, determine how long it will take to fix it. If a serviceman can't get to the unit for three days, transfer the frozen food to a commercial locker plant or to a neighbor's freezer. If this doesn't work, buy dry ice and keep it in the freezer. About 50 pounds of dry ice will keep the temperature down to 15 degrees for about two days. Look for dry ice at a local dairy or cold-storage warehouse. If power outages are frequent in your area, be prepared for a power interruption by doing the following:

- Run your freezer colder than usual, down to 20 degrees below, if possible. The extra cold temperature will keep food longer after power stops.
- Find a source for dry ice before you need it.
- Select a freezer with better than average insulation.
- When all else fails, keep food canning equipment and supplies on hand and be prepared to can thawed food to save it.

MONEY SAVERS TO REDUCE LOSSES OR DAMAGE FROM EMERGENCIES

Only the eternal optimism of the human race or an unwillingness to face the prospect that some disaster might strike keeps you from taking a few, inexpensive precautions against emergencies. The big area-like calamities strike rich and poor alike. But, you can borrow a motto from the Boy Scouts and — "Be Prepared." A few precautionary steps may save you thousands of dollars. Some of the hints included —

- A checklist you can use to find potential fire hazards in your house.
- Methods for reducing the fire dangers in your home.
- Installing fire extinguishers and learning how to use them — just in case.
- Installing built-in alarms for both fire and burglar protection.
- Recognizing potential damage from floods and how to avoid damage.
- Being prepared for the storm that knocks out power to your house.

11

Keep The First Cost Of Landscaping To A Minimum And The Maintenance Cost To Practically Nothing

Sink $10,000 in landscaping for your home? You could do it — easy. But, you'd find it difficult to see the $10,000 value. You could get much the same result for 1/25th as much. Gardening, lawnkeeping, and general outdoorsmanship around your house are personal. Landscaping reflects time, attention, and effort as much as money. Maybe you maintain your lawn and plantings because "everybody in the neighborhood does." You want to keep up. And, there's always one in an area that sets the pace — makes it tough for the rest. Whatever your interests or needs, you can dress the outside of your house in green (and not the kind with past presidents and numbers on it) by —

- *Learning the rudiments of landscape planning — then doing your own.*
- *Growing your own deep seedbed for your lawn — instead of hauling in a carpet of "black dirt."*
- *Picking the plants you need at bargain or "no cost" prices.*
- *Scrounging for plants from cuttings and from wild areas.*
- *Following the farmers to the good buys in fertilizer.*
- *Controlling weeds and insects effectively at low cost.*

"People who buy a finished landscape must be planning on living only one year," a neighbor remarked after watching full-size plants going in and turf being rolled onto lawn areas. There's no question that well-planned landscaping enhances the appearance and market value of your house. Yet, landscaping can cost up to 30 per cent of the value of the house — or practically nothing. What accounts for the difference? Patience and gardening know-how — yours!

What Do You Want in Landscaping?

Is gardening a hobby with you or anyone in your family? Does puttering around the plantings, trimming the lawn, and talking knowledgeably about plants with their Latin names genuinely absorb much of your time? Or, do you consider every minute spent on your lawn and grounds as time that could be spent more enjoyably on the golf course?

Landscaping affects your home's market value, of course, but not in proportion to costs. Suppose you spent $8,000-$10,000 on a professionally-designed and installed landscape around your house. If your house is valued at around $20,000 without such expensive landscaping, you would receive little credit in an appraisal for a mortgage loan. You would find the house easier to sell, and the sale price may be slightly higher. But, you would recover only a small part of the money spent on landscaping.

If your lawn is weedy and plants are scraggly around the house, the appraisal suffers little; the house still receives primary attention. But, you will find selling more difficult, and the price you settle for may be less. Real estate agents, loan arrangers, and appraisers consider plantings and lawn a personal thing with the owner. A good gardener can make almost any home a beauty spot. A disinterested owner can allow beautifully landscaped home grounds to revert to weeds in a single season.

The price you pay for landscaping can vary widely — more than any other single expenditure around your house. Why? Because how you plan your landscaping, the money-saving shortcuts you use, and your scrounging abilities can cut the cost of landscaping to practically nothing.

Here's how to do it —

Learn How To Be Your Own Landscaping Planner

There's no substitute for know-how! You've got to know what is good and what is bad when planning your landscaping. Don't depend on the thin advice of a door-to-door plant salesman. Don't hem and haw when talking with a nurseryman about plants. Even if you are not a gardening buff, learn the essentials before lifting a rake or buying even one little seed.

Search Out Sources of Free Advice — Gardening attracts garrulous persons who love to lean on a shovel and talk about their plants. If you are new to an area, strike up an acquaintance with the owner of that beautifully kept house on the next street. Ask him how he keeps his lawn so green — and why his plantings around the house look so healthy. Such an opening is bound to start an outpouring of practical advice. Most nurseries supply advice along with seed and fertilizer. Tap this source for answers to specific questions. Don't hesitate to ask what may seem like stupid questions. You'll be pleasantly surprised at how much you learn from the answers. In addition to these common sources, look further for information.

• Magazines, particularly those with regional editions, such as SUNSET, AMERICAN HOME, and BETTER HOMES AND GARDENS, are loaded with ideas and suggestions for planning your landscaping. Search out back issues for March, April, September, and October for seasonal planting ideas.

• Library shelves are loaded with books on landscape planning and gardening. Check with your local librarian for books that are keyed to your local conditions. Frequently, local garden clubs or a university's botany department publishes pamphlets or booklets on plants particularly adapted to the soil and rainfall conditions in your area.

• Garden clubs abound in most communities and are a valuable source of free advice. Members are knowledgeable and voluble. You don't have to join to gain access to their expertise. Simply attend their meetings, listen to the informal discussions, and ask questions during the coffee hour.

• Newspaper garden editors usually write a column for the big Thursday home editions and the Sunday garden page. Garden writers are wells of information on local conditions. You can tap this fund of knowledge by writing a question which may be answered in the newspaper or by telephoning. Most editors welcome questions as cues for topics to cover in their columns.

• Radio stations have followed the newspapers and added gardening experts on their "open line" programs. Use your telephone to talk directly with a guest expert over the air.

Plan Your Landscaping for Low Cost and Low Upkeep — If your grounds are barren and ready for a complete landscape treatment from ground zero, or are tired and need rehabilitation, start first with a plan. Here's where your interests come to the fore. Maybe you are a true gardener and plan to raise prize roses or dahlias. But, if you are interested in planting a good-looking, easy-to-keep lawn and shrubs for restrained elegance, aim in that direction from the start. Attack your landscape plan in three steps —

• Lay out your house and lot to scale (Fig. 11-1). Draw in all permanent buildings, walkways, drive, and play equipment. Mark any slopes, prevailing winds, or view direction.

• Block in general areas according to your planned use (Fig. 11-2). Locate items to be built, such as a barbecue patio and oven.

• Locate trees, planting beds, tall plantings for privacy, shrubs around the house to soften the lines between ground and building, and cultivated areas for a home garden (Fig. 11-3). Don't crowd plants; reserve enough space for each type when it is fully grown.

• Use these brief, basic principles in your planning to achieve specific results:

1. Narrow, upright shrubs increase visual height and minimize length or width.
2. Horizontal lines brought about by low, spreading shrubs diminish apparent height and emphasize length or width.
3. Large trees planted to the side of or behind a house minimize its height and add stability.
4. Houses with high foundations have greater need for foundation plantings than houses built close to the ground.
5. Plants that stand up above others, or contrast in some way, draw attention to entrances, picture windows, fireplaces, and changing building lines.
6. Tall shrubs used to break up a blank wall should break it into unequal spaces.

Draw on your stock of accumulated know-how when choosing plants. If your area tends to be dry in summer, select native plants that have learned to cope with arid periods. Also, choose plants that will withstand the winters in your area. Here is where buying plants from a far-away nursery can be dangerous — and costly. Don't be shy about asking your neighbors with good-looking established plantings which plants are best suited to local soil and climate conditions. Don't rush through this step. Try several alternatives. Let out the reins of your imagination. Moving plants around on paper is a lot easier than digging holes and hauling real plants around your yard. When picking plants, consider the many chores of spraying and dusting to control insects and plant diseases. Exotic roses and other hybrids require regular attention; native plants get along largely by themselves.

• Schedule the planting for each area. You won't be able to put all of the lawn and shrubs in at one time. You might wait several years before planting certain areas. Or, you may postpone some planting until a patio, retaining wall, or a building is complete. If you are like most homeowners, you'll start with a lawn because it covers large areas and establishes the grade for other plantings.

Money-Saving Ideas For Planting

Scrounging, planning, and patience pay big dividends. Hiring a contractor to come in and do all the work sounds great — but it's costly. Also, with your eye on later maintenance — in terms of both time and cost — you'll plant your lawn and shrubs differently than most landscape contractors. So, look ahead; build easy maintenance in from the start.

Grow Your Own Topsoil — You can have the best-looking lawn in the neighborhood at one-third the usual cost by following this proved method for building lawns on barren lots. If your present lawn is sick, you follow the same process to rebuild it completely. Instead of hauling truck loads of so-called "black dirt" at $3 to $4 per cubic yard and plastering a two- to three-inch cover over the clay and sand left by the builder, build a deep seed bed the way the farmers do.

Here's How to Do It: Good growing soil contains about equal portions of clay, humus, and sand. "Black dirt" is soil rich in humus, but still mostly dirt. Why add more dirt to your lot? Instead, follow these steps in sequence—

• Determine whether your soil is mostly clay or mostly sand. There will likely be little humus because the dirt will have come from basement or foundation diggings. If you want a scientific analysis, send a soil sample to your state university's extension service. Find the exact address by calling your local county agent or extension service office.

• Hire a tractor and operator to grade your land. Depending on the natural topography of your lot, you may need to plan a drainage pattern. On a flat lot, the builder will have sited the house to permit a gradual slope away from the house in all directions. If your house is on a side-hill, develop a surface drain pattern that prevents water from flowing toward your house. Final grading should leave the surface about four inches below finish grade.

• If the dirt that's left is mostly clay, haul in enough washed garden sand to spread a layer about three inches deep evenly over the lawn area. Soil with too much clay will pack down, accept little water, and limit root growth.

• If the dirt is mainly sand, haul in enough clay to build a mixture of half sand and half clay. Soil that is too sandy will not hold humus, fertilizer, or water.

• Add humus to both types of soil. If you are lucky enough to be near a source of pure humus (peat, composted garbage, etc.), spread it at least two inches thick over the sand or clay layer. If pure humus is not available, use any cheap local organic material, such as sawdust, bran, cottonseed hulls, ground corncobs, or chipped hardwood. Rent a heavy-duty rototiller to churn the whole mixture at least eight to ten inches deep. Add a balanced fertilizer (10-10-10) at a rate of about five pounds per 100 square feet.

• Plant field rye (not rye grass) at almost any season. If you plant rye in the spring, cut it at intervals until fall, then plow it under. Do not — repeat — DO NOT use a rototiller. A plow turns the surface completely over and brings new, untreated dirt to the surface.

• Spread another layer of fertilizer. Plant another crop of field rye the following spring, and repeat the cycle. If you plant the first crop of rye in the fall, allow it to go dormant during the winter, turn it under in late spring, and plant another crop. Growing and turning under field rye adds what the farmers call "green manure."

• After plowing — not rototilling — under the second crop of field rye, grade and smooth the lawn areas. Successive planting and plowing will have killed out the weeds in the soil. Instead of a seed bed two inches thick, you'll have a deep, porous loam that invites grass roots to grow deep into the soil. Except during very dry, prolonged drought, you may never need to water the lawn through the summer.

• Plant your finish lawn in the fall. Grass planted in the spring competes with all kinds of weeds. A fall-planted lawn gets the jump on weeds and develops deep roots. With a good start, lawn grass can crowd out many of the annual weeds that begin growing the following spring. Since you have killed out most of the weeds by the successive plowings, make sure the seed you buy is weed free. Also, check the price you pay for seed according to the comparison in Table 11A.

Money Savers When Acquiring Plants — With the lawn in or after finish grade is established, begin planting shrubs and perennials to fill out your basic landscaping plan. Here's where scrounging, imagination, and gardening skills pay off big.

• Buy small plants and watch them grow — Call on time as an ally and be patient. Shrubs grow faster than you think. So, buy small two- or three-year shrubs in small pots. You often save one dollar per plant when you buy the three-year size rather than the four-year size. Within two or three years, they will grow rapidly and fill in the spaces left for growth. You save by buying small plants several ways — 1) Small plants have spent less time in the nursery, so they are priced at only a fraction of the cost of the same plants two or three years older. 2) Small plants are less expensive to haul, to stock, and to keep alive in pots until sold. Large shrubs require balling and rolling in burlap to keep a chunk of natural earth around roots. All this effort adds to the expense. 3) Transplanting small plants from pot to your garden is easier, and the plants have a much greater chance of living.

• Buy your plants from a supermarket nursery or discount nursery outlet. These stores haul in large quantities of plants during the season they can be transplanted best. But make sure you buy quality — tips a soft green, pots or cans kept wet, dense growth near ground level (for low-growing bushes), and lush top growth (for tall growing shrubs). Many shrubs have similar common names; only the long, hard-to-pronounce botanical names identify the plants you want for sure. Know what you want before you shop in a nursery. Don't buy on impulse because a certain shrub happens to be on sale. Don't expect to get much help from the salesmen at supermarket lots; they are not trained nurserymen.

• Buy plants on sale near the end of the season. Plants are perishable, and the supermarket or discount nursery that buys potted or balled-and-burlapped (B & B) shrubs must sell them or take a total loss. But, remember, the longer plants remain out of the soil in pots, the less chance they have to survive. Be picky about the plants you select at end-of-season sales. Make sure soil is damp and has remained around roots in burlap balls. Don't buy plants with dried leaves at the tips of limbs. Continue to look for plants with strong growth indicators — not spindly, scraggly, or unshapely plants. When you plant these end-of-season shrubs, give them an extra chance to live by dipping the root ball in rooting hormones, and mix transplant fertilizer liberally in the planting hole. Make sure each plant has plenty of water. Prune top growth to lessen the load on roots while the plant is getting started.

• Look for plants at local garden club sales. Unique and hard-to-find species are frequently offered for sale at fund-raising sales by garden clubs. You'll find the plants in good pots, well rooted, and fresh, ready for planting. Also, prices are less than you'd pay at commercial nurseries for comparable plants. These sales are particularly good if you are looking for small vigorous plants.

• Don't buy plants and shrubs from a door-to-door salesman. A distant nursery spends a sizable chunk of money to ship your plants by mail. Often such shipments are delayed, roots dry out, soil may shake loose from root balls, or tops may be broken during shipment. Also, the plants may be unsuited to your soil and climate. Costs are likely to be high to pay the huge commission earned by smooth-talking salesmen. Finally, to save shipping costs and to improve chances of survival, shrubs are likely to be small. Sometimes, the salesman offers to draw a planting plan for your house. Such plans are likely to call for expensive, exotic shrubs that require babying and extra care.

• Don't buy plants by mail from newspaper or magazine advertisements. Many of the same problems of buying from a door-to-door salesman apply to the purchase of plants by mail — high selling costs, shipment by express from a distant nursery, small sizes, and the possibility of buying plants unsuited to your soil and climate conditions.

Money Savers — No-Cost Plantings and Shrubs — Cut your cost for shrubs to almost nothing by one of the following —

• Trade rooted cuttings from your favorite plants for similar starts from plants grown by your friends. There's no better way to acquire a variety of shrubs than by bartering. Develop your own trading stock by cutting slips from your plants and rooting them in flats of rooting soil mixed 50-50 from sand and peat moss. Check your garden book for the best time to cut slips from each of your plants and where the break should occur to assure good rooting. Dip the cuttings in a rooting hormone and plant them about two inches apart in a flat. Keep the flat moist at all times; one way to assure constant moisture is to keep a porous clay pot near the center filled with water. As the soil in the flat dries, water from the pot seeps through the porous clay and wets the soil. Another way to develop rooted plant starts is to bury a long branch in earth near the tip. Keep the area damp and the space back of the tip covered with earth. In a few weeks, the branch will have developed roots of its own. Cut the branch loose and transfer the new plant to a pot. Air layering is still another method for rooting starts. Roots develop in a wad of peat moss around the limb held by a plastic cover. Once the moss is moistened, the plastic cover keeps it from drying out. When this is properly done, roots develop rapidly. The new start is then snipped off the parent shrub and potted for further growth. Later, you transplant it in your garden. Plants that normally propagate by sending out runners over the surface are a cinch to separate and plant in pots. Simply dig up one of the new growing starts, snip off the runner from the parent, and repot. Seedlings grow through the surface from underground roots. These small plants can be similarly liberated from the parent with a sharp trowel and potted separately. Once this array of new starts from your plants and shrubs is growing healthily in pots, you're ready to trade. Cost to you? A little time, a little gardening know-how — and large dollops of patience.

• Dig out seedlings and spreading plants from neighbors' or friends' gardens for use around your home. Instead of hoping others will develop their own trading stock, scrounge excess starts from a mature garden. Bulbs of all kinds require digging up and separating every few years. When your friends are at this task, offer to take some of the new bulbs. When plants spread by runners or underground seedlings, the mature garden must be thinned and these extra starts eliminated. Be prepared to offer them a new home in your garden — at no cost to you but the digging.

• Start your own plants from slips or cuttings. Rather than grow new plant starts from your own shrubs and trade them for others, ask your gardening friends for slips or cuttings from their plants. You start them in flats as noted above. When the slips or cuttings are rooted, transplant them to pots or to a sheltered section of your garden. Allow them to grow one or two years before setting them out according to your planting plan. By growing your own shrubs, your garden changes constantly, increasing its variety and richness. You substitute patience and planning for dollars.

• Dig your own small native plants from wild areas. Rather than wait for no-cost plant starts from slips or cuttings, you dig up small native plants and shrubs from field or forest areas. Of course, state and national parks do not permit digging of plants. However, if you live near one of the national forests, ask the local ranger where you can dig. Or, watch for land with native plants on it being converted to highways. Natural areas to be bulldozed away contain many small plants that can be transplanted to your garden. Timing is important. Get there before the bulldozers move in. Take a big ball of natural earth with each plant. For large plants or small trees, be prepared to wrap the root ball with burlap pinned around the trunk with nails. For small plants, carry empty pots. Fill the pot with earth and soak it as soon as you arrive back home. Learn to recognize the plants you want from their foliage, needle pattern, blooms, or berries. If you can choose the time, pick the season that is best for each plant. Check your garden book. Trees can usually be moved most easily during the winter. Flowering plants are best moved just before and when they are in bloom.

Maintain Your Yard and Landscaping for Less Cash

Fertilizer, water, and labor for mowing and trimming lawns,

weeding planted areas, pruning or clearing shrubs and spraying or dusting for insects or diseases can drain your pocketbook right through the season. Borrow these money-saving tips from the professionals —

Buy Fertilizer Right! — You must feed grass regularly for it to remain healthy with a deep green color. Shrubs need food too, but of a different kind than grass. Again, your gardening know-how pays off.

What to Do:
• Buy fertilizer by analysis. Look for the three numbers on fertilizer bags. The numbers, 10-10-10, for example, indicate that the fertilizer contains 10 per cent nitrogen, 10 per cent phosphoric acid, and 10 per cent potash. These are the three basic plant foods. The percentage analysis figures are always in the same order. Lawn plant food contains a high nitrogen content. But a high-nitrogen fertilizer causes flowering plants to grow stalky and produce few flowers. For shrubs and flowering plants, you need high phosphorous-potash fertilizers. So examine the percentage figures to know what you're buying. You can spread a 10-5-5 fertilizer half as thick on a lawn as a 5-5-5 fertilizer and still provide the same amount of nitrogen.

• Buy your fertilizer in a farmer's or professional grower's market. When you compare prices on a pound-for-pound basis, you pay handsomely for the small, gaily printed sacks of fertilizer at your local hardware store. Instead, buy fertilizer in 100-pound bags at a store that sells by the ton to farmers.

• Mix your own fertilizer for specific needs. Suppose you buy large bags of a balanced fertilizer from a farmer's market. You waste phosphorous and potash if you apply a balanced fertilizer to lawns where extra nitrogen is needed. So buy small bags of ammonium sulfate from filling stations to boost the nitrogen content. Ammonium sulfate is 20.5 per cent nitrogen. Add 25 pounds of ammonium nitrate to a balanced 5-5-5 fertilizer and you nearly double the nitrogen content. Simply mix the ingredients dry with a shovel on a smooth, dry, concrete surface, then load the mix into your lawn spreader.

• Don't fertilize blindly. Have your soil tested to find out scientifically what kind and how much fertilizer it needs to grow grass or specific shrubs. Watch out for special events at garden centers. As a special promotion, a soil tester is on hand to check your soil sample for the three main ingredients while you watch. The quick chemical test indicates which plant food is lacking. Or, you can send samples of soil to your agricultural university or extension service center. Ask your county agent or extension service agent for the address. You will pay a nominal charge, usually about $1.50, for a complete analysis of your soil. When selecting samples, take a few spoonsful from various locations, mix them together, and send about a cup full in a plastic container. If you want lawn, vegetable garden, or shrub planting areas tested, send a separate sample from each area. Enclose a note with the sample indicating the kind of planting intended for each area. The report will advise you which type of fertilizer to apply. If your soil is deficient in trace minerals or is too acid or alkaline, these conditions will be noted too.

• Buy fertilizer for plant nutrient content, not simply bulk. Chemical fertilizers provide more plant nutrient per dollar than organic fertilizers. Nitrogen from ammonium sulfate will make grass just as green as nitrogen from organic sludge. If you prepared your soil with large quantities of sawdust, wood chips, or ground corncobs, apply the equivalent of four pounds of nitrogen per cubic yard to support bacterial decomposition. With plenty of humus in the soil, buying fertilizer for humus content costs you extra. Buy fertilizer for plant nutrient, not as a soil conditioner.

• Schedule applications of fertilizer for maximum utilization. Don't, for example, apply heavy doses of fertilizer to lawns early in the spring. Grass naturally grows fast and lush during early spring. Extra fertilizer is simply wasted. Later in the spring, apply a medium dose to carry the growth into summer. Early in the fall apply a heavy dose of fertilizer with phosphorous and potash in addition to nitrogen to encourage deep root growth. A heavy application too late in the season could be entirely wasted if cold stops growth. During the winter most of the excess nutrients leach out of the soil and wash away. Fertilize shrubs according to their best growing period. Normally, a good shot of fertilizer is needed right after blooming. Some plants and shrubs require frequent treatments because of small root patterns. Study the nutrient needs of each plant from data in your garden handbook.

• Watch for special sales of fertilizer if you don't have ready access to a farmer's market. Late season sales frequently cut fertilizer prices in half. Stock up for a later season; fertilizer won't deteriorate as long as it remains dry. For example, buy a good lawn fertilizer at a late fall season to have on hand for the next spring when prices are at their peak.

Save on Watering and Weeding with Mulches — Cover bare ground around shrubs with a mulch of ground bark, sawdust, leaves, grass clippings, or a compost of several ingredients. Don't buy expensive, exotic materials, such as peat moss, for example. Use common inexpensive mulch materials readily available in your locality. Or better still, use the free leaves and grass clippings you would burn or throw away anyway. Mulch does two jobs — 1) Keeps the weeds from growing or leaves them easier to pull. 2) Prevents ground moisture from evaporating rapidly during hot, dry days. So you use less water to keep plants green — sometimes, no extra water at all because the mulch tends to draw ground water nearer the surface.

Sawdust also makes a good mulch. Cedar or cypress sawdust will take years to decompose, but hardwoods, like alder, birch, or maple, decompose readily and lighten heavy soils when dug into top layers. Add 17 pounds of ammonium sulfate or 11 pounds of ammonium nitrate per cubic yard of sawdust to accelerate decomposition.

Learn When and What to Spray — Chemical sprays and dusts greatly simplify garden maintenance. But if you had selected plants indigenous to your area, you would probably not have to spray or dust at all for insects or plant diseases. If your plants require regular chemical treatments, learn how to spray them yourself. Professional spray services charge mostly for labor — very little for the actual chemicals used.

What to Do:

• Find out specifically which spray to use for controlling insects or diseases on your plants. Ask your local extension service for bulletins and pamphlets that cover your area and its pests. Or call the garden editor of your local newspaper for specific advice. Don't spray randomly. Since public agencies seldom advise the use of products by trade name, learn to recognize generic terms, such as chlordane, DDT, and others. Read the label to find the ingredients in each of the concentrated spray products, and buy the one that contains the chemical recommended.

• Pick the right time for spraying. Dusk is a good time for controlling many insects because they are active then. Dusk is a good time to spray for weed control too, because pores of the leaves open up in the evening and quickly absorb chemicals. Spray for weed control during the season when plant growth is rapid. Find the right season for controlling specific insects according to your locality and the pest.

• When spraying, add a small amount of stick-um additive so the spray will not roll off waxy leaves. Or add half a teaspoon of detergent per gallon of water-mix spray to help wet the surface.

• When dusting, do it early in the morning while leaves are damp, to keep the dust in contact with the plant.

Weed Control — Chemicals such as 2,4 = D have long been helpful in controlling dandelions and other broad-leaf plants. Crabgrass is a little more persistent, and other weeds make life miserable for the home gardener in specific areas. However, new chemicals are available for control of nearly every unwanted plant from Bermuda grass to poison ivy. Consult Table 11B for the chemical treatment best suited to eradicate your specific weed pests.

Another inexpensive way to control weeds around shrubs is to lay black polyethylene film around shrubs, along border plantings, and under trees. Punch holes in the plastic film every six or eight inches for water to drain through. For permanent use, apply the plastic film and cover the area with four to six inches of mulch to hide the film.

Looking at the price per pound of seed only can cost you extra. Instead, read the label and compare the true cost of pure-live seed as follows:

TABLE 11A Comparison of Grass Seed Costs

	LOW-QUALITY SEED	HIGH-QUALITY SEED
	90¢ per pound	$1.00 per pound
Germination	80 per cent	90 per cent
Nongrass seed and filler	15 per cent	2 per cent
Pure grass seed	85 per cent	98 per cent
Germination x purity	(80)(85) + 68%	(90)(98) = 88%
Pure-live seed	68 per cent	88 per cent
Price ÷ pure-live seed	$\frac{90c}{68\%} = \$1.32$	$\frac{\$1.00}{88\%} = \$1.14$
Actual cost per pound of pure-live seed	$1.32	$1.14

Unless you consider label facts, you could pay more for pure-live seed by buying the low-quality seed.

TABLE 11B Chemicals for Weed Control

WEED	GENERAL	SPOT TREATMENTS
Nutsedge	2,4-D, repeated heavy rates	2,4-D, methyl bromide, SMDC, DMTT
Bermuda grass	dalapon	dalapon, methyl bromide

TABLE 11B Chemicals for Weed Control (Continued)

WEED	GENERAL	SPOT TREATMENTS
Crabgrass	DCPA, DMPA, R-4461, trifluralin	
Goosegrass	DMPA, R-4461	
Dallis grass	DSMA	Stoddard solvent, DSMA
Nimblewill	DMPA, repeated heavy rates	DMPA
Plaintain	2,4-D	2,4-D
Dandelion	2,4-D	2,4-D
Ground-ivy, Chickweed, Henbit, and Knotweed	silvex	silvex
Pigweed	2,4-D	2,4-D
Lambsquarters	2,4-D	2,4-D
Dodder		DCPA, CIPC
Wild garlic	2,4-D	2,4-D
Purslane		DNBP, CIPC
Red sorrel	dicamba	dicamba
Spotted spurge	silvex	silvex
Mugwort		amitrole
Poison ivy	2,4,5-T	amitrole
Virginia creeper		amitrole, ammate
Honeysuckle	2,4-D	2,4-D
Hardwood seedlings	2,4,5-T	2,4,5-T
Orchardgrass, Tall fescue, Timothy, and Broomsedge		Stoddard solvent
Woodsorrel	silvex	silvex
Ragweed	2,4-D	2,4-D

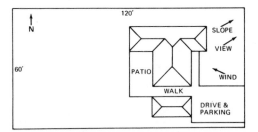

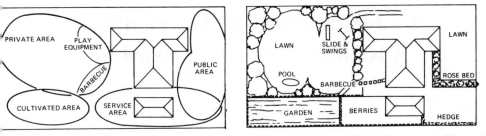

FIG. 11-1 — Layout of House and Lot Drawn to Scale.
Note Dimensions, Location of Fixed Improvements, and Other Data

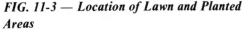

IG. 11-2 — Plan of Functional Areas for
se in Planning Landscaping

FIG. 11-3 — Location of Lawn and Planted
Areas

MONEY SAVERS WHEN YOU'RE SPENDING FOR LANDSCAPING

Don't pay the price for "instant landscaping." Patience pays off in plantings whether it's a lawn or a collection of exotic plants. You can go either of two routes when it comes to landscaping your house —

1. Plan and plant low-cost, low-maintenance shrubs so they take less time away from your golf, sailing, or what have you —

2. Develop an outdoor showcase for your personal interests in plants, shrubs, and flowers. Your garden is your hobby.

Whichever route suits you best, you can save bundles of boodle from the tips and hints you learned in this chapter, such as —

- Recognizing the positive or negative value of well-landscaped lawns and grounds when buying or selling.
- Developing your resourcefulness and ingenuity when it comes to planning, propagating, and planting plants and shrubs around your house for little or no cost.
- Working with nature to start new plants, dig up extras, and natives from wild areas, planting small and waiting — all guaranteed to save you money.
- Looking to future savings by planting your lawn in a seedbed such as a farmer would develop for his cash crop.
- Buying the fundamental nutrients you need in a fertilizer at a saving — instead of a pretty, colorful bag.
- Cost and labor savings go together when you plan and follow through on a schedule that works with, not against, nature.

12

Understanding The Economics
Of Home Owning And Renting

Buying a home is popular — the "in" thing to do. Our beneficent federal government smiles on the homeowner and gives him a boost with easy money and a break on taxes. So, many families buy a home wherever they touch down — as many as half a dozen or more houses during a nomadic lifetime at the direction of industrial giants. But, despite the popularity of home ownership, few families really understand the basic economics affecting the housing part of their spending plan. When you're dealing with up to 25 per cent of your income, it pays to know what the dollars are buying. Some of the know-how you need includes —

- How to make a breakeven analysis of whether to buy or rent.
- How to figure how much housing you can really afford.
- Your attitude when buying a home and its effect on financing.
- How to analyze the pocketbook effects of mortgages, payment plans, interest, and "fine print" clauses.
- How to clamp down on closing costs.

Not buying a home in the United States is almost unpatriotic. Just look at all the government has done to encourage home buyers —

- FHA and VA mortgage insurance programs to keep mortgage cost low.
- Income tax deductions for house taxes and the interest on mortgage payments — both substantial amounts in a home-owner's budget.

However, the costs of buying and selling a house frequently offset any savings realized from equity buildup or income tax reduction. The important figure to consider is the actual net cost per year for housing.

Is your family the one out of five that will change locations this year? Many large corporations with widely spread operations move their work force around like checkers on a countrywide or worldwide board. If you are subject to frequent company-dictated moves, you may be lining the realtor's pockets — but stripping your savings account.

Do You Really Save Money by Owning a Home?

The old "handful of rent receipts" syndrome has really gotten to many families. Of course, there are many reasons for owning a home rather than renting. Let's disregard the psychological, nostalgic, and ephemeral, and zero in on cost. What are the dollar considerations of buying vs. renting?

Breakeven Analysis — One way to determine whether you should rent or buy is to make a breakeven analysis. When you buy, consider that you may also have to sell — the complete cycle known as exchange costs. If you move often, exchange costs may exceed the lower operating cost of owning your house. Consider the example facts in Fig. 12-1. Whether you are interested in a $15,000 house or one costing $50,000, the analysis technique remains the same. All you need to do is supply appropriate estimates that apply to your situation.

If you have never considered the effect of exchange costs, you might be surprised at the total — including the two realtors' commissions. You pay one commission directly as the seller. The other you pay indirectly in the buying price. Also, there's the expense of maintaining a house. Whether you buy a new home or an older one, you must consider maintenance expenses as follows:

• New home — Actual maintenance expenses for plumbing repairs, painting, etc., are likely to be small for several years on a new house. In fact, a builder's warranty may cover debugging costs for one or more years. But, to balance the low maintenance expense, you will want to plant a lawn and shrubs, build a patio, add shelves in the garage, install wall-to-wall carpeting — possibly build on small or large additions to the basic house.

• Older home — If you buy an older home, possibly one that has been around for 50 to 75 years, you can figure maintenance costs at an average of 1 ½ to 2 per cent of the house value per year. Even houses that are four to five years old begin to need regular repairs.

Look at two other items in the list of Annual Costs:

Down payment: 10% ($2,000)
Mortgage: $18,000 at 6% interest

BUYING AND OPERATING COSTS

Closing Costs for Mortgage Loan

Mortgage processing fee (1½%)	$270	
Sales tax (1%)	200	
Recording fee (0.1%)	20	
Title insurance ($5/$1000)	90	
Inspection and appraisal fee	35	
Credit report	10	
Survey and plat	35	
Legal opinion	30	
	$690	$690

Annual Owning and Operating Costs

Insurance	$130	
Taxes	320	
Maintenance (1¾% of value)	350	
Interest loss on down payment (5%)	100	
Mortgage interest + interest loss on accumulating equity	1,296	
Less income tax saving on taxes and interest	312	
	$1,884	$1,884

SELLING COSTS

Real estate sales fee (6%)	$1,200	
Three month's loss on unoccupied house	415	
Prepayment penalty (1½%)	270	
	$1,885	$1,885
TOTAL EXCHANGE COSTS		$4,459

FIG. 12-1—Calculations for Breakeven Analysis

• Loss of interest on down payment — The money you use as a down payment, if invested, would earn interest or dividends. In the example, you could have invested the $2,000 down payment and drawn at least 5 per cent interest. The $100 per year loss in earning power represents a cost to you of owning the house.

• Income tax effects — Taxes and mortgage interest are deductible from your gross income in figuring the net income on which your income tax is based (providing you use the long form with itemized deductions). How much these deductions are worth to you varies according to your tax bracket. At 20 per cent in the example, the $312 represent your gain if you paid taxes and interest of $1,560 rather than spent the same amount for rent.

Determine the breakeven point in years and 10-year cumulative costs relative to varying monthly rents (Table 12A). Pick off the breakeven point from the chart in Fig. 12-2. Obviously, your decision to buy or rent will be influenced by the housing market in your living area. If a number of houses are offered for rent, the price is likely to be lower than if the demand for rental houses greatly exceeds the supply. Exclude the cost for utilities, as these are a cost whether you rent or buy a house. In an apartment, however, heat, water, and rubbish or garbage removal may be included in the basic rental.

TABLE 12A Comparison of Owning Vs. Renting Costs

	BUY*		RENT*							
			$160/Month		$180/Month		$200/Month		$220/Month	
Year	Cumulative Cost	Average Cost/ Year	Cost/ Year	Cumulative Cost	Cost/ Year	Cumulative Cost	Cost/ Year	Cumulative Cost	Cost/ Year	Cumulative Cost
1	$4,459	$4,459	$1,920	$1,920	$2,160	$1,920	$2,400	$2,400	$2,640	$2,640
2	6,343	3,172	1,920	3,840	2,160	4,320	2,400	4,800	2,640	5,280
3	8,227	2,742	1,920	5,760	2,160	6,480	2,400	7,200	2,640	7,920
4	10,111	2,528	1,920	7,680	2,160	8,640	2,400	9,600	2,640	10,560
5	11,995	2,399	1,920	9,600	2,160	10,800	2,400	12,000	2,640	13,200
6	13,879	2,313	1,920	11,520	2,160	12,960	2,400	14,400	2,640	15,840
7	15,753	2,250	1,920	13,440	2,160	15,120	2,400	16,800	2,640	18,480
8	17,647	2,206	1,920	15,360	2,160	17,280	2,400	19,200	2,640	21,120
9	19,531	2,170	1,920	17,280	2,160	19,440	2,400	21,600	2,640	23,760
10	21,415	2,142	1,920	19,200	2,160	21,600	2,400	24,000	2,640	26,400

*See Fig. 12-1 for analysis of exchange associated with buying and owning a house.

How about the profit from house appreciation over the years? You've heard about the homeowner who bought a house for $12,000 right after World War II and sold it ten years later for $20,000? The homeowner who bought prior to World War II and sold in the 1950's probably gained an even larger profit. Long-term investment gains in housing in terms of current dollars were common a few years ago. In constant dollars, house prices have remained remarkably stable.

Note: Consider — Rent or buy a home priced at $20,000.

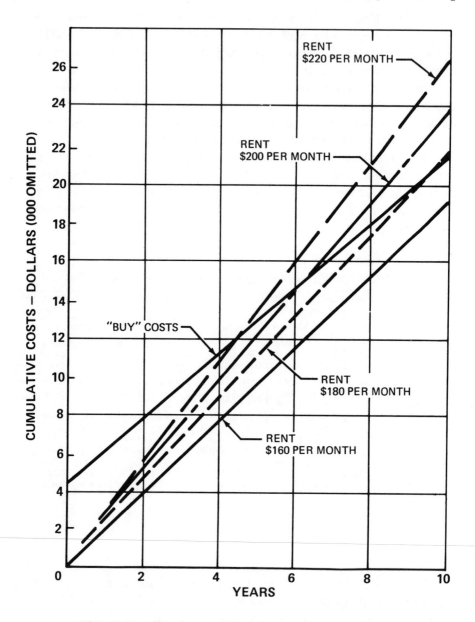

**FIG. 12-2 — Breakeven Point Analysis — Buy Versus Rent.
(See Fig. 12-1 and Table 12A for Data)**

Rather than increasing in value, houses depreciate with time. New materials, improved planning, and rapidly improving appliances and equipment tend to obsolete an older house. You may find that the market value of your house at any specific moment may be less than the amount you owe if you bought with a minimum down payment and a long repayment period. The FHA estimates, for example, that for a 35-year loan following a minimum down payment, an owner will owe more than the value of the house for at least 20 years.

Inflation, however, definitely affects house prices. If a house cost $10,000 when a dollar was worth 100 cents, the same house might be priced at $20,000 if the purchasing power of a dollar decreased to only 50 cents. Inflation is behind the gradually increasing market value of older homes. So, if you should net a small, long-term investment gain after owning a house for five or six years, you will probably find that prices have increased by an even greater margin when you rebuy. Only if you should move from a booming area where housing is short (and prices high) to a stable or depressed area where housing is long (and prices low) can you expect an exchange gain.

You may find it difficult to rent a house that offers the same living standards as one you can buy. In areas where a number of houses are on the market, try converting a seller to a renter if your breakeven analysis indicates an advantage for renting. After a house stands vacant for several months, the owner may be open to a lease proposition, particularly if he has been so ill advised as to buy another house before selling his old one. If the realtor showing the house won't consider a lease, approach the owner directly.

Apartments or town houses offer advantages for the family on the move. Consider such trade-offs as an apartment project swimming pool instead of a big grassy lawn. The new apartment complexes may have hobby rooms and shop areas for building furniture, toys, or boats. Apartments also tend to be rented by families like yours — new to the community, a knowledge that you may be moving in a year or two, few friends in the community, and similar interests. So, for a family on the move, renting may offer more advantages than simply a reduced cost of housing.

How Much Housing Can You Afford?

You are the only one who can decide how much of your income to spend for housing. You will already have considered the effect of your "housepower" (see Chapter 1). The only logical way to determine exactly how much money you can devote to housing is to develop an over-all Spending Plan. Chapter 9 of a companion book, HOW TO LIVE BETTER AND SPEND 20% LESS,* details the steps for such an analysis. The result limits how much of your income can be spent for housing. Fig. 12-3 summarizes such an analysis and compares that figure with averages from two other families' spending plans.

Rules of Thumb — One of the frequently used formulas calls for spending about 2 ½ times the annual income for housing. So a family with an income of $10,000 yearly could afford to buy a house costing $25,000. Many mortgage lenders consider this formula as a top or maximum expenditure. Some agencies limit the ratio to not more than twice the annual income.

A second rule-of-thumb limits spending for all housing costs — including mortgage, utilities, taxes, and maintenance — to 25 per cent of your income. So, if your annual income amounted to $9,600, you could afford to spend $2,400 per year on housing or $200 per month. Remember, however, that the 25 per cent figure includes all housing costs. Mortgage payments amount to only about half the total expenditure for housing (see Fig. 12-3).

What's Your Personal Situation? — Disregard rules of thumb that, by trying to fit everyone, fit nobody. Instead, consider some of the following factors —

• Your life cycle position. If you have been married for a few years and have one or more small children, you are still headed uphill in housing requirements. If you live in a crowded apartment or a minimum house, you're soon going to need more room. Your need for additional housing is likely to continue for 10 to 20 years. With inflation ahead, you might consider spending somewhat more on housing (and less on other items in your Spending Plan) as a hedge against an increase in housing costs later.

On the other hand, if your children have flown the nest, gardening and house maintenance are taking too much time and effort, or you are thinking of retirement, you could be thinking of less, rather than more, space.

• Your earning cycle position — Suppose your foot is on the bottom rung of the ladder, you are young, and you have completed a sound program of schooling. You can look forward to a steadily increasing income. Rather than buy small, sell later and rebuy again

---

*Merle E. Dowd, *How to Live Better and Spend 20% Less* (West Nyack, N.Y.: Parker Publishing Company, 1966).

	Dollars allocated	Per cent of income	Per cent spent by urban family with $10,000-$12,000 yearly income	Per cent spent by urban family with $12,000-$18,000 yearly income
Food	$2,086	21.6	22.5	20.1
Clothing	1,150	11.9	11.7	12.2
Transportation	1,524	15.8	16.7	14.9
Medical	589	6.1	6.2	6.1
Fun (Total)	1,314	13.6	13.3	13.9
Personal care	270	2.8	2.8	2.8
Tobacco	116	1.2	1.5	1.0
Alcoholic beverages	174	1.8	1.7	1.9
Recreation	455	4.7	4.8	4.7
Reading	106	1.1	1.0	1.3
Education	193	2.0	1.5	2.2
Miscellaneous	261	2.7	2.3	4.0
Household operation	919	9.5	9.5	9.5
Insurance	107	1.1	1.0	1.1
Taxes	193	2.0	1.9	2.1
Maintenance	242	2.5	2.6	2.5
Other	377	3.9	4.0	3.8
Home furnishings and equipment	521	5.4	5.5	5.4
SUBTOTAL	$8,364	86.6	87.7	86.1
Available for current spending	$8,364		$7,690	$10,952
Available for mortgage and interest %		13.4	12.3	13.9
$	$1,296		$1,079	$1,768
*TOTAL	$9,660		$8,769	$12,720

* Disposable income left after income tax and FICA have been deducted.

FIG. 12-3—Spending Plan Analysis

— possibly repeating the cycle several times, consider overspending on housing relative to your current income. Later, when your income moves up, housing costs will take a relatively smaller bite from your income. Over several years your investment will probably grow (relative to inflated dollars). You will likely save one, possibly two or three, series of exchange costs.

But, if you are past 50, your chances for steadily increasing earnings may be dim. Think twice about assuming a stiff mortgage. It is unlikely that increasing income will pull your housing costs down to a reasonable percentage of your take-home pay.

Income Available for Housing		6% Interest Loan Period — Years				6½% Interest Loan Period — Years			
Monthly	Yearly	20	25	30	35	20	25	30	35
$50	$600	$4,763	$5,114	$5,360	$5,534	$4,634	$4,957	$5,179	$5,333
60	720	5,715	6,137	6,431	6,640	5,561	5,949	6,215	6,400
70	840	6,668	7,160	7,503	7,747	6,488	6,940	7,251	7,467
80	960	7,620	8,183	8,575	8,854	7,415	7,932	8,287	8,533
90	1,080	8,573	9,206	9,647	9,960	8,342	8,923	9,322	9,600
100	1,200	9,525	10,228	10,719	11,067	9,269	9,915	10,358	10,667
110	1,320	10,478	11,251	11,791	12,174	10,195	10,906	11,394	11,733
120	1,440	11,430	12,274	12,863	13,280	11,122	11,898	12,430	12,800
130	1,560	12,383	13,297	13,935	14,387	12,049	12,889	13,466	13,867
140	1,680	13,335	14,320	15,007	15,494	12,976	13,881	14,501	14,933
150	1,800	14,288	15,343	16,079	16,601	13,903	14,872	15,537	16,000
160	1,920	15,240	16,365	17,150	17,707	14,830	15,864	16,573	17,067
180	2,160	17,146	18,411	19,294	19,921	16,683	17,847	18,645	19,200
200	2,400	19,051	20,457	21,438	22,134	18,537	19,830	20,716	21,333
220	2,640	20,956	22,502	23,582	24,347	20,391	21,813	22,788	23,467
240	2,880	22,861	24,548	25,726	26,561	22,244	23,796	24,860	25,600
260	3,120	24,766	26,594	27,869	28,774	24,098	25,778	26,931	27,733
280	3,360	26,671	28,640	30,013	30,988	25,952	27,761	29,003	29,866
300	3,600	28,576	30,685	32,157	33,201	27,806	29,744	31,075	32,000

Note: To use Table 12B, you must first determine how much income you can spend for housing (see Fig. 12-3). The figures show how large a loan can be carried for a specific monthly allocation for housing. The monthly allocations include an allowance of 4 per cent of the loan value to cover taxes, insurance, and maintenance. You must also figure this 4 per cent allowance for the value of your down payment. For example, if you paid $3000 down, 4% of $3000 would amount to $120 yearly or $10 per month.

How Much Housing Can You Afford?

7% Interest Loan Period—Years				7½% Interest Loan Period—Years				8% Interest Loan Period—Years	
20	25	30	35	20	25	30	35	20	25
$4,510	$4,807	$5,007	$5,143	$4,390	$4,663	$4,842	$4,962	$4,274	$4,524
5,412	5,768	6,008	6,171	5,268	5,595	5,811	5,955	5,129	5,429
6,314	6,730	7,009	7,200	6,146	6,528	6,779	6,947	5,984	6,334
7,216	7,691	8,011	8,228	7,024	7,460	7,748	7,940	6,839	7,239
8,118	8,652	9,012	9,257	7,902	8,393	8,716	8,932	7,693	8,144
9,020	9,614	10,013	10,285	8,780	9,325	9,684	9,925	8,548	9,048
9,922	10,575	11,015	11,314	9,660	10,258	10,653	10,917	9,403	9,953
10,824	11,537	12,016	12,342	10,536	11,190	11,621	11,910	10,258	10,858
11,726	12,498	13,017	13,371	11,413	12,123	12,590	12,902	11,113	11,763
12,628	13,459	14,019	14,400	12,291	13,056	13,558	13,895	11,967	12,668
13,530	14,421	15,020	15,428	13,169	13,988	14,527	14,887	12,822	13,573
14,432	15,382	16,021	16,457	14,047	14,921	15,495	15,880	13,677	14,477
16,236	17,305	18,024	18,514	15,803	16,786	17,432	17,864	15,387	16,287
18,040	19,228	20,027	20,571	17,559	18,651	19,369	19,849	17,096	18,097
19,844	21,150	22,029	22,628	19,315	20,516	21,306	21,834	18,806	19,906
21,648	23,073	24,032	24,685	21,071	22,381	23,243	23,819	20,516	21,716
23,451	24,996	26,035	26,742	22,827	24,246	25,179	25,804	22,225	23,526
25,255	26,919	28,037	28,799	24,583	26,111	27,116	27,789	23,935	25,336
27,059	28,841	30,040	30,856	26,339	27,976	29,053	29,774	25,645	27,145

Suppose you can spend $120 monthly for housing and you can pay $3000 down. You then have $110 left to pay off the mortgage and cover taxes, insurance, and maintenance. From the figures in Table 12B, you'll see that $110 will cover a $10,478 mortgage loan over a 20-year period with an interest rate of 6%. The same $110 would cover a 35-year loan up to $12,174 at the same interest rate. However, if a 7% loan is the best you can find, your $110 will only permit you to carry a $11,314 loan over 35 years.

• Resources available from savings, investments, or other tappable money supply — You might take on a higher than rule-of-thumb mortgage if other resources can carry you through an emergency. In accumulating these resources, you have probably established spending patterns that enable you to handle a heavier-than-usual mortgage.

The other side of this coin is the family with a backlog of debts rather than savings. Such a family's spending pattern is also a habit. It manages its financial resources poorly — therefore, taking on a big mortgage could be enough to sink the whole ship.

How much housing you can afford depends on how many dollars you can spend every month for mortgage payments plus insurance, taxes, maintenance, utilities, and furnishings. Depending on the mortgage, down payment available, and other financing arrangements, your monthly housing allocation will buy differing amounts of housing. Table 12B provides a quick guide for converting dollars per month into mortgage amounts. Your next consideration is financing.

Understanding House Financing

Nearly every family buys a home with some kind of borrowed money for either or both of two reasons:

• Many families simply don't have enough cash to buy a home outright.

• Other families that might have the cash to buy a home prefer to use their cash for some other purpose and take advantage of readily available low-cost financing. These same families may also wish to use the deductions available from taxes and interest.

Two different family attitudes affect mortgage costs:

• Families that want to buy a house — eventually to own it free and clear. To these families, owning a home is a form of security.

• Families that consider mortgage payments as a cost of housing, not as a means of building an equity and finally owning the house.

If you aim to own your house, you will find it prudent to shorten the mortgage period, to reduce the number of payments by repaying principal when extra money is available, to shop diligently for a low-interest mortgage, or to make a substantial down payment. But, if monthly house payments are viewed as only a regular cost-of-living item, you will be less concerned about time and interest and more concerned about keeping the down payment and monthly payments as low as possible. Examine your attitude and place yourself in one or the other of these categories before studying the following data on mortgage costs.

Mortgage Costs — Two major factors affect mortgage costs — repayment period and interest rate. Table 12C briefly sorts out these effects for a principal amount of $1,000. These figures are for an amortized loan. That is, a part of each monthly payment goes for the principal and a part goes for interest. Over the stated period of the mortgage, payments cover all interest and repay the total amount borrowed. Interest is simple interest — not installment interest. Early in the mortgage period, payments are mostly for interest. But, as small amounts of the principal are repaid, interest drops and the portion

Effect of Interest Rate

Rate	Monthly payment required to repay $1000 in 25 years	Total interest during 25 years for each $1000
4½%	$5.56	$668
5	5.85	755
5½	6.15	845
6	6.45	935
6½	6.76	1028
7	7.07	1121
7½	7.39	1213
8	7.72	1306

Effect of Repayment Period

Years of monthly payments	Monthly payment to repay principal & interest @ 5½%	Total interest paid during period for each $1000 @ 5½%
10	$10.86	$ 303
15	8.18	472
20	6.88	651
25	6.15	845
30	5.68	1045
35	5.38	1260
40	5.16	1477

TABLE 12C Factors That Affect Mortgage Financing Costs

paid toward principal increases. This is the reason that equity builds up so slowly in the early years.

Table 12C highlights two major effects any home buyer should remember:

• Repayment time has a greater effect than the interest rate on the size of monthly payments.

• Repayment period greatly affects the number of dollars paid for interest.

Down Payment Effects — Money speaks with a loud and authoritative voice. Despite the many offers to sell a house with "No Money Down," most lenders expect you to assume part of the risk of owning your home. The risk you assume is measured by your down payment. Other factors may also affect the size of your down payment. Factors you should consider are:

• You pay no interest on down-payment money. If your aim is to own your home, you pay less interest over the life of your mortgage if you borrow less — and pay more down. As noted in the breakeven analysis, however, you lose any income from the money paid down.

• How much you pay down affects the mortgage you can get. Veterans Administration financing permits you to buy a home without any down payment, if you qualify. The Federal Housing Administration permits buying homes with as little as 3 per cent down payment on houses up to $15,000 and with 25 per cent of certain portions of a more expensive house. Conventional mortgages may be limited to 75 per cent of the appraised value of a house. The difference between the mortgage amount and the agreed purchase price becomes your down payment.

• Table 12B details how large a mortgage specific monthly payments will cover at a variety of interest rates. A high down payment can be traded for low monthly payments. For example, suppose your spending plan allows $160 per month for mortgage only. At an interest rate of 6 per cent, and a loan period of 25 years, $160 monthly would cover a mortgage of $16,354. But the house you want costs $25,000. If you buy, the down payment amounts to $8,646. To buy a more expensive house, you would need to: 1) Locate a mortgage with a lower interest rate; 2) Extend the loan period; 3) Allocate more of your monthly income to housing; or 4) Increase your down payment. Alternatives 2 and 3 will increase the total, long-term cost of your house. Alternatives 2 and 3 will increase the total, long-term cost of your house. Alternatives 1 and 4 will decrease the cost of the more expensive house — over the repayment period.

Prepaying a Mortgage — Related to a big down payment are the considerations for prepaying a mortgage. Both will save interest over the loan period. For example, suppose your mortgage is for $22,000 at an interest rate of 5½ per cent for 25 years. Interest plus loan amortization payments total $135.10 monthly. Prepaying the 25th through the 36th months' principal portions, for example, would cost $470.66, save $1150.54 interest, and shorten repayment period to 24 years. The 25th payment includes $96.86 interest and $38.24 to pay on the principal. By contrast, the 37th payment is divided to pay $94.70 interest and $40.40 on the principal.

Prepaying a mortgage amounts to investing money at the interest rate of your mortgage. So, when you pay off that $1,000 ahead of time, you are really investing $1,000 for the remaining years of the mortgage. If your aim is to own your house, prepaying a premium makes sense. If mortgage payments are simply a regular cost of housing, prepaying a mortgage only increases your housing costs.

The relative cost of money also affects your decision to prepay. Loans on real estate cost near minimum interest. Rather than prepay a mortgage, consider investing the free cash you have in some other dynamic investment, such as a well-selected stock portfolio, or a mutual fund. Such a plan diversifies your investments — equity build-up in real estate through regular payments and a build-up in stocks or mutual funds through purchases when cash is available. Both are good hedges against inflation.

Shopping for a Mortgage — Many organizations, mainly insurance companies, make their money by lending money for mortgages. Other sources of home loans are savings and loan associations, savings banks, fraternal organizations, credit unions, and individuals. Check them all before you sign up, because there are differences in cost and interpretations of your ability to repay.

Conventional, FHA, VA, and privately insured mortgage loans are also different. Conventional loans usually require higher down payments than either FHA or VA loans because conventional mortgages are not insured by an agency of the U.S. Government. Conventional loans frequently carry higher interest rates than either FHA or VA loans but do not include "points" — lump-sum payments by the builder to increase the lender's actual earnings. Buyers can usually obtain a conventional loan quicker than an FHA or VA loan. The red tape in getting an FHA or VA loan can be frustrating to builder, buyer, and seller. FHA and VA loans can usually be obtained for longer repayment periods, particularly if you are buying a new house. VA loans are usually the most liberal and may be obtained with no down payment and only nominal closing costs on some houses.

To borrow under FHA, you and the house you intend to buy must meet a number of requirements. Reviewing these rules and how they apply to each transaction eat up time and tangle the bureaucratic red tape. If you are shopping for a loan, have a quiet chat with a savings and loan company officer authorized by the FHA or VA to make insured loans.

Investigate other sources of mortgage loans, too. Your realtor can suggest one or more firms. But don't depend only on realtor referrals. Check the classified section of your local telephone book; you'll find every type and shape of mortgage lender listed.

Interest rates, loan periods, "point" cost, closing costs, and many other elements in a mortgage can make factual comparisons about as confusing as a house of mirrors. Attack each task in succession with the aid of a "Mortgage Comparator" like the one shown in Fig. 12-4. Use it to compare the cost of financing a specific house — not mortgages in general. Make sure you obtain the information you need without signing a loan application. Also, check mortgagor plans for such small-print items as:

• Prepayment penalty — Will the mortgage obligate you to pay an additional amount if you pay off the mortgage early? If you should sell during the period in which a prepayment penalty applies, what will the costs be? Prepayment clauses have been calling for steep penalties during the last several years of high interest rates to prevent refinancing if interest rates should fall — so watch this one closely.

• Taxes and insurance escrow account — Will the mortgage company require you to deposit a monthly amount equal to 1/12 of the estimated taxes and premium for insurance? This is money that seldom draws interest; you might prefer to manage it yourself.

• Insurance — Will you be required to buy fire and extended damage insurance from the mortgage company? Will the mortgage company accept a homeowner's policy that includes basic fire coverage to protect the company's interests plus other coverages that protect your furnishings and provide liability coverage? Will the mortgage company require you to carry a term life insurance package to retire the mortgage in case of your death? Ordinarily you should avoid buying any insurance from the mortgage company. You can probably buy equivalent protection from other sources for less cash (see Chapter 4).

• Late-payment penalty — Will the mortgage agreement include a grace period for making payments? If payments fall outside the grace

	Lender #1	Lender #2	Lender #3
Name of Potential Lender			
Address			
Person Contacted			
Down Payment Required			
Loan Amount			
Interest Rate			
Monthly Payment (Principal + Interest)			
Escrow Payments (?) (Taxes + Insurance)			
Type of Mortgage			
Total Mortgage Cost (Monthly Payments × No. of Months)			
Dollar Cost of Interest (Total Cost — Loan Amount)			
Appraisal Fee			
Survey Fee			
Title Search & Insurance			
Revenue Stamps			
Recording Fees			
Credit Check			
Mortgage Finder's Fee			
Mortgage Service Charges			
Other Costs			
Total Loan Costs			
Open End Mortgage			
Prepayment Penalty			
Insurance Required			
Appliance Package			

FIG. 12-4 — Mortgage Comparator

period, what penalty will be assessed — if any?

• Interruption provisions — Will your mortgage include short-term provisions to protect your investment in case you are hospitalized or unable to work for a short period? Some mortgages include automatic extension privileges to cover valid interruptions of income and ability to pay.

• Open-end provisions — Will the mortgage permit borrowing later for improvements without refinancing?

• Points — Another name for a discount loan, "points" are a one-time cost leveled against either the seller or buyer by the lender. One point is simply 1 per cent of the loan amount. For example, if a loan is set up for $10,000, each point amounts to $100. A lender who charges three points deducts $300 from the $10,000 loan amount and arranges an amortized payment schedule for the full amount. Points increase your effective rate of interest. How much your interest rate is affected depends on how long you continue to pay on the loan. If you were to pay three points on the example $10,000 loan to be paid off in 20 years at a nominal 6 per cent interest rate, your effective interest rate is 6.13 per cent. However, if you pay off the entire loan after only five years, you pay an effective nominal interest rate of 6.51 per cent. Table 12D summarizes the effect of points paid on interest rate. This table is abstracted from a full set of 55 tables covering rates from 5% through $7^1/_2$ % by 1/4 per cent increments over periods of 10, 15, 20, 25 and 30 years for up to 10 points.* Compare interest costs among lenders according to how many points they plan to charge — not the quoted nominal rate.

Closing and Other Costs — In addition to checking out the fine-print clauses, compare the so-called "closing costs." These costs are payable in cash at the time you take title to the house. Some of the important closing costs:

• Title insurance is a policy issued by an independent company that certifies the deed you receive when you purchase a house is a good title. There may be exceptions noted, such as an easement. Should a controversy arise about your ownership, the title insurance company is obligated to defend your title in court and, if you lose, to pay you damages up to the amount of the policy. Usually, the cost of a title search is included in the policy costs, but check before signing.

• Land survey is another service required by the lender. An engineer with metal tape and transit determines the corners of your

Influence of Mortgage Points on Interest Rates, (Box 576, South Bend, Indiana 46624: Carleton Financial Computations, Inc.).

property and checks the actual land against the plot plan and legal description. Usually, a survey for a lot where known corners are clearly marked runs from $30 to $50. However, if you should be buying an irregular, large chunk of land where sight lines are impeded with trees and topography is hilly, a survey could run into several hundred dollars.

*TABLE 12D Effect of Mortgage Points on Interest Rates**

20-Year Mortgage Period

Nominal Interest Rate	No. of Points Charged	Effective Nominal Interest Rate if Loan is Repaid after			
		5 yrs.	10 yrs.	15 yrs.	20 yrs.
6%	1	6.25	6.16	6.13	6.13
	2	6.50	6.31	6.26	6.25
	3	6.76	6.47	6.40	6.38
	4	7.02	6.64	6.54	6.51
	5	7.28	6.80	6.67	6.65
	6	7.55	6.97	6.82	6.78
6½%	1	6.75	6.66	6.63	6.63
	2	7.01	6.82	6.77	6.76
	3	7.27	6.98	6.91	6.89
	4	7.53	7.15	7.05	7.02
	5	7.79	7.31	7.17	7.16
	6	8.06	7.48	7.33	7.30
7%	1	7.25	7.16	7.14	7.13
	2	7.51	7.32	7.27	7.26
	3	7.77	7.49	7.41	7.40
	4	8.04	7.66	7.56	7.53
	5	8.30	7.83	7.77	7.67
	6	8.57	8.00	7.85	7.81

*Summarized with permission from *Influence of Mortgage Points on Interest Rates,* Carleton Financial Computations, Inc., South Bend, Indiana.

• Finder's or placement fee is charged by the mortgage company as a service charge for arranging the mortgage. A fee of 1 ½ per cent of the mortgage amount is common, but this percentage may vary from 1/2 to 4 or 5 per cent.
• Inspection and appraisal fee is optional, but covers the cost of appraising the property for the lending institution. An inspection fee covers the cost of a structural engineer's inspection for dry rot or termite damage. These fees vary widely, possibly from $25 to $100, depending on the house.

• Sales tax, recording stamps, and registration fees are legal requirements that vary by state, sometimes by city and county. Sales tax may run 1 per cent of the sales price (not mortgage amount), but stamps and fees seldom exceed .1% of the mortgage amount.

• Credit report is a routine charge that may run $10 to $20.

• Attorney's fees vary widely from as little as $25 to as much as $300 and depend on the problems encountered.

• Prorated payments for taxes, insurance, and any other prepaid or accrued costs are settled as of the date of closing. For example, a buyer who takes over property for which taxes are collected at the end of the year may receive an allowance for that portion of the year in which he did not own the property.

Any closing costs that fall outside of these general categories should be investigated. Sharp lenders are known to tack on fees and unidentified charges as a part of the closing to increase their income from the property sale or lending of money. Make a detailed study of the closing statement, preferably ahead of time with the aid of your Mortgage Comparator (Fig. 12-4).

Land Contracts — Property may be sold and financed with a land contract that is similar to but distinctly different from a mortgage. Some of the major differences are:

• Title to the property remains with the seller in a land contract. Ordinarily, in a sale with a mortgage, title passes to the buyer subject to satisfaction of the mortgage. In a land contract, the seller "contracts" to convey a valid title upon completion of the terms of the contract — mainly paying off the balance due.

• Down payment is frequently quite small. Rather than a down payment of 20 or 25 per cent on a conventional loan, the land contract payment may be 5 per cent, or as much as 10 per cent. A small down payment compensates for the lower risk assumed by the seller (since he still has title to the property and can sell again if the buyer defaults).

• Higher interest payments are another offset to the small down payment normally required on a land contract.

• High monthly payments result from high interest and small down payment. Also, land contracts are usually written for a short period, say five years. During this period, the high monthly payments build equity fast and permit the buyer to obtain a mortgage that he uses to pay off the land contract.

MONEY SAVERS FROM AN UNDERSTANDING OF HOME FINANCING ECONOMICS

Leverage, or the multiplier effect of equity, affects the price you pay for housing — the monthly or yearly price you pay for sheltering your family. Your equity in a house is usually small. In fact, you don't buy a house — the mortgage company buys the house and you buy it from the mortgage company a bit at a time. Learning the economics of house buying, renting, or selling the hard way, from the mistakes you may experience, can be mighty expensive. The money-market pros make few mistakes. So, to protect your pocketbook, this chapter covered such fundamentals as —

- *Analysis of the real costs of owning a house — exchange costs and repetitive costs.*
- *Understanding the real effects of inflation and depreciation on housing prices and costs.*
- *How to develop your spending plan to find how much of your income you can spend on housing — then how to buy the housing you want for that money.*
- *Managing your housing loan costs — down payment, prepayment, and interest effects.*
- *How to shop for a mortgage and how to protect your investment.*
- *Understanding the variations in closing costs.*

13

How To Shop For A Home And Pay Less When You Buy

When it comes to fun and games you play with your own money, it's hard to beat "let's buy a house for less." The payoff can be in the thousands of dollars. You may lose by default, skinned so neatly even you aren't aware of the slick job. What makes the "buy-a-house-for-less" game so fascinating is the multiplier effect from the equity — total cost relationship. A 1 per cent saving on a $20,000 house is $200 — and you can easily save five — even ten times that amount and still get the house you want. How? By knowing and practicing some of the tactics realtors and house appraisers know best. It's your money — learn how to stretch it to cover the housing you really want by —

- *Analyzing the trade-offs between older homes, builders' tract homes, prefabs, shell houses you finish yourself, trailers — and others.*
- *Systematizing your search for the house that best suits your needs.*
- *Check-rating a neighborhood.*
- *Living with a floor plan.*
- *Checking the advantages, disadvantages, and costs of building your own, very special, new house designed by an architect.*
- *Shopping tactics and know-how when searching for a house.*
- *Negotiating the dollars you pay for the house you want.*

You can't squeeze 'em like tomatoes in the market — or look for their government inspector's grade mark, like T-bone steaks. Houses are different. And, they are about the biggest-ticket item you're ever likely to buy. So, you ought to know what you're doing.

Are you looking for a place to sleep — some place to keep the rain off, to hang your slacks — minimum shelter?

Or, are you looking for a house that shouts — "I've got it made!" — a place that commands attention, that reflects your good taste, and affords a stage for entertaining?

Either way, you want the most for your money.

Which Kind Of House?

Immediately you must choose — old house, one peoplecoop in a tract, custom design, prefab, trailer, or a shell house? Each has its place. Don't make your decision until you've considered all the alternatives—

Older Houses — You'll find older houses in established neighborhoods where schools are stabilized, utilities are built (and possibly paid for), streets have been paved for years, and the character of the area is fixed or changes slowly. Take established location for example. Old-timers appreciated a view too. So, they built their homes on view sites. But an established location may be so old that blight has set in. Big houses may have been cut up for small apartments; streets may be so narrow and lots so small that parking space is limited and traffic is congested. The established location may be in the middle of an industrial area where air is polluted. Schools and utilities may be substandard. Sewers may be in and paid for, but they may be too small and back up when overloaded. Weigh possible advantages of older houses against possible disadvantages. For example—

• Space — Houses with more rooms, kitchens with pantries and eating spaces, bedrooms with enormous walk-in closets, etc., were common years ago. The extra space you buy in an old house may also be more expensive to heat, impossible to air-condition, and full of dust and drafts to make housekeeping dificult.

• Charm and tradition — Truly charming homes in the tradition of New England and Williamsburg offer a nostalgic link with the past. They invoke fond remembrances of how great things were in the "good ol' days." Where there is a strong emotional attachment between homeowner and shelter, the charm of an old house may very well overbalance an electrical system that is underwired, worn plumbing that is too small to accept garbage disposers, or a hot water system with a capacity too small for automatic dish- and clothes-washers plus baths and showers.

• Stability — When you buy in an established neighborhood, you can see what you're getting into — the schools are built, the local government has matured (possibly decayed), community facilities are in and likely to remain unchanged — for good or bad — for years.

Little need be imagined or planned for; it's there. If you like what you see, you can expect it to remain relatively unchanged. But if you see problems, you are unlikely to change them appreciably.

New Tract Homes — Since World War II large areas of farmland have been converted to millions of homes. Many of these developments were poorly planned. However, they offer relatively clean air, a long commute, and a chance for many families to start new communities. Examine these factors about new homes, particularly those built on a tract:

• Location — Living away from the center of things is the price you pay for living in suburbia. Check not only the availability of transportation, but the price. You can put a price on distance by adding the cost of transportation to your monthly housing budget. A far-out location with a large commuting bill simply reduces the amount you can spend for a house. Industry is moving to the suburbs. You may be living closer to your job in the country than you would be in the city. But, know the price you will be paying for transportation.

• Growing instability — Facilities that are taken for granted in the city must often be set up from scratch in the new communities. Police and fire protection, water, sewer, garbage collection, schools, local government, recreation districts, transportation — all may be only partly developed in the new, fresh tract of homes that attracts your eye. The low taxes and low utility rates quoted may simply mean that they haven't yet totaled the price for a new town hall, new schools, new roads, and all the other things and services you expect in a new community. Over the horizon may be a series of bond issues, higher taxes, and double-shifted schools until new facilities are provided with your money.

• Getting settled costs — Along with the unrestrained job of occupying a house no one else has lived in, you will need to consider the cost of landscaping (see Chapter 11), frills the builder left off, such as water softener, storm doors and screens; carpets, equipment, such as lawn mower, wheelbarrow, and a variety of small tools; and a seemingly unending list of things from garbage cans to light bulbs. There are also shelves to be installed, painting to finish, things to be fixed (unless your builder was unusually conscientious), floors to be waxed and polished, and plans made for finishing off a basement or expandable upstairs. It has been truly said that "a house is never finished."

Shell Houses — Lowest in cost is the shell house — an unfinished house that is mainly enclosed space. Depending on the builder, the shell home may include only a minimum of underground plumbing and a source of electrical power. There may not even be a way to heat the house. Or, the shell house builder may include plumbing and fixtures, basic electrical wiring, and a heating system. However, there may be no ceiling, insulation, interior walls (except those necessary for structure and to hold plumbing runs), finished floors, cabinets, or paint. These are the finishing touches you agree to complete for a 20 to 30 per cent reduction in price. By finishing off a shell house, you add a "sweat equity" from your own labor.

If you consider a shell home, make sure you understand the size of the finishing job. Time and your labor are not the only ingredients needed. Figure also the cost of lumber, wallboard, paint, flooring, hardware, and fixtures, Evaluate the problems of living in a space that will regularly be contaminated with sawdust, plaster dust, and paint spills, the need to clean rough floors, and the lack of time for socializing. And, take it from one who did, finishing off a shell house takes much more time and energy than you expect. But, you can build enough equity into the house to pocket enough of a down payment to buy the house you really had in mind in the first place. Such a scheme takes planning. However, if you are skilled, finishing off a shell house for sale amounts to a form of moonlighting with a break on income tax.

Custom-Designed-and-Built House — Most expensive and most satisfying is the house built just for you. Custom houses are expensive because they are one of a kind and because they are built to a higher standard of everything from kiln-dried lumber to top-grade plumbing and lighting fixtures. The architect will design every part of the house and write specifications controlling the quality — and cost — of every item in it. Builders, on the other hand, select fixtures and equipment specially designed for mass production and competitive cost.

Prefabricated House — Formerly a term synonymous with cheap houses, prefabrication has proved economical and effective in applying factory methods to house-building. Prefabrication may mean a variety of things. Some prefabricators build whole sections complete, much like a trailer, then truck the sections to a site and simply fasten them together. Other prefabricators simply build components, such as 4-foot-wide wall sections and roof trusses. The site builder assembles them to form nearly any floor plan he or you select. If you plan to buy a home near a prefab factory, you can probably buy more house for less money in a prefab than you can from a conventional builder. If your site is a long truck haul from the factory, if your lot is not level, or you want something just a little unusual, a prefabricated house may cost you more than a house specifically planned and built for your site. When checking alternative costs, include all elements furnished in a cost comparison. Prefabricators usually include more equipment, such as dishwashers, in a package than individual builders.

Prefabbing formerly offered a few floor plans with little variety. But no longer. Modular units, selected elements, and varied equipment packages can be combined into a plan with varied space to suit almost any requirement. However, most plans are ordinary and offer little of the flair and originality available in a custom-built home.

Trailer or Mobile Home — Completely factory built, the mobile home offers the benefits of mass production with built-in equipment and mobility. But the running gear and structure necessary to provide mobility cost extra. Weigh these factors when considering a trailer:

- Mobility — If your job moves around, a mobile home may solve the problem of packing up and moving from one rented house or apartment to another. Instead, you put the trailer together, hire a professional tow truck and move to another mobile home park. Lots for mobile homes are usually small — another cost saving. Rent for mobile home space complete with sewer, water, and electrical hook-ups is only a fraction of the cost of rental housing. Modern mobile home parks occupy view sites and are accepted like row houses or apartments. Moving your big trailer from one spot to another (40c to 75c per mile) will probably cost much less than the exchange costs in selling and buying a home plus the cost of packing up belongings and moving.

- Financing — Buying a mobile home frequently requires more cash for a down payment and higher monthly payments than a house. Terms for mobile homes frequently require 25 or more per cent down, with the remainder financed over periods no longer than seven to ten years. Offsetting the higher finance costs are: 1) You buy only the home, not the home plus land. 2) Total cost of a suitable mobile home will probably be less than similar accommodations in a fixed house. 3) More of your payments go to retire the principal of the loan, so you acquire an equity more quickly than for a long-term house loan.

Co-operative Apartments — Co-op apartments offer some of the advantages of owning (acquisition of equity, break on taxes) along with the lower cost of multiple housing. Laws vary in different states, but the term "co-op apartment" usually means you do not actually own your own apartment. You do own a share in a corporation or trust which, in turn, owns the apartment house. There are a number of advantages:

- More living space for your money — By eliminating the landlord's profit and by taking advantage of low-interest, FHA-guaranteed loans, you can usually buy more space per buck in a co-op than you can in a straight rental.
- Tax benefit — Since you actually own a part of a housing corporation or trust, you benefit by deducting interest payments and taxes when computing your income tax.
- Guarantee against rental increases — Most renters roll with the punches of inflation by absorbing rent increases and costs as prices go up. Once you buy a co-op, the owning portion of your payment remains fixed. However, the variable portion of your payment that covers taxes and communal upkeep may increase.

Co-ops also have a number of disadvantages you should be aware of:

- Possible selling difficulties — When you buy a share in the co-op corporation, the agreement may call for your neighbors' approval of any potential buyer, renter, or subleaser. Check your rights on this point carefully and know your possible recourses.
- Uncontrollable costs — If all apartments are occupied in a co-op, you can estimate monthly payments and operating costs quite closely. However, if some of the co-op owners become delinquent, move out without selling, or some of the apartments remain unsold, the remaining owners must assume a higher share of total costs.

Condominiums — More popular every day are condominium apartments. Enabling state laws permit ownership of blocks of space rather than areas on the face of the earth. In a condominium, you actually own your own apartment under an exact definition of space, much as a building lot is legally described. You can sell it, rent it, lease it, or leave it empty without affecting the surrounding apartments. Of course, your neighbors can do the same. Before you buy, retain a lawyer to look for legal loopholes in the condominium you may be considering.

Row Houses — Conservation of land leads to the building of row houses — those individual homes set alongside each other, many with common walls, and all with a minimum lawn or yard. Limited landscaping and yard upkeep is one plus for the row house. Row houses combined with green space available to all owners is a new idea being practiced to get away from street after street of "peoplecoops."

Row houses are popular in areas where old buildings near the center of a city have been torn down as part of rehabilitation projects.

What To Look For When Shopping For A House

Evaluate Lot and Location — Real estate agents will tell you the three most important elements in buying a house are location, location, and location. A house and its lot are inseparable — buy one — buy them both. And you can't consider a lot or building site by itself; you must evaluate it relative to the lots around and the neighbors. Even Confucius recognized the value of a lot when he said, "The value of thy property dependeth upon thy neighbor."

Whether you buy an empty lot or one with a home already built on it, look for certain elements:

- Size, shape and topography — is the lot big enough for the house or so big that yard maintenance will be a chore rather than a relaxing pleasure? How about drainage? Is the shape right for the house that's there or the one you have in mind?
- Value — What is the price of the empty lot relative to the price of the house. Generally, an improved lot with utilities and street improvements in and paid for should cost about 10 to 15 per cent of the total cost of house plus lot.
- Neighborhood — Remember, your lot will be a part of a much larger community. How does it stack up? Are the other houses well kept, painted, lawns mowed, etc.? Do the other owners take pride in their homes? Or, is the area on the down-grade with families moving out and less desirable groups moving in, possibly attracted by cheaper prices? How about noise and air pollution? Transportation? If the area is completely new, what are the zoning provisions that protect your well-built home from ending up alongside a trailer or a shack? Check on taxes, plans for building highways, and existing or planned community facilities, such as schools, churches, municipal fire and police protection, and recreational opportunities. Don't depend on a realtor; visit the town hall and school administration headquarters yourself.

Use the Lot and Location Checklist (Fig. 13-1) to make sure you consider every element. Once you buy a location, it's there to stay. You may move, but the lot and house stay. Always consider the problems you may have in selling a house before you buy it. Money lenders do!

Check Out the Floor Plan — Traffic pattern, arrangement of rooms, separation of living and activity areas from sleeping areas,

When rating potential lots for building or the lot with a house built on it, use a point-rating system where:

Excellent = 3 points
Good   = 2 points
Fair   = 1 point
Poor   = 0

	Point Score
NEIGHBORHOOD	
General trend — building up or deteriorating	
Noise and traffic	
Street layout and standards — sidewalks	
Public transportation availability	
Type, service, frequency	
Cost	
Travel time to and from work	
Accessibility to shopping areas	
Proximity to industry and air pollution sources	
Local government — incorporated or area-wide	
Zoning regulations — enforcement of codes	
General services	
Police, courts	
Fire protection	
Health	
Public recreation programs and facilities	
Street lighting	
Sanitary sewerage	
Storm sewerage	
Rubbish and garbage removal	
School system — rating — evaluation	
Recreation — commercial facilities	
Churches	
Amusements	
SPECIFIC LOT* IN NEIGHBORHOOD	
Siting — effect on outdoor living	
Shape and topography — any problems with building?	
Soil conditions — rock, clay	
Drainage	
View or potential view — potential view blockage	

*Rate either for potential building site or as part of over-all house and lot combination.

FIG. 13-1—Lot and Location Check List

	Point Score
Privacy or potential privacy	
Size of lot relative to others in neighborhood	
Cost of lot relative to size and cost of houses	
Utilities — general	
Water — from system or well?	
Sewer connection available — cost?	
Gas service mains in?	
Distance to fire plug	
Electric power availability	
Taxes — without house	
— with an existing house	

TOTAL

FIG 13-1—Lot and Location Check List (Continued)

possibilities for arranging furniture — all are functions of the floor plan. Does the front door open directly into the living room? Or into a hall from which your guests can choose to move to the living room, kitchen, upstairs, or to the bedroom section without passing through the rest of the house? All of these features are present in some degree in every house. A floor plan may be easy to live with according to your living pattern, family make-up, or existing furniture. The same plan may be completely wrong for another family. There is no ideal floor plan. Check every house yourself, following the check list in Fig. 13-2.

When you find a house that seems to suit you best, spend some time going through the motions of living in the house. Walk through the motions of a day — or a week in the house. For example, move from the bedroom to bath, to kitchen, and out to the garage to simulate the activities you normally go through at the beginning of each day, getting your family up, feeding them breakfest, and getting them (and possibly yourself) off to school or work. Follow through with a similar examination of activities for entertaining. Is there a closet for coats inside the front door? If your parties end up in the kitchen, is there room for more than two or three? Can you separate dining room and/or kitchen from the living area? Or, do you prefer to have an open plan with one area flowing into another without sharp breaks? In effect, run the house through a shakedown cruise to see that it fits your living pattern.

Size of rooms and total floor area are a major concern in comparing houses. As part of your rating (Fig. 13-2), see if the master bedroom will handle the king-size bed you prize, or whether there is space for your long, low, and modern divan. Check for adequate storage space in kitchen and bedrooms. Consider the total house area and compare its cost on a square-foot base. Here's how — Find the total living area from the basic dimensions. For example, if the house is 24 feet wide and 36 feet long, one floor covers 864 square feet. If it has a garage or carport 20 x 20, that's 400 square feet, but it is not living area. Apply a 1/4 factor and add 100 square feet to the total. If there is a basement, apply a 1/2 factor to the actual space, because it is potential living area. Second-floor rooms finished and livable get a full factor; if they are unfinished, apply the 1/2 factor. For the example house, take 864 basic, 100 for garage, plus 432 for a basement, and there is no upstairs. This totals 1,396 square feet of equivalent living area. If you buy the house for $17,250, that figures out to be about $13.30 per square foot. Use such a figure as a rough guide only. Houses fitted out with carpeting, expensive built-in appliances, and on a highly desirable lot will cost more than a bare, minimum-equipped house on a tiny tract lot. The price per square foot of equivalent livable area can prompt questions about why one house may be higher per square foot than another.

Follow point-rating plan of Fig. 13-1: Excellent = 3 points, Good = 2 points, Fair = 1 point, Poor = 0

	Point Score
GENERAL PLAN	
Separation of living, sleeping, and working areas?	
Hall arrangements and accessibility	
Does front door open into living room?	
Does front door open into a hallway?	
Is door to kitchen close to garage or driveway?	
Do bedrooms open to hallway near bath?	
Stairways to upper level or basement handy?	
Relation of garage and driveway to street	
Guest parking available	
Are storage areas strategically located?	
Guest closet near front door	
Children's closet and boot storage near back door	
Bulk storage — garage, attic, or basement	
Linen storage near bedrooms	
Privacy — from street	
— from abutting neighbors	

FIG. 13-2—Floor Plan Check List

	Point Score
Outlook — oriented toward street	
— oriented toward new or outdoor living area	
Siting relative to — prevailing summer breeze	
— winter storms	
— sun for both winter and summer	
Could floor plan be expanded to include more rooms?	
LIVING AREAS	
Living room relation to traffic into and through house	
Relation of living room — oriented to street	
— oriented to view	
Size and shape — fit family?	
Living room open to or separated from kitchen?	
Window treatment	
Shades and draperies	
WORKING AREAS	
Kitchen — relation to dining room	
— relation to back door and garage	
— relation to family room	
— cabinets — storage space	
— working counter	
— traffic pattern while cooking	
— open to rest of house	
— close to bath and play areas	
— relation to patio or outdoor living area	
Laundry — relation to bedrooms and baths	
— upstairs or in basement	
— relation to drying yard (if no dryer)	
— sorting and folding space	
EATING AREAS	
Separate dining room	
Family eating space — in kitchen	
— in family room	
Traffic pattern between kitchen and eating areas	
Size and traffic pattern in dining areas	
SLEEPING AREAS	
Number of bedrooms for family	
Relation of bedrooms to baths	

FIG. 13-2—Floor Plan Check List (Continued)

	Point Score
Any rooms without access directly to hall	
Convertible space available for guests	
Bedrooms separated from living and working areas	
Room for study and quiet play in bedrooms	
BATHING AREAS	
Enough bath facilities	
Relation of baths to bedrooms	
Relation of baths to living areas	
Relation of baths to play areas	
FUN AND RECREATION AREAS	
Family room near kitchen	
Play areas separated from sleep areas	
Relation of outdoor living areas to kitchen	
to driveway	
to main hallway	
Are outdoor play areas private — from house	
— from neighbors	
TV zone away from play areas	
from living areas	

TOTAL

FIG. 13-2—Floor Plan Check List (Continued)

Evaluating the Whole House — You have already looked at two of the most important factors in selecting a house — location and floor plan. Some of the other important factors to consider include:

- Materials — Are interior walls plasterboard, paneled, papered, or painted? What kind of kitchen counters are built in? How about floors — tile, hardwood, or carpeting? On the outside, is the siding wood, metal, composition? What kind of roof? Look for signs of potential maintenance or repair expense both inside and outside.
- Basement or attic? Either of these two areas may offer expandable living space if you foresee a need for additional bedrooms. Or, they offer storage space that relieves the pressure on closets and garage.
- Outdoor siting — Depending on whether a house is planned individually by an architect or planted in a row by a tract builder, a house may fit its environment or not. Check, for example, whether the outdoor living area (that yard or patio space just off a

family or dining room) includes privacy. Is it on the south or west to put you in the warm sun if you live where evenings are cool or in the shade if evenings are hot and muggy? Do the driveway and garage permit easy access from the street? How about guest parking space? Is there yard room for children's activities? Consider all of these exterior features when check-rating a house (Fig. 13-3).

- Structurally sound? — Unless you are well versed in house construction, ask for help on this one. But make a preliminary check yourself. For· example, look for cracks in plaster, doors that bind in their frames, noticeable slopes to a floor, peeling paint outside, signs of water leakage inside, damp or wet basement floor, and loose window panes or windows. You probably won't find a house that is perfect in every detail. But, if some clue triggers a question, find out the answer *before* you buy. If you see something that obviously needs fixing, a contractor will give you an estimate of the cost. Also, a seller when faced with the facts of a fault in the house, may be easier to dicker with.

- Operating expenses — Since heating or air-conditioning costs are the biggest items among various utilities, check two or three years' heating bills (gas, oil, electricity) and strike an average. If the owner hasn't kept records, check with the gas company or his oil supplier; they may have records. Check also on sewer charges, rubbish removal (are costs paid for in taxes — or separately), electrical power, water, and taxes. All of these costs become a part of your housing bill along with regular payments on a mortgage. A house without insulation and a high heating bill may not be so good a buy as a well-built house priced higher but with lower operating costs.

Building A New Home

For families who are home-oriented, building their own house — just like they want it — is a dream and a goal. A custom home can be individual, can suit the living pattern of the family that built it — and usually costs considerably more than a tract house. If you decide to build your own home, look for these ideas to get your dream house for less cash:

Use an architect? — Like many professional people, an architect prospers only if he can contribute to his client. An architect will study your living pattern, probe into your home-oriented imagery, and determine the specific and important items you want in a house. Then,

Point values: Excellent = 3 points, Good = 2 points, Fair = 1 point, Poor = 0

Point
Score

GENERAL CONSTRUCTION

Foundation — basement walls straight, cracked
           — leakage streaks
Crawl space — ground sealed against moisture
Framing — sound, without cracks
         — surface finish
         — interior walls cracked, bowed, or crooked
         — joists and rafters sound — no rot or termites
         — floor firm, quiet, without sags or grade
Roof — condition from outside
       — any apparent leaks in attic or ceilings
       — condition of gutters and downspouts
       — overhang adequate
Insulation — in attic or ceiling
         — under floor
         — storm windows and doors
         — weather-stripping
Porches or decks — any rotting, flaked paint
         — construction sound

WIRING AND HEATING

Size and power capacity of main junction box
Arrangement of lights and outlets
Separate outlets for kitchen appliances
Furnace size okay for house
Fuel compatible with area
Registers or radiators strategically located
Blower or pump operation okay
Are ducts or hot-water insulated?
Noise during operation of heating system
Filter condition (hot-air system)

WATER AND SEWER

If water supplied by area system, cost?
Is water hard?
Water softener? Type?
If water comes from well, reliability?
  Rate well can supply water?
Hot-water heater — size — sign of leaks?

FIG. 13-3—House Construction Check List

Point
Score

Sewerage system installed and operating?
  If not, what are plans?
  Assessment probable?
Septic tank
  Operation of drain field satisfactory
  Relation of tank and drain field to house
Operation and condition of plumbing fixtures
Faucets — leaks — noise during operation
Any water hammer or chattering in water system?

INTERIOR

Kind and condition of floors
Door operation
Wall surface condition
Windows operate easily?
Are lights and fixtures adequate?
Built-in appliances — dishwasher, oven, range top,
  other
Condition of tubs and showers
  Tile clean, joints sound
  Joint between tub and tile leak-tight?
Storage cabinets — finish and operation okay
Kitchen counter tops — type, condition

TOTAL

FIG. 13-3 — House Construction Check List (Continued)

he will design a house to fit those needs exactly — after a little negotiation. You should pick an architect with the same care you pick a doctor, because the relationship will be close and personal.

An architect charges from 8 to 15 per cent of the cost of the house as his fee for designing, drawing working plans, helping you select a builder, and representing you during construction. If you are knowledgeable about building and can deal with a contractor on a businesslike basis, you might save from 3 to 5 per cent of the architect's fee by not buying the supervision and inspection service. Many architects, however, combine all activities into a single package, including inspection. So, check before you sign the architect agreement. An architect will probably not save you enough during construction to pay for his fee (despite his claim) — but the house you get is more likely to satisfy your unique needs than a stock plan you attempt to modify yourself.

Buy and Use a Stock Plan? — Magazines and plan services offer a wide variety of plans for homes. Stock plans are usually designed by architects and carry a registered architect's seal (required to obtain a building permit in many states or cities). They work like this — A magazine editor will select a home that offers something new and different — often an idea that starts a trend. The architect sells his rights to the plan for a royalty, and the magazine offers copies of complete blueprints for $5. to $7.50 per set — and you'll need at least four sets of plans for bidding and construction. Along with the plans are specifications covering such things as the size of electrical wire used in each section of the house, plus a materials list that simplifies estimating the cost of the house. Stock plans are also available from companies that sell plans from a catalogue by mail.

But, a stock plan represents a house designed to suit someone else. If the plan should suit your family, will fit your lot shape and orientation, and meets the specific and peculiar building code requirements in your community, then you can save yourself several hundred dollars compared to the services of an architect. You have to choose a package. You can't pick a front profile from one design, the floor plan from another, and add a couple of bedrooms to still another one.

Combine Design and Building into One Contract? — Frequently, a builder will offer a package — custom design and building. He builds a house designed specifically for you. Sounds Great! You have to deal with only one person. But, a good architect may be a poor builder, and an efficient, good-quality builder may simply adapt a stock plan to your ideas. Often, a builder simply offers to build a stock house on your lot. If the designer is also the builder, you must make the decisions on quality of lumber, plumbing fixtures, and the myriad details an architect normally performs for you. Also, the designer who is also the builder can cut many corners on cost to his advantage without your knowledge. If you pay the architect separately, he is your man; he protects your interests during building. Again, if you know lumber, plumbing and electrical specifications, and how houses go together and have the time necessary to inspect the building as it goes up, you may save money by combining the design and building into one contract.

Dollar Stretchers — Individually designed homes offer greater variety and flair — often at an increase in price. You want a home uniquely suitable for your family's needs at the best possible price — not the cheapest nor the highest, but the optimum mix of quality, space, and dollars. Some of the ideas to watch for whether you are working with an architect, selecting a stock plan, or designing your own home include:

- Eliminating as many corners, odd shapes, and differences in elevation as possible. A simple square design encloses the maximum space for the least wall area, but a rectangle or some other shape may suit your floor plan or lot better. Evaluate the cost-effectiveness of the added wall length and complication vs. the space you need in the right arrangement.
- Keep bathrooms together, either back to back or stacked directly on top of each other in a two-story house. Such arrangements permit using one vent stack for more than one use. Also, plumbing runs are simpler and you use less hot water if the hot water tank and kitchen are close to the bathrooms.
- Keep the exterior design details simple and in good taste. Designs with highly pitched roofs, geegaws in decorative construction, and use of odd materials or colors to achieve a "gee-whizzer" effect can severely affect the loan available from a mortgage lender. Remember, the house may be exactly right for you, but the mortgage banker considers how he can sell the house if you don't make the payments. If a house is so odd or unusual that resale value may be affected, your down payment will be larger than if the house is more reasonable — therefore, resaleable.
- Look ahead and eliminate double building, such as expensive hardwood floors under wall-to-wall carpeting or finished plasterboard walls covered with wood or hardwood paneling. Finish off floors to be carpeted with smooth (and inexpensive) plywood, for example. If you plan to install paneling, either leave the studs blank (if permitted by code) or nail up plasterboard but eliminate the joint-taping expense.
- Do spend money where later reductions in operating expense will pay for the extra cost. Insulation is a prime example. Installing effective insulation when the house is built and walls are open can pay for the slight extra cost within a few years of operation. Or, install an effective drain system outside a basement footing to carry away ground water rather than try to stop seepage after the house is built.

Shopping For A House

For most families, buying a house is a major purchase. Unless you are a chronic mover, in which case you should probably not be buying a house (see Chapter 12), you'll be living with your house for a long time. So, don't end up living with a mistake. Here's how —

Shop Widely and Intensively — If you recently moved to a city or area, find some kind of temporary housing. Don't be stampeded into buying a house because you must have some place to live. Take time to search out neighborhoods (using the checklist in Fig. 13-1 as a guide), drive over alternate routes to your work, investigate school systems, pick up a feel for trends — which areas are headed for blight, which areas are building prestige, and which areas will be convenient to the activities that interest your family. Remember, location is all-important.

Evaluate Houses, Builders, and Local Designs — Land use and house designs vary widely from one section of the country to another. For example, don't expect to locate a trim Cape Cod cottage in a desert area abounding with sweeping views. Look at as many houses as several realtors will show you. Despite multiple listing services, different realtors show different houses — along with many of the same houses. Only after studying the market thoroughly will you begin to sense a pattern of values and prices. Remember, it's your money you'll be spending for a number of years.

Look at Housing for Yourself — Don't depend entirely on realtors. Drive around desirable neighborhoods on weekends. Look for owners who are selling houses for themselves. Examine the classified sections of local newspapers intensively to locate houses for sale by individuals. Examine company bulletin boards, study in-plant newspapers and trading posts for leads to houses that could be priced below the market, and ask among your friends or associates at work for leads. The "market" is a changeable thing that exists mainly in the minds of realtors and is determined only in part by actual purchases. Find out for yourself why different houses carry varied price tags. Don't hesitate to ask your friendly banker or mortgage lender about specific areas, possibly even specific houses and why houses are priced as they are. You'll sense these patterns from the mass of data you collect only if you keep at the shopping and if you allow enough time for conclusions to emerge.

Look into the possibilities of buying a foreclosed FHA or VA home from the United States government. When buyers pay a minimum or nothing down (for qualified VA buyers), a house may actually be worth less than the money owed for a number of years. Therefore some buyers walk away rather than to try to sell their homes. The government, as the loan insuring agency, gets the houses back. Contact the local FHA or VA office in your community for information on foreclosed homes for sale at a saving.

Shopping for a house is much like shopping for a used car — you'll probably never find one that satisfies all your requirements. But, look for the one that most closely meets your needs within the price range you have already established (see Chapters 1 and 12). After you have developed a feel for the market, use a check-off chart like the one in Fig. 13-3 to narrow your choice. Use the numerical score you come up with only as a guide; don't buy a house by the numbers. But using such a chart will prevent you from putting too much emphasis on some single element.

Closing the Deal — Actually negotiating for a house involves even more of the David Harum-type of practical horse (read "house") trading than does the buying of a car. None but the naive owner or realtor expects to sell a house at the asking price these days. Such a price is simply a point of departure from which to start bargaining. Realtors, when asked, "How firm is the price?" will usually adopt a serious mien and reply, "Quite firm." *Don't believe it.* Remember, the realtor derives his commission from the seller — the greater the price, the more his commission. Sometimes, an owner will establish a rock-bottom price (considerably below the asking price) and allow the realtor to retain the difference between this rock-bottom price and whatever he can wheedle out of a buyer. There was a time, right after the war, when housing was short, that realtors could be hard-nosed on price — could sell on a "take-it-or-leave-it" basis. Not so any more. With few exceptions, it's a buyers' market. Don't be hoodwinked into paying more than the owner really expected to get for his house. When closing the deal for the house you have selected, remember —

• A realtor cannot refuse any bona fide offer. He must transmit any offer he receives in writing to the owner for his decision. The realtor can comment, he can recommend that the owner not accept the offer, but he cannot refuse to show it to the owner. The owner — not the realtor — is selling the house.

• A house that has been on the market for several months may be ripe for a cut-to-the-bone offer. But make sure you know why the house has not sold. Many times the owner simply refuses to place a realistic value on the house. Realtors stop showing a house after a number of prospects balk at the price. But an owner's resolve deteriorates with time. He gets impatient. He may have been so imprudent as to buy another house before his first house is sold. Such an owner is ripe for a low-priced, cash offer.

• The "ridiculous" offer frequently buys the house. When you see many houses standing vacant in an area, you can be sure that, despite realtors' efforts to maintain housing values, only the bargain houses sell. When you have thoroughly cased the market and selected the house you want, don't hesitate to make a "ridiculous" offer. A figure 20 per cent below the asking price may be accepted by a desperate owner — particularly one who has moved out of town. If you don't make the offer, you'll never know. Don't be stampeded into a high offer by a realtor who suddenly hears of another offer being considered by the owner. From your study of the market, you will know whether houses are selling quickly or not. If you have settled into temporary housing, you can afford to wait out a low offer — and it's surprising how many are accepted. Remember, it's your money — don't give it away just to be a good fellow.

• Deal directly with the owner who is selling his house without the aid of a realtor. Many owners attempt to sell their own house in order to save the 5 or 6 per cent commission "earned" by the realtor. If such an owner is at all knowledgeable, he will have established his asking price higher than the price he expects to sell for. But he will usually plan on saving the realtor's commission. He may have arranged for financing or offer to transfer his mortgage (providing you, as the buyer, are acceptable to the mortgage company). When making an offer to an owner selling his own house, figure (from your analysis of the market) how much the house is worth less the realtor's commission. A sharp seller may figure there's no point in giving away the entire commission, but, you can probably gain at least 3, possibly 4 per cent, allowing the seller to retain 1 or 2 per cent of the commission. He has little choice. If he gives up and retains a realtor, he loses the entire 4 or 6 per cent commission. He knows the probable selling price. By allowing him a portion of the commission, he may be tempted to sell, and you gain an extra several hundred dollars.

Learn the Facts Yourself — There's absolutely no substitute for facts when shopping for and buying a house. As a buyer you have no professional representative looking after your interests. You and you alone must take full responsibility. At some time in the future, there may develop a need for an agent to help the buyer locate and buy a home that best suits his family and on the best terms. In court lawyers represent both sides of a case. Why not professional help for the buyer? In the meantime you must use every stratagem available to protect your interests and your money.

MONEY SAVERS WHEN SHOPPING FOR AND BUYING A HOUSE

Caution, family councils, and a searching analysis of the area, available homes, alternatives, and costs all figure into a good buy. Don't be too hasty in making up your mind and committing two or three years' earnings for a house. Patience pays off handsomely — so do the many shopping and negotiating tactics bunched together in this one chapter, such as —

- *Matching your family's real needs in housing to the kinds and variety of houses you're likely to find. A haphazard approach won't do.*
- *Considering all of the effects on value through an organized check list that assigns point values to many of the factors you might ignore.*
- *Looking at a house with the idea that you will be selling it some day — so you buy something that is marketable.*
- *Evaluating the neighborhood, the lot, and the house.*
- *Learning how to stretch your dollars if you build a new, custom house.*
- *Shopping for a house in a new area — the ins and outs of buying what you really need for less.*
- *Negotiating for the hard-line price that suits you best — not the owner or the realtor.*

14

Get More Housing Value For Your Dollar By Remodeling

Remodel, or sell your present home and buy another? Maybe your need for more space in a prestigious neighborhood has blinded you to some of the economic facts — that selling and rebuying can cost you all or most of the equity you've built up in your present house. Or, that you can get the bigger, better house you need and want for a tremendous saving by remodeling. Money and emotions can get pretty mixed up without some kind of guidelines to use in your trade-off analysis. So, consider the following — and see how remodeling may be the low-cost answer to your needs by—

- *Examining the dollar exchange costs if you should sell and rebuy. The answer can be a shocker.*
- *Studying the possible pitfalls of remodeling as it applies to your family's housing situation.*
- *Planning your remodeling — which projects pay off, which projects are likely to cost more than they are worth.*
- *Building your dream house in steps through remodeling — at a cash saving.*
- *Shopping for the lowest-cost financing that fits your remodeling needs.*

You've got to move. You've made up your mind. Why? Any number of reasons —

- Expanded income — you can afford more and better housing.
- More children — you need more space.
- Job promotion — you need an upgraded neighborhood to reflect your improved status.
- Parents — they've come to live with you, and you need space.
- Hobbies — Your yard and grounds offer no further challenge to

your green thumb, or you need a big workshop.
- You're just plain sick and tired of the old house and WANT to move.
- Any number of other reasons — only you can think of them.

But wait! Hold on! Consider whether you could answer your needs for less cash by remodeling your present home instead of selling and rebuying. True — emotional or nonfinancial factors may outweigh the dollars-and-cents look. How many dollars are these subjective factors worth to you? Before you move, evaluate alternative plans and assign a cost to each, the way big business does. Convert all data to one common denominator — dollars. With these facts, fancies, and estimates in hand, you're ready to make a rational decision — emotions and dollars all considered.

Cost Impact Of Selling And Rebuying

Don't make an impulse decision without looking at the cost alternatives. If you sell and rebuy, you face the same exchange costs as those detailed in Fig. 12-1. Remember, you pay twice — once when you sell and a second time when you buy. Each transaction can take as much as 10 per cent out of the pot or 20 per cent total from a sell-rebuy exchange. And those dollars come out of your equity. As an alternative, consider how much remodeling you could do with the equivalent bundle of cash. Refer to Fig. 12-1 for details on how you can calculate your own exchange costs.

If you are looking mainly for more space, consider adding rooms onto your house. For example, you might add on a new dormer area to a second floor, finish off existing space in an attic or lower level, convert a garage into living space and rebuild the carport or garage — even build on an entirely new wing with its own plumbing and heating systems. Compare the estimated remodeling cost to your exchange loss if you sell and rebuy. Most likely your loss in the exchange would pay for all or most of the remodeling. Low-cost home improvement loans can supply the added money needed. But, before you jump into remodeling, analyze the following:

Overbuilding — Picture your remodeled house in relation to your neighborhood. If you add on extensively to a small house on a small lot in a neighborhood that is stabilized at a fixed price level, you will probably lose most of the value of your remodeling if you should sell later. For example, suppose you spend $5,000 to add two rooms and modernize the kitchen. Before remodeling, your house and others in the block were worth about $20,000. If you were to sell a few years later, your house might sell for $21,000.

But, if you own a small house on a big lot surrounded by houses worth considerably more than yours, remodeling to bring your house up to the neighborhood level may not only be desirable, but you stand a good chance of recouping most of your investment if you should sell later.

Recognize that neighborhoods fall into price classes. Don't continue to add on to and remodel a small house in a small-house neighborhood until it becomes a castle among huts.

Location — Selling a small "interim" house and rebuying in a prestigious location may be worth the added expense. Your improved job status may demand a bigger home in a "status" neighborhood. No amount of remodeling brings with it a prestigious address. But, make sure of your motives before committing a major chunk of future income to achieve a higher housing status. Only you can evaluate this element.

Uprooting — Moving to a new bigger house in another neighborhood may force you and your family to cut friendly ties with neighbors, community, and school. Make no mistake — the wrenching readjustments that come with a disruption of friends, particularly your children's friends and their school environment, can be upsetting. Here is where you need to bring the entire family into the discussion.

Looking Ahead — Much of the pain and strain from trying to decide whether to remodel or sell and rebuy can be avoided if you look ahead when you first buy. If your housing needs are due to expand, look for a house with space to add rooms on a second floor or in a basement. Or, for the same money, choose a larger house with expansion possibilities over a smaller house full of costly gimmicks. The gimmicks can be added later, but in the meantime, you have the space you need.

Designing And Planning Your Remodeling

Make your changes with a pencil — they're cheaper than changes made with a hammer and saw. Elementary? Of course. But families with the urge to get started frequently change their plans after the carpenter has built part of a new room or other addition. Planning, sketching, borrowing good ideas — all contribute to low-cost, satisfying results from a remodeling project. Remember, planning, with big dollops of dreaming, imagination, and great expectations, is the cheapest part of remodeling. So, as with any low-cost ingredient in a stew, use lots of it. Before picking up a hammer, plan — *plan* — PLAN!

- Study magazines and books — Your public library stacks rows of books on how to plan houses, remodeling projects, and ideas for redoing everything from a basement to a whole house. Read through back issues of AMERICAN HOME, BETTER HOMES & GARDENS, HOUSE BEAUTIFUL, HOUSE & GARDEN, and others. Consult special fall issues of POPULAR MECHANICS, POPULAR SCIENCE, MECHANIX ILLUSTRATED, and SCIENCE AND MECHANICS for plans and ideas to improve your home. The first batch of magazines noted are usually heavy on ideas. The mechanical magazines include more information on actual construction. These magazines are aimed at the homeowner who may be doing all or most of the work himself. Look in the special magazine columns for leads to special booklets to aid planning by American Plywood Association, Western Lumber Association, and many others.
- Consult an architect — Consider hiring an architect if the cost of your remodeling project approaches half the cost of the original house. For example, you may have bought a summer house on a waterfront lot or an old, small house because of the view or site. A thorough remodeling may cost as much as the original house. After remodeling, the original house may be unrecognizable. An architect can help avoid the "added-on" look by integrating the new into the old when you build.
- Work with a builder — When remodeling includes such projects as converting a garage to a family room, finishing off living space in an attic or basement, or adding wiring or heating to a home where the basic exterior dimensions are unchanged, a contractor or builder can help — and you save an architect's fee. But don't select just any builder. Avoid particularly those remodelers who advertise widely, particularly in the TV section of your newspaper, offer free gifts, or promote seasonal specials. Remodeling requirements are so varied that the way is open for crooks and builders who supply shoddy materials, cover up poor workmanship, and charge high fees — particularly add-on costs as work progresses.

    Ask your banker or a trusted friend at one of the lumber yards for a recommendation. Then, check a potential builder's references — and the local Better Business Bureau for any complaints against that builder. One of your best bets is to hire a small builder, possibly one who works by himself as a carpenter, to handle the main job and to help you select plumbing and wiring subcontractors to tie in with their work. Also, if you are handy, you can work with him or do part of the job yourself, such as painting or laying floor tile.

- Meeting Building Code Requirements — Check with your building inspector for requirements. You may need a fairly detailed set of drawings before you can get a building permit. Or, if your project is extensive and you plan to borrow from a mortgage lender, you will need drawings and possibly a detailed set of specifications to define the work. If you are not qualified to detail such drawings, look for a talented student, teacher, or draftsman working in an office to help you out at night. These capable assistants are often interested in moonlighting to pick up a few extra bucks.

Like any activity, knowledge of what is needed, and your own basic know-how will keep costs down and assure you of getting what you want. So, read — study — observe buildings going up — talk to knowledgeable people and specialists. Build your own stock of know-how before embarking on any extensive remodeling. The time you spend studying can pay off handsomely.

Which Remodeling Projects Pay Off? — Earlier in this chapter, you examined the cost trade-off between remodeling and sell-rebuy. The other cost trade-off to examine is — which remodeling projects increase house value? Of course, any worthwhile remodeling increases a house's value to the family living there. But, what about resale value? Usually, the market value of a house does not increase by as much as the cost of a remodeling project. But some remodeling projects increase market value more than others. For example—

- Kitchens — Recent major improvements in kitchen equipment, layout, decoration, and floors tend to obsolete older kitchens. Therefore, a newly remodeled kitchen is likely to increase the market value of your house and/or improve its saleability. Plastic laminate counters, a dishwasher, an easy-to-maintain floor, and more cabinet storage are relatively easy to install and could increase the market value of your house by as much as you pay for the remodeling. However, don't spend this kind of money just to improve a house's market value in anticipation of selling. Such major expenses are a real gamble (see Chapter 15). But, it's comforting to know that the money you spend on kitchen remodeling will also increase its resale value by some undetermined amount.

- Bathrooms — Living standards, particularly relative to the number and luxury of bathrooms, have increased steadily during the last 20 years. A large house with only one bathroom is almost impossible to sell. So, remodeling to add another full or half bath will usually increase a house's resale value. Again, each house is different. Adding a third bath or another half bath to a house already equipped with two or three baths will add little to resale value. Also, spending a wad to apply ceramic tile and new fixtures to an existing bath are doubtful value-raisers.

- Added rooms or space features — Along with higher incomes today, families want more space — a room for each child, a den for home business activities, and, most of all, more closet and storage space to put the many things we all buy in. So, added bedrooms (with baths), and increased storage in a new wing or expanded upstairs add value — but not so dramatically as added baths and upgraded kitchens.

- Special features related to locality — Air-conditioning, preferably a central system, is becoming standard for homes in the humid southern states. So, a used house drops dramatically in value without the modernity of central air-conditioning. Installing such a system not only improves your comfort, but increases house value at selling time. Decks, patios, screened porches, lanais — all keyed to the trend toward outdoor living — are easy to sell, so they improve a home's value in areas where weather extends the outdoor living season.

Home Improvements That Don't Pay Off — Don't cancel a planned improvement that is important to you and your family just because it may not improve resale value. But, study its cost effect. Some of the improvements that are doubtful value raisers include:

- Luxury items — Expensive additions that may be out of key with the rest of the house and the neighborhood seldom pay off at resale time. For example, a swimming pool back of an $18,000 three-bedroom house may actually stop a sale. However, if other houses in a neighborhood sport a swimming pool, your house could suffer by comparison if it lacked one. Expensive patios with a built-in barbecue pit and smoke oven, finely paneled den or imported carpeting are marginal items, and are related to overbuilding a house for its neighborhood.

- Landscaping — Probably nowhere around the house can money disappear with less to show for it than professionally executed landscaping. You can spend almost any amount of money on your grounds, but the credit will seldom exceed the bare minimum of having a lawn with a few shrubs.
- Hidden improvements — Improved wiring, extensive foundation or framing repairs and upgrading, better than average painting or staining, replacement of doorway and window trim, or replacement of a heating system are not likely to be noticed and appreciated by a quick-looking potential home buyer. On a car, it's the styling, colors, and interior upholstery that catch the buyer's eye rather than the mechanical improvements under the hood. So it is with a house. It's the easy-to-see, easy-to-identify-with, surface items that increase a house's value.

House Bargains Through Remodeling

The existing stock of badly used, run-down, undersize, poorly planned houses in the United States is almost beyond understanding. Sharp builders, homeowners, young couples, and real estate operators are converting this stock of inadequate housing into first-rate, modern homes. Old houses have several valuable attributes — voluminous space, first-come location, sound structure, nostalgic charm, and monstrous challenges. A prime building lot may be worth less with a run-down, possibly even dilapidated house on it than if the lot were vacant. In many cities land is so valuable old houses are simply bulldozed away. But in many others the marginal value of a building is just enough to keep a choice site out of most builder's hands. These are the places ripe for remodeling. Take a look at some of the outstanding examples:

- Downtown apartments — Increasingly, people are moving to close-in locations with access to the cultural core of the city. But, instead of living with creaky floors, cramped bedrooms, and Victorian plumbing, builders gut the interior of a stone or brick building. Then, they build a modern, air-conditioned apartment inside. Up to the front door, nothing appears changed. But, inside! Once you pass through the door, you're in a pad reminiscent of the latest high-rise. Total package price can be much less than similar diggings in a new building because the location and structure come cheap relative to new construction from the ground up.

- Waterfront cabins — Early city dwellers in many locations around the United States built summer homes on the shore of a nearby lake, river, or seashore. Since these cabins were only part-time houses, they were built small and cheaply. But they still sit in many localities — ready for complete remodeling. Again, as in the old, run-down city apartments, much of the basic house is there — sewer and water connections plus a bit of structure. Rather than simply buy the choice waterfront lot and tear down the cabin, plan to use the structure and engulf it with a new, remodeled house. For such projects, the services of an architect usually pay off.
- White elephants — old houses sit astride much valuable real estate. But these old houses are expensive to heat, have tiny bathrooms, depend on kitchens designed for a multiplicity of maids, are taxed at luxury rates, and may include so much lawn that full-time gardeners are needed. Such houses might properly be museums. Properly remodeled, they can provide low-cost, spacious housing. Sometimes, zoning permitting, they can be remodeled to provide several housing units (already accomplished in many, many areas), or portions of the property can be sold off for building lots. Bathrooms are the biggest problem — too old and too few. Small rooms or large closets can be converted into additional baths. A kitchen can be remodeled to one-cook size by relocating sink, stove, counters, and refrigerator, and blocking off some of the space for closets or pantry. Here again, such major remodeling can profit from the professional advice of an architect.

Do-It-Yourself Remodeling for Double Savings — Opportunities abound for crafty homeowners to increase their net worth through remodeling. The home handyman can use his spare time to build in those extra rooms, replace plumbing fixtures, push out a dormer for extra space, and redo the exterior. Many a handyman can turn his skills and spare time into cash by completely remodeling a run-down house and selling it. For example, houses that need paint, show an ill-kept lawn with weedy plantings, and disclose an interior with broken tile in the bath, dirty walls, and grubby floors sell only at a big discount. Combine poor condition with outdated plumbing, too few rooms, and pioneer kitchen and a house is practically unsaleable (see Chapter 15). The skilled all-purpose handyman can buy such a lemon, fix it up, and sell for a handsome profit. Here's how —

Each house is a separate challenge. Figuring with a sharp pencil and an eye to value will determine whether to remodel kitchen and bath completely. These two rooms are likely to be the key. Another key is the number of rooms and baths to serve them. Perhaps a new addition will bring the house up to today's standard. These are big-money decisions, but not so big as they could be, if the handyman does the work. Also, the sharp shopper can pick up most of the materials, such as plumbing fixtures, furnaces, shutters, stairways, and basic materials such as pipe, lumber, and bricks, from a house wrecker at a fraction of their ordinary cost. And, because freeway construction is clearing out new houses and apartments in some areas, these reclaimed materials may be practically new.

Tax advantages accrue to the do-it-yourself remodeler too. Any increase in the house value is taxed as a capital gain (if he owns it at least six months) when sold. Also, the interest he pays on the loan during the time he owns the house and the taxes accrued are deductible expense items. So don't overlook remodeling as a way to increase your housepower.

Financing Home Improvements

Depending on the extent of your planned remodeling project, money could be a problem. For minor refurbishing, you might use your own savings account — or pay for a series of small changes out of current income. But, major improvements run into big money. How you finance your remodeling project can affect the total cost as much as how you do the work or the kind of materials used. Before plunging, investigate various sources of money. Look at several factors — true interest rate, repayment period, possible limitations on how the money is to be used, and whether ancillary costs, such as term life insurance, will be added to basic loan costs. Major sources of funds for home remodeling, listed roughly according to their potential cost, are:

Open-End Mortgage — Your existing mortgage may include provisions to borrow additional money at the same basic rate — an add-on privilege. However, if your mortgage does not already include this clause, you won't be able to change it without rewriting the entire mortgage. Some open-end clauses limit your later borrowing to the amount of principal paid up to that point. Interest rate for the add-on portion continues at the previous rate. Because mortgage interest rates are among the lowest, open-end, add-on money could be your lowest source of remodeling funds.

Insurance Policy Loan — Your paid-up insurance is another source of low-cost funds, possibly lower than open-end mortgage costs. Check with your insurance agent for the amount you can borrow. While the interest costs are low, the amount you can borrow may be less than you need for a major remodeling project. There's no problem in borrowing against life insurance, but two cautions should be observed:

- Outstanding loans against an insurance policy will be paid out of the proceeds in case of the insured's death.
- Insurance companies rarely press for repayment of policy loans. So, even though the interest rate is relatively low, without a strict repayment schedule, interest continues, possibly for several years. In the end, the total dollars paid out in interest could be several times the amount paid at a higher rate but with a definite repayment schedule imposed.

Collateral Loans — Banks or other lending institutions are likely to lend money at lower rates when their risk of loss is also low. So, if you put up quick collateral, you may obtain a loan for 6 to 8 per cent true interest. The most common quick collateral deposited is negotiable stocks or bonds. You pay interest only on the outstanding principal.

FHA Home Improvement Loan — Title I FHA home improvement loans are theoretically available to qualified borrowers in amounts up to $3,500 for repayment over periods as long as five years. Interest ranges from 5 per cent (installment interest — not simple interest) on the first $2,500 to 4 per cent on the amount from $2,501 to $3,500. Table 14A details the monthly payments, equivalent simple interest rates, and the amounts a loan will cost over the repayment period. Note that the actual interest rate is close to 9 per cent for these FHA insured loans. (See Chapter 5 for a method to convert installment interest rate to equivalent simple interest.) While FHA improvement loans are attractive in cost, few lending institutions make such loans because of the involved paperwork and the low rate of return.

Bank or Personal Loans — Chain and local banks have come up with a variety of their own plans for financing home improvements. Usually, such plans call for interest rates higher than those permitted by the FHA. Bank plans may also be more flexible to allow modernization of heating plants and appliances in addition to brick and mortar changes. Interest rates will range from 10 to 16 per cent (true interest rate), but may be called 5 to 8 per cent (installment interest rate). You may also be asked to carry term life insurance on the declining balance.

Nominal Interest	Amount of Loan	1 Year Monthly Payments	1 Year ERI*	2 Years Monthly Payments	2 Years ERI*	3 Years Monthly Payments	3 Years ERI*	4 Years Monthly Payments	4 Years ERI*	5 Years Monthly Payments	5 Years ERI*	6 Years Monthly Payments	6 Years ERI*	7 Years Monthly Payments	7 Years ERI*
5 1/2%	$ 500	$ 44.10	10.8%	$ 23.17	10.7%	$ 16.19	10.7%	$ 12.71	10.7%	$ 10.61	10.7%	$ 9.22	10.7%	$ 8.22	10.7%
	1000	88.19	10.8%	46.34	10.7%	32.38	10.7%	25.41	10.7%	21.22	10.7%	18.43	10.7%	16.44	10.7%
	1500	132.29	10.8%	69.51	10.7%	48.57	10.7%	38.12	10.7%	31.83	10.7%	27.65	10.7%	24.66	10.7%
	2000	176.37	10.8%	92.67	10.7%	64.76	10.7%	50.81	10.7%	42.44	10.7%	36.86	10.7%	32.88	10.7%
	2500	220.46	10.8%	115.83	10.7%	80.95	10.7%	63.51	10.7%	53.05	10.7%	46.08	10.7%	41.09	10.7%
4 1/2%	3000	264.09	10.4%	138.56	10.4%	96.71	10.4%	75.78	10.4%	63.23	10.4%	54.87	10.4%	48.88	10.4%
	4000	351.35	10.0%	184.00	10.0%	128.21	10.0%	100.31	10.0%	83.58	10.0%	72.43	10.0%	64.45	10.0%
	5000	438.61	9.7%	229.45	9.7%	159.71	9.7%	124.85	9.7%	103.93	9.7%	89.99	9.7%	80.03	9.7%

*Equivalent (True) Rate of Simple Interest

Dollar Cost of Financing Loan

Amount to be Financed	Loan Period							Discounted Interest Rate
	1 Year	2 Years	3 Years	4 Years	5 Years	6 Years	7 Years	
$500	$29.10	$55.96	$82.82	$109.69	$136.55	$163.41	$190.27	5.5%
1000	58.20	111.93	165.65	219.37	273.10	326.82	380.55	5.5%
1500	87.30	167.89	248.47	329.06	409.65	490.23	570.82	5.5%
2000	116.40	223.85	331.30	434.75	546.19	653.64	761.09	5.5%
2500	145.50	279.81	414.12	548.43	682.74	817.05	951.36	5.5%
3000	169.06	325.12	481.17	637.23	793.29	949.35	1105.41	5.5 & 4.5%
4000	216.18	415.74	615.28	814.84	1014.39	1213.95	1413.51	5.5 & 4.5%
5000	263.30	506.35	749.40	992.45	1235.49	1478.55	1721.61	5.5 & 4.5%

TABLE 14A Repayment Schedules for FHA Home Improvement Loans

Credit Union — Don't overlook such semipaternal organizations as your company's credit union, the lodge you belong to, or a union fund for remodeling. Company credit unions usually deduct regular repayments from your paycheck — so, with less risk, interest costs are relatively low. Don't hesitate to ask lodge officers or union representatives for ideas on where to borrow funds for remodeling. You may find sources you hadn't thought of on your own.

Contractor Credit — Two possible sources for financing are — 1) the dealer who sells materials, or — 2) the builder who contracts to do the whole job. Lumber yards, for example, sometimes have time-payment plans that permit you to pay for purchases over a year's time. Such credit is mainly of help if you plan to do most of the work yourself. Contractors may include full financing as part of their remodeling package. They borrow the money from some source, of course, and frequently use financing as a selling tool. So, look out! Study the cost of a remodeling project with and without financing included by the contractor. You may find the "interest" cost for contractor credit to be in the 18 to 30 per cent bracket (true interest rate). Also, you may find yourself paying for extras that are not properly called interest — term insurance, financing fee, credit check, and other "services" that run up the cost of borrowing. Be sure to investigate alternative sources of credit. Take two precautions — 1) Keep clear of remodeling contractors who solicit business door to door, and — 2) Check with your local Better Business Bureau before signing a contract that calls for financing.

Refinanced Mortgage — If you own a fairly large equity in the house you plan to remodel, consider refinancing your present mortgage to raise funds to pay for remodeling. The new mortgage pays off the old and sets up a new schedule of monthly payments. But the new interest rate may be several points higher than the old mortgage rate.

Second Mortgage — If your present mortgage is closed-end (no add-on borrowing permitted), you might find it less expensive to negotiate for a second or junior mortgage rather than refinance the existing mortgage plus the amount needed for remodeling. Second-mortgage interest rates may run as high as 24 per cent. As risk increases, so do interest rates. Study the trade-off in costs between a small second mortgage and a larger refinanced first mortgage.

MONEY SAVERS WHEN REMODELING

Your greatest saving may come from your decision to remodel rather than sell your present house and buy another. Resist that tendency to "wipe the slate clean and start over." Instead, examine the real cost-saving possibilities of upgrading your present house with the money you'd spend on realtors' fees, closing costs, and moving expenses. You really learned to stre-e-tch your housing dollars in remodeling by —

- Analyzing the dollar trade-offs between the sell-and-rebuy plan vs. the fix-it-up remodeling projects — now and when you might sell later.
- Calculating the long-term, cost-price impact of specific remodeling projects — now and when you might sell later.
- Completely rebuilding a small, run-down home to develop the kind of home your family wants, rather than buying it all ready built.
- Applying your own know-how and "sweat equity" through remodeling.
- Looking at the tax advantages of remodeling, particularly your labor contributions to the final project.
- Examining the alternative avenues for financing your remodeling projects.

15

How To Collect More Cash For Your House When You Must Sell

Put yourself on the other side of the desk. You're selling, not buying. Apply what you learned about buying for less in reverse to selling for more. With the many company-directed moves these days, you need to know how to protect the equity you've worked so hard to build up. Learn how to avoid the traps that cost many homeowners so dearly. Since you're not likely to sell a house often, you have little opportunity to learn from experience. So, study every facet of selling and profit from the experience of others. Here you learn how to—

- *Appraise and value your house objectively; how to determine its true market value.*
- *Analyze the pros and cons of selling your house yourself or through a realtor.*
- *Work closely with a realtor to get the most cash when you sell.*
- *Transfer the title to your house on terms profitable to you.*
- *Put your house up for sale with its best look forward. That first impression really counts.*
- *Spend a little money and effort to gain a big dash differential.*
- *Stay clear of the dumb mistakes many home sellers make.*

Now you're the seller. Switch your hat 180 degrees and look at the whole sequence of buying and selling a home from the other side. What's good for the buyer may not be in your best interests as a seller. In fact, when you're ready to sell, just hope your buyers haven't read the other 15 chapters in this book.

You've got one chance in five of moving and selling your house this year, according to statistics. When your turn comes, will you know how to get full value from your house? Do you know how to protect your equity? Don't forget the equity leverage — a $1,000 difference may be only a 5 per cent variation on the total price, but it could mean a 50 — even a 100 — per cent difference in the net cash you realize from a sale.

Look at a selling transaction like this — Your house is worth about $20,000. You still owe the mortgage company $16,800. So, if you sell at $20,000, you have $2,000 left after paying off the mortgage and the $1,200 realtor's fee. Just to keep the figures simple, we'll ignore the possibility of a prepayment penalty and the adjustments for assigned insurance and tax accruals. But, suppose you actually sell your house for $21,000 by following many of the ideas you'll find in this chapter. Your net take increases to $2,940 — a 47 per cent increase — despite an increase in total price of 5 per cent. On the other hand, suppose you are forced to sell cheap — at $19,000. Your net take falls to $1,060, for a decrease of 48 per cent. So, the difference of 5 per cent up or down from the nominal $20,000 market value covers a range of $1,880 net difference of cash in your pocket. Worth considering? You bet!

Learn How Much Your House Is Worth

If you price your house too low, it will probably sell right away. But then it's too late. The house is gone. If you price your house too high, it won't sell. Soon, realtors will quit showing it. Later, you may have to accept a ridiculously low offer just to get out from under. So price your house competitively, realistically — unemotionally. Don't hold out for the last penny and drag out a sales campaign for many months. To find the "right" price for your house, use any or all of these methods:

Realtor Appraisal — Ask your realtor's aid in setting a price. Some realtors may give you the "drive-by" appraisal, a price set after a slow drive past your house. Other realtors will examine your house in detail, ask their associates for an opinion, then settle on a consensus. One of the real services a realtor can provide is a realistic appraisal of your house, the neighborhood, the money market, price trends, and many other factors — some of which may be purely subjective. But beware of the realtor who attempts to flatter you by setting an unreasonably high price.

Shop Competitively — Become a potential house buyer, and examine other houses like yours. Then mark your house up or down according to the differences between other houses for sale and yours. Use the checklist in Fig. 13-3 as an aid.

Order an FHA Appraisal — For a fee a lending agency working with the FHA will arrange for an official FHA appraisal. Most FHA appraisals are brutally objective. They also tend to be conservative. In many areas, houses sell for several thousands of dollars more than the FHA appraisal. Here's how this works — Say the FHA appraises a house at $16,000. The FHA would insure a mortgage on such a house at 90 per cent of its appraised value, or $14,400. But, the seller may find a buyer willing to pay $18,000. The FHA would still only insure a mortgage for $14,400. The buyer must then cough up $3,600 to complete the deal. So, a low FHA appraisal may be a drag on the price because a potential buyer may hold out for the FHA appraised value. If such an appraisal is excessively low, first find out the reason. Second, keep the information to yourself. Third, arrange for financing without an FHA-insured mortgage. Otherwise, the FHA appraisal, once made, will stick.

Pay for an Independent Appraisal — Professional appraisers work mainly for government agencies, insurance and financing institutions, banks, and others. But they will also work for you in a purely professional capacity. An appraiser will make a detailed examination of your house and neighborhood and write a report that details the potential selling price and some of the reasons backing such a price. If your opinions vary sharply from those of the professional appraiser, lean in his direction. Your opinions are probably prejudiced.

Market Value — The "market" exists in the minds of realtors and varies daily, weekly, monthly, and yearly. The market value of your house is the price you can sell it for. Plan on adding about 10 per cent onto a realistic market value to find the "asking price." You don't really expect to sell your house for the asking price. A serious buyer will not consider the asking price as the sale price. So you are both playing a game. If you should be tempted to price your house at the market value and plan to "hold the line" — *don't*. Allow yourself some maneuvering room — but not so much that you scare away potential buyers.

Sell Your House Yourself? — Or Through A Realtor?

Your biggest expense in selling and rebuying another house is the total fee extracted by the two realtors involved. The usual fee in most areas now runs 6 per cent. There's a big bonus to be made if you sell your house yourself and pocket the realtor's fee. Some people on the move sell their own house each time. But, there are hazards. Some of the functions handled by a realtor you must perform if you sell yourself include:

Finding a Buyer — Realtors spend millions of dollars advertising the houses they have for sale, mainly to contact families in the market for a house. Once they find a potential buyer, the realtor shows him through many houses — including yours if you are listed. Through a multiple listing service, other realtors show your house. And, frankly, many lookers prefer to have a realtor haul them around than to spend the time and trouble looking for a house themselves. But, you can find a buyer by one of the following means:

- Set up a sign that announces your house is for sale. Rather than say "By Owner," state "Inquire Within." Don't attempt to hand letter your own sign. Build the board, then pay a professional to paint it. A messy sign sets the wrong tone.
- Use your company's bulletin board, in-plant newspaper, or home-listing service to attract potential buyers. Frequently these communication media are free to employees. Also, leave a typed card with the personnel department.
- Advertise in the local "shopper" or neighborhood newspaper. Ads in big daily classified sections are costly. By choosing the local papers, you reach a group of potential buyers who may have already decided on an area.
- Put up neatly lettered cards describing your house on neighborhood bulletin boards. Many communities offer free listing services near the post office, certain supermarkets, or other gathering places.
- Include notices in a lodge, club, or organization bulletin sheet. Again, these are frequently free.

Arranging Financing — Shop various money markets to arrange financing before you have a potential buyer on a string. Check the classified section of your telephone directory under "Mortgages." Talk to the loan officer of your bank. Try several outlets and find out where you can bring a prospective buyer for a mortgage. Check whether the house would be eligible for an FHA mortgage if a buyer wants to go that route.

Legal Details — Realtors are experienced in handling the many details of transferring the legal title of your property to a buyer. You can engage a lawyer to help you manage the sticky details according to law. Every state and locality seem to follow differing procedures. Some of the legal steps you will need help on are:

- Purchase agreement — This is the first piece of paper, and one of the most important, involved in a sale. Make sure it protects you. Basically, the purchase agreement establishes the price and sets the conditions for the final sales contract. The buyer puts up an earnest money deposit to hold the property while financing and other paper transactions are completed. You agree not to sell the property to anyone else and to sell it according to the specified terms. If the prospect backs out of the deal, he forfeits his earnest money deposit. On your end you must sell the property according to the terms of the agreement or face a suit. So, setting down all the terms precisely calls for legal handling despite the availability of pre-printed purchase agreement forms.

- Mortgage papers — Most of this work is handled by the financing institution, but you may need legal advice at some stage in the red-tape mill. Otherwise, you may still be held liable for some financing details even after the sale — as in the case where a buyer takes over your existing mortgage.

- Deed and transfer papers — Here you will definitely need a lawyer familiar with local customs to draw the deed in strict accordance with the terms agreed upon in the purchase agreement. Properly signing and filing the deed actually transfers ownership subject to mortgage or other liens recorded.

Timing and Distance — Most families sell their house because they are moving, usually to a distant city. A reporting date on the job establishes a time schedule. When time is a factor in selling a house, the owner trying to sell by himself is at a serious disadvantage. Also, don't try to sell a house yourself if you have moved away. Only someone on the spot can handle the many visits and answer the many questions necessary to consummate a sale.

If you are planning a move to another house in the same city without a specific timetable, you're in a better position to save the 6 per cent realty fee by handling the sale yourself. Without the necessity of moving, you can dicker on price and other terms more effectively.

Pros and Cons of Hiring a Realtor — Saving at least a part of the 6 per cent realtor's commission is a very real possibility for some owners selling their own house. The commission is a pile of bucks. You can probably do better selling your own house if you—

- Understand the mechanics of attracting prospects, know the techniques of selling, and obtain good legal and other advice when needed.
- Can arrange for financing at a reasonable cost.
- Have the time necessary to find a buyer.

On the other hand, selling a house can be a frustrating business at best. Realtors *do* provide a service — some more and better than others. You will probably be happier selling your house through a realtor if you—

- Can't be bothered with the picky details of talking with mortgage companies, drawing up agreements, and handling the closing details.
- Must move on a fixed time schedule which allows little time to find a buyer and complete the sale.
- Are planning a move to some distant location.
- Don't like selling, are not generally persuasive, and prefer not to submit to the frustrating series of contacts with prospects and the nitty-gritty details of what goes with the house, what stays, and the minor changes in price that may or may not occur with such decisions.

Listing with a Realtor — Three basic ways of working with a real estate agent are recognized by the National Association of Real Estate Boards. There may be slight local variations, but generally you work with an agent through one of these methods:

- Open listing — You may tell as many real estate agents as you like about your house and commit yourself to pay the agent who sells it the agreed-upon commission. You may also try to sell the house yourself. Agents are less likely to spend much effort or advertising on your house, because some other agent could turn up a buyer and take the commission. With an open listing, the selling agent takes all the commission.
- Exclusive listing — Just the opposite of the open listing, the exclusive listing limits the sale of your house to one agent. You can sell the house yourself, but you will still have to pay the commission. Make sure your exclusive agreement spells out the commission, the time limit for the contract, the level of effort expected, sales price, and your limits on working with any other realtor. With an exclusive listing, a realtor can afford to advertise the house, set up open-house arrangements on week ends, and

generally spend more effort selling your house because he is certain of the fee if the house sells within the prescribed time limit.

- Multiple listing — Most real estate boards use a system of trading information whereby a house listed with one real estate agent is listed with all member agencies in the area. The commission from the sale may be split — one half going to the listing agency and one half going to the agency that sells the property. If the agent who lists the property also sells it, he gets the total commission. You benefit from a multiple listing because more agents are working to sell your house. With a multiple listing, you must still pay the commission even if you sell your house yourself.

- Cooperating with a realtor — While not technically a listing, another form of working with real estate agents is known as "cooperating." Such an arrangement may be informal or agreed to in writing. Cooperation works like this— You are selling your house yourself. However, a realtor may have a client interested in your house. Rather than take a chance that the prospect will deal directly with you, the realtor works out a cooperation agreement. He may sell the property for whatever price he can get and turns over to you an agreed-upon sum. Or, the agent may take his normal commission, but usually from a higher price than you planned. As an owner you gain from a cooperation agreement when selling because you may still get the price you want or the agent may take less than his usual commission rather than lose the sale entirely. On the other side of the coin, an agent may "sell" the prospect a different house — one on which he earns the full commission.

Title Transfer

Whether you sell your house yourself or work through a realtor, you may choose among several options for actually transferring title to your property:

Cash Payoff — Cleanest of all methods is where the buyer obtains a new mortgage or pays full cash to you at the closing. You, in turn, use the money to pay off your mortgage and any outstanding liens. You deed the buyer your property, and he assumes full responsibility for any new mortgage, all outstanding taxes, etc. If you have owned the property only a short time, you may be subject to a prepayment penalty for paying off the mortgage ahead of time.

Assume Your Mortgage — Depending on how your existing mortgage is written, you may transfer your mortgage to a buyer who agrees to take over payments and pays you for your equity. Such an arrangement may be advantageous to the buyer if your mortgage is close to the sales price (so less down payment money required) and carries a low rate of interest. VA loans at 4½ per cent and a high loan ratio are prime targets for such mortgage takeovers. However, the mortgage company may refuse to accept a buyer for several reasons — poor credit rating being the most common. The mortgage holder may also prefer to rewrite the mortgage at a higher interest rate if the company is not bound by the contract to permit a mortgage assumption. While allowing the buyer to assume your mortgage may speed the sale, you should exercise caution unless — 1) The equity payment represents at least a third of the sales price, 2) The buyer is responsible with a good credit rating, and 3) You are prepared to take back the property in case the buyer fails to fulfill his obligations. Even when the buyer agrees to assume full responsibility for your mortgage and the mortgage holder agrees, you, as primary mortgagee, are still responsible. If the buyer fails to make payments, the mortgage company will hold you responsible.

Land Contract Sale — Rather than actually transfer the property, you may agree or contract to sell the property later. Such a transfer is known as a land contract. With such an agreement, the title to the property remains in your name. You, in effect, agree to transfer the property under the stated terms when the buyer is able to pay enough down payment and obtain a mortgage — or some other condition. Land contracts can be tricky. Before you sign one, consult your lawyer about your responsibilities and the chances you may be taking.

Trade-In Sale — One realtor can handle both ends — selling and buying — if you use the trade-in approach. Usually, such antics are applicable only if you are moving from one house to another in the same locality. Trade-ins generally work out like this— You are interested in a new house, but you can't buy until your present house is sold. So, the realtor agrees to take your house in as a part of the deal for buying the new house. The realtor seldom takes title to your old house or applies your existing equity as a down payment on the new house (as is common in trading for new cars). Usually, the realtor will guarantee a minimum selling price for your house but will try to sell it at a higher price. You may be shocked at the price a realtor is willing to guarantee on a trade-in deal. But, at least you know where you stand. Due to the risk involved, the guaranteed price may be unacceptably low to you. Consider whether you might be better off to sell through regular channels, and then buy your new house without the drag of a trade-in. In any event, check out alternatives. Taking the easy way out through a trade-in may cost you a hefty piece of your equity, even though the actual difference in sales price is reasonable.

Getting the Most From Your Old House

Buyers react favorably to any product that looks good, gives the appearance of loving care, and promises easy maintenance. A house that looks good may be no better buy than the house that needs paint, exhibits a ragged lawn, and promises the new owner an endless run of Saturdays to be spent on cleaning and refurbishing. However, the bright, cheerful, good-looking house sells quicker and for a higher price than the run-down house. A house in the $22,000 to $30,000 bracket can easily sell for as much as $2,500 more if it is primped for sale rather than sold "as is." Remember, any difference in sale price affects your equity with brutal leverage. For example — suppose your house is priced at $25,000. Your unpaid mortgage stands at $20,000. If you were to sell at $25,000 and pay the realtor his 6 per cent commission, you pocket $3,500 ($5,000 equity less $1,500 realtor commission). But, if your house needs attention and is hard to sell (as explained later), it may sell only for $24,000. At this price you pocket only $2,560 ($4,000 less $1,440 commission). On the other hand, if you present a readily salable package, an astute realtor may sell your house for $26,500. At this price you pocket $4,910 ($6,500 equity less $1,590 commission). By preparing your house for sale and getting the higher price, your net take is almost 92 per cent greater (difference between $2,560 and $4,910 expressed as a per cent). Not a bad prize worth working for! Here are some proved ideas for getting the top dollar for your house when you're ready to sell—

Create a Warm First Impression — A potential buyer's mental reaction to your house the very first time he or she sees it is crucial. Make sure that vital first impression is a positive one. A realtor may point your house out to a buyer as he drives by. Unless the first impression from the street is inviting, they may never come back to examine your house in detail. Remember, what a prospect actually sees is only part of the story. What the looker may not see can be just as important. A potential buyer sees how neatly a lawn is trimmed, how carefully the paint is preserved, and the absence of splits or cracks. From these visual cues he concludes that the owner is interested in his house and that the things he can't see will have received the same tender loving care. Try to look at your house like a buyer — pick out the little things that are wrong, look for items that create questions in your own mind, then make a list of the things you would work on if you were a new owner. If you do this job objectively, you will automatically find the weak points in your house. You can correct most of the deficiencies with large applications of elbow grease and a minimum of cash.

Attack the Outside First — Unless your lawn and house exterior are inviting — unless they say, "This house looks like a place I might want to live in" — a potential buyer may keep right on rolling past your house. So, attend to these details that, taken together, make your house a more attractive package—

- Keep lawn and plantings in tip-top shape — Even if you normally pay little attention to your lawn grounds, keep the grass clipped and edged, spray out or pull weeds, and sprinkle enough fertilizer to bring the lawn color to a deep, healthy-looking green. The husband who sees such a neatly clipped lawn thinks, "Well, I won't have to spend much time on the lawn; it looks good." Immediately he begins thinking about finding a golf course or some other diversion. Apply the same attention to your shrubs or flowers. Pull the weeds, then cover the ground with a light mulch of bark or leaves. Cut off any dead shoots or branches and trim the other plants to bring out their best. If you are selling in an off season, rake up any debris or remove collections of old leaves, stalks, or cuttings.

- Clean up the yard and grounds — Remove any wind-blown debris, newspapers, old wagons, junk hauled in by the kids, or stuff you meant to do something with but never found the time. Any loose boxes, old lawn-mower parts, or other unnecessary junk should be hauled away to the dump. Leave the area clean, and the new owners will find their job of moving in easier.

- Paint the outside or not? — Usually the cost of painting the entire exterior of your house is not worth the added price your house may bring. However, if the paint is dingy, flaking off or badly blistered, if you have put off painting in anticipation of moving, or you have made some recent repairs, a one-coat paint job could do wonders for your house's appearance. If you can do the job yourself, the cost of the material alone is probably a good investment. Also, any expenses for fixing up your house within 90 days of the sale can be added to the basic price of the house when figuring capital gain tax on any profit. If painting the entire exterior appears too expensive, consider washing dingy siding with trisodium phosphate to remove smoky grime or mildew and to bring out the color of existing paint. Or, you might paint the trim only, including shutters, porch columns, etc. Doors take such a beating that you might paint the doors only — especially the front door.

- Watch interior items that are visible from outside — First, make sure the windows are clean all around the house. If windows are curtained, arrange them so they are symmetrical and are easily visible from outside. If your windows include roll shades, leave them open, or drawn to the same level in each room. If drapes are pulled and windows are visible from the street, keep furniture neatly in place. Clean out the garage or carport. If there are outdoor storage cabinets, shelves in the garage, or other storage areas for such gear as lawn mowers, bicycles, etc., remove the collections of junk and either pack them for the move or haul them away. Cleared-out storage areas where husband and wife can visualize storing their own stuff becomes an open invitation to move right in.

- Fix anything broken — Cracked and uneven concrete on walkways or badly tipped bricks or stepping stones can be straightened or cracks filled with mortar mix for little cost to gain a big improvement in appearance. Broken fence slats should be replaced, crooked shutters straightened, and other such items you may have dismissed as unimportant should be corrected before showing your house. Consider your impression if you saw such things as a broken fence, broken shutter, etc. Such items spell WORK. Moving is bad enough, but a list of things to repair immediately cools whatever buyer interest a realtor may have developed in your house.

Tackle the Inside — Clean — clean — clean is the word for the interior of your house when you want to sell. Elbow grease again is the needed ingredient.

- Woodwork and walls — New cleaning materials from trisodium phosphate to new aerosol-can products make the job of cleaning woodwork, floors, walls, and ceilings easier than ever — and more important. Remove fingermarks, cobwebs, dingy spots on floors — anything that spells WORK for the new wife. Use a wax cleaner on varnished woodwork. Ordinarily, it's not a good idea to repaint walls and woodwork because the new owners may want to select their own colors to match their furniture. But, a clean, well-scrubbed look invites confidence that any repainting will go easily. Follow up such cleaning with a polish job on hardware, using a metal polishing cream or spray — doorknobs, cabinet handles, and metal light fixtures.

- Check out things that must "work" — Replace all burned-out or broken light bulbs and make sure they operate from switches that work easily — quietly if possible. Reset latches on doors that vibrate from the least wind and quiet windows that rattle. Oil noisy hinges, sliding doors, and switches or actuating handles on windows. Oil the furnace fan and pump for quiet operation.

- Correct any plumbing problems — Easiest to fix are leaking faucets. If previous dripping has rusted a bowl, clean with ZUD, or a weak muriatic acid wash. If plumbing bangs and rumbles every time a faucet closes, water hammer is the cause and can be corrected by draining air columns back of faucets or by installing vertical standpipes if none now exist. All faucets, toilet bowls, and drains should work properly.

- Clean kitchen from top to bottom — Key target for a prospect's wife is her primary work station in the kitchen — so make it as appealing as possible. Make sure the oven is sparkling — several kinds of oven cleaner make this chore easier than ever. Remove any grease from range top and brighten with a metal cleaner. Counters, sink, and appliances can be brightened with a wax cleaner to build eye-appeal. Attack dirt or greasy spots on the floor with steel wool and cleaner; then wax until the floor shines. Do the same with cabinets. Clean out as much of your own stuff from cabinets as possible and wash shelves or replace dingy shelf paper. Clean, open shelves help the prospect's wife to plan how she will store her own stuff when she moves in. Make sure stove, oven, refrigerator, dishwasher, garbage disposer, and any other equipment that will remain with the house work properly when you demonstrate them. Do as much as you can to brighten the kitchen without spending money for anything other than cleaning products. However, if the kitchen floor is impossible to clean, shows badly worn spots or holes, you might consider relaying a new, low-cost linoleum floor covering in the kitchen area.

- Clean out closets and storage areas — Most homes have too little storage space, so make the space you have seem larger. Pack up the stuff you plan to move and clean out the stuff you will be throwing away. Leave only the essentials you need to continue living in the house until moving day. Develop the idea that space is plentiful by showing empty closets, a clean storage area in the attic, or empty shelves in the basement or garage. Families on the move know they have lots of stuff to store, and making a place for it will help more than you might think in selling your house. When clothes and other gear must remain in storage spaces, hang or store them neatly.

- Fix things that are broken, cracked, or missing — Nail pops, cracked plaster, or opened seams in plasterboard tend to worry potential buyers. So, since repairing them is so simple, work on such items pays handsome dividends. Replace any tile that may be missing, and invest in a new caulk job around tub or shower to prevent leaks. If wallpaper is torn, badly wrinkled or exceptionally dirty, you may be better off to remove it and cover the wall with a quick one-coat paint job. Broken woodwork, damaged cabinets, doors that won't operate — any of these things discourage buyers quickly, so get them fixed before showing your house.

- Light up — clean up the basement — If your house is blessed with a basement, make the most of it. Install enough lights to turn it into a bright, cheerful, useful area — don't show it with one bulb weakly trying to light the whole area. Clean the floor and remove any rubbish from storage areas. Sometimes, a quick coat of a light-colored basement wall paint will add cheer to what often is a black hole. Indicate how spaces have been or can be used for play areas. If the laundry facilities are located in the basement, clean them till they sparkle, and light the way from stairway to laundry. Remove any signs of previous water leaks around the walls. You may find it profitable to spruce up a dingy, hard-to-sweep floor with a coat of rubber-base concrete paint. But, above all — clean any basement thoroughly and keep it clean until the house is sold.

Don't Remodel Before Selling — Despite what you consider as obvious shortcomings in your house — don't spend much money remodeling if your only idea is to increase your house's sale price. The money you spend seldom pays off in a higher selling price. For example, don't do over the kitchen by installing new cabinets, a new sink, new counter tops, etc. You're better off financially to spend time and effort but a minimum of cash on scrubbing up, cleaning out, and improving the appearance of your house.

Several exceptions to the general rule apply, however. If something is broken or a major fault really needs to be fixed, you're generally better off to repair the problem yourself than to lower the price of your house to compensate. Suppose your screened-in porch is badly rotted around the bottom edges. Any reasonably alert prospect will notice such a problem, figure the cost of repair, and hammer down the price by at least that amount — probably more. You're better off to rebuild the rotted portion and sell your house in good condition. The same logic applies if you have an obviously leaking basement, structural weakness somewhere in the foundation or joists, or termite damage. In fact, in areas where termites are frequent pests, you may as well order a termite inspection and offer the report as evidence that your house is free of termites. However, if you should discover termites, repair the damage and, again, get an inspection report that permits you to offer your house free of termites.

Be Prepared With Answers — Serious prospects begin asking a raft of questions about your house, so be prepared ahead of time to answer such questions as— How much are heating bills? How much are taxes? What are water rates, electric rates, costs for rubbish removal, sewer charges — and the like? Old bills, particularly for taxes and utilities, help answer such questions. Be prepared to talk about schools, even if you have no children or they are no longer in local schools. Also, can you rattle off such information as the dimensions of your living room, total living area of your house minus the garage or carport, timetable for local bus transportation, how old the house is, and scads of other information of interest to a potential buyer? Don't depend on the realtor to supply this information; he has too many houses to worry about, although some of the data will be copied on his listing sheet.

MONEY SAVERS WHEN YOU'RE SELLING YOUR HOME

Having to move and sell your home can be a traumatic experience. Don't make it a costly one to boot. Realtors and the sharp-money boys grow fat in the house-selling game because so many homeowners know so little about the home market and how to keep from getting fleeced. In this chapter you learned about the mistakes that cost so many home sellers a sizable chunk of their accumulated equity. You learned to avoid many of these mistakes by —

- *Pricing your home right on target — not so low that you lose part of your equity — not so high that it doesn't sell.*
- *Selling your house yourself, if the market is right and you know how to handle the many transfer details.*
- *Helping the right realtor sell your house at a profit if you don't know enough about selling it yourself.*
- *Preparing your house for sale so it sells at the highest possible price.*
- *Recognizing the multiplier effect on your equity by working for that price differential that puts extra cash in your pocket.*

16

The Law And Your Home—
How To Avoid Costly Losses

Few sections of the law are so varied and so deeply rooted as those laws that affect title to land. As a property owner, you can't afford to ignore the many and complicated laws that apply to you and your property. Not knowing the law can be costly at best — disastrous at worst. So, as a windup, know where you stand and the mistakes to avoid by —

- *Recognizing the need for insuring the title to your property, the risks and the potential costs.*
- *Protecting yourself against frauds and honest "mistakes."*
- *Learning your rights if your property is condemned.*
- *Knowing where you stand on fences, drainage, and property lines.*
- *Saving money on taxes of all kinds relating to home and property.*

The guy who said — "My home is my castle — and ye shall not tread therein" — didn't understand the law. All you need for that castle to come tumbling down is a superhighway plan that plunks a double yellow line right through your living room. Or how about the owner of your land two or three transactions back who forgot he had been divorced *after* he bought the land, and now this long-lost divorcee wants a piece of the action on your lot. Too bad! The law of titles sometimes leads to disaster. And, then there are taxes — always taxes. So, although you may say — "This is my castle, begone," you really ought to know your limitations — and your rights under the law.

House Deeds Can Cause Trouble

"Title" to a piece of property can be defined as — "The sum of all the facts on which ownership is founded, or by which ownership is proved." "Title" is really your legal right to possess and use a piece of property within the restrictions imposed by law or limitations on its use. Land is wrapped up with a bundle of laws not applicable to any other kind of property. Every bit of land is described somewhere in the records, but the records are not always complete. In fact, it is the complication of records that makes it almost imperative that you protect your land and any improvements on it with *title insurance.*

Title insurance is a simple contract that makes good a loss arising through defects in title to real estate. The record of past deeds, mortgages, liens, and other possible encumbrances on a piece of land can become so complicated that not even an experienced lawyer can say for certain that "You own this property free and clear." The title insurance company says, in effect, "We have examined your deed and are willing to guarantee that you own the described property. If some defect in the title shows up, we will defend any court action, and if we lose, we will pay you the value described up to the limit of the policy coverage."

Ooh — that was a mouthful! First, what's a defect — specifically, what's a title defect? There are two kinds — 1) Defect of record — any encumbrance on a title which is made a part of the public record. Defects of record include: court judgments, mortgages, liens, easements, etc. 2) Hidden defect — any encumbrance on a title that is not apparent from an examination of the public records. Forged signatures on some previous title instrument, a secret marriage, unknown heirs, a minor's signature, etc., are examples of hidden defects. An encumbrance is any right to or interest in land which may be held by third parties to the lessening of the value of the title to real estate. Abstractors can easily be tripped up by hidden defects, so title insurance was developed to provide assurance to homeowners, mortgagees, insurance companies, and the like. Here's how it works—

Suppose you buy a house for $20,000. You are really buying the land and everything on the land. The grantor (seller of real estate) conveys the land to you, the grantee, with a deed. A title search indicates the grantor is the owner and in a position to sell the land to you. Then, just to ease your mind — and satisfy the mortgage company — you take out a $16,000 title insurance policy to cover the mortgage company's interest. You live happily with your house, you pay the mortgage company its bit monthly, you pay taxes regularly — though grumblingly. But, out of the blue, a frump of a woman turns up with a legal instrument that says your property was transferred to her as part of a divorce settlement. Your lawyer, after duly examining the papers and court records, agrees. You have a problem. Your home isn't really your castle at all.

But the title insurance company steps in and defends your title in court. The company and you lose! You have to give up your land and house. But, because you were insured, the title insurance company pays off — $16,000. If you had paid the principal of the mortgage down to $15,000, you get $1,000 after the title insurance company pays off the mortgage company's interest. You're out the difference between the $1,000 you collect and the added $4,000 value of the property. You get nothing for your equity. You can learn two things from this not uncommon example —

1. Even title company searches may overlook hidden defects.
2. The title insurance company only pays off to the limit of its liability.

In this case, you bought a $16,000 face-value policy. You co-insure any value above that — in this case the $4,000. For full protection, you would buy a policy that covers the full value of your home.

Official title abstracts, deeds warranting clear title of the grantor, lawyer's searches and examinations, contracts that the title is "good," or your own knowledge of the deed and property are not invincible. Even the title insurance company's search may not uncover some hidden defect, but it is willing to put its money on the line and guarantee its search results. The companies aren't wrong often.

Frauds — And Your Protection

For many years the idea prevailed that once you took title to a house it was yours — no guarantee, no call-backs to fix unsatisfactory workmanship by a builder — nothing. Many states now modify this stand that you buy a house "as is," and the federal government, through the FHA, guarantees a certain level of quality. Here's how the law may protect you from fraud or poor workmanship —

Guarantee on New Homes — Contractors selling new homes in some states must, by law, correct deficiencies that pop up within one year after the sale. What is a deficiency? Well, the wording and interpretation vary in different states. Also, one contractor may view his responsibilities differently from another. But, generally, if water pipes leak, a toilet fixture fails to work properly, the heating system breaks down, or big cracks appear in one or more walls, the contractor must correct the faults — at no cost to you. Check with the consumer protection department, attorney-general's office, or with the local building inspector in your state to determine the extent of protection afforded by your state.

Protection Under the FHA — Houses built to standards and specifications issued by the Federal Housing Administration are inspected periodically during construction to qualify for FHA-insured financing. This inspection during construction is your first protection. However, if you bought a house built after September 2, 1964, the FHA will help you pressure the builder to correct faults. Your first call is still to the builder. But, if your complaint is a real one and the builder fails to correct the fault, the FHA can and will step in and do the job. This protection does not extend to used houses, even though FHA may appraise the house and approve a mortgage to be insured under FHA provisions.

Protection for Used Houses — "Sorry, old chap, but you bought the house 'as is.'" Such a rejoinder is likely to meet any complaint you may have about a defect you discover after buying a used house. An appraiser may point out defects or problems during his appraisal. If an FHA man found the faults, the FHA may hold off approving financing arrangements until the faults are fixed. But, once you buy the house — it's yours — faults and all.

What You Can Do: But, all is not lost. For example, suppose you buy a used house with the understanding that it is insulated. But, in cutting through a wall to add a dryer vent, you discover there is no insulation in the sidewalls. If you can prove the buyer specified there was insulation in the walls before you bought the house, you may collect damages or force the seller to install the insulation.

The sure way to protect your purchase is to write such understandings or warranties into the purchase agreement. As part of the purchase agreement, you might specify something like — "the heating system is operable," the "house includes two inches of insulation in all exterior sidewalls and four inches of insulation in the ceiling," the "roof is in good condition," and the house is "warranted to be free of termites, carpenter ants, and powder-post beetles." If the house depends on a well for water, you might specify that the water has been tested for purity and palatability. If your waste system connects to a septic tank, you might include the provision that the sewer system functions without leakage or backup. A seller who objects to including such written guarantees in the purchase agreement tips his hand that something is wrong or that he is deliberately misrepresenting the house.

Condemnation

Local, state, and federal governments exercise a "right of eminent domain," to take your land if it is needed for public purposes. The "due process of law" in our Constitution protects you from willful loss and unfair treatment. But the facts are that your home and land can be snapped up for a superhighway, a school site, or any other public purpose that can be proved "necessary,"

Do you have any defense? Of course, you do. You are entitled to a fair price for your property based on market value — not value as assessed for tax purposes. However, sitting on your land with a shotgun across your knees defying the bulldozer will get you nothing but trouble — and your picture in the paper. Appraisers make mistakes, and if you don't agree with their figure, don't be browbeaten into signing. If you have a justified complaint, hold out for a court case to present your ideas.

Tract houses are fairly easy to appraise. However, if you have added extra rooms, expensive landscaping, and improved mechanical systems, you may not get full credit for such improvements. A custom-designed, custom-built home is more difficult to appraise because it includes many hard-to-price goodies. The policy among most government agencies when taking over your property is to give you a fair price — not so low that you suffer a real financial loss—not so high that you make a windfall profit. Prices are likely to reflect current inflation.

You may have more of a problem if your property isn't taken for a highway — or if the state wants only a part of your land. If you are left alongside a noisy, exhaust-filled highway where you once enjoyed the quiet and tranquility of woods or open space, you have little recourse. You may try a suit for damages on the basis that your land and house are now less valuable than before, but such suits fail more often than they win. If only part of your lot is needed, you are usually paid a fair price for the portion taken, plus damages for the remainder. The problem of part damages is sometimes so difficult that the government will take all of your land even though they use only a part.

What To Do: If your land lies in the path of some public project, you may not know it until the negotiator knocks on your door with a purchase agreement to sign. At various stages of the process, you may—

• Block or change the plan — Not likely unless you learn about a project very early, while it is in the planning stages. If you wait until the public hearing (usually required by law), the plans may be so rigid (cast in concrete is the cliche) you can't break them, even with concerted group action. The time to act is while the plans are relatively fluid — changeable. Then, if you muster a group and do a little alternate planning of your own, you can sometimes convince highway, school, airport, or other planners that an original plan is too costly — or has other defects, and your plan offers benefits. The key element here is *early action.*

• Point out items of value about your property if you have an opportunity to influence an appraiser. Ordinarily, independent appraisers are hired by the state or other government agency to set a fair value on your property. Appraisers evaluate the entire tract to be taken and then work on each parcel individually. An appraiser may set a value on your property without your being aware of it. But, if you have a chance, you can point out a view, more than normal interior building, or special equipment, such as an electrostatic precipitator or central air-conditioning.

• Deal with the negotiator. Depending on the state, negotiators have a varied range of freedom in dealing for your property. Sometimes, they can offer only the one price set by the appraisers. Or, they may have limited discretion about recognizing value overlooked by the appraiser. Sometimes, they cannot make changes on the spot, If you remain objective about points of added value that may have been overlooked by the appraiser, you may achieve a second look without going to court.

• Don't be bamboozled into accepting a lower-than-market value for your property. Some negotiators may attempt coercion. They may point out the greater value to the community of the improvement planned on your land. But, while the community gains — you lose. Stand firm. If you don't get a fair price, hold out and prepare for a condemnation suit. Some states permit one other step — a group of landowners, appraisers, and state negotiators might consider informally, as a kind of kangaroo condemnation court, whether you have a case. If you're right and the offer is too low, the state may change its offer to avoid condemnation. But, if negotiations break down and no agreement appears possible, the court suit is the last step.

• Prepare for your condemnation suit by hiring an independent appraiser, preferably one with court experience, one who has established a gold-plated reputation for integrity — one whose opinions are valued in court. If your independent appraiser concurs with the offer you have for the property or the offer is only slightly higher, weigh the cost of a court fight vs. any probable gain. After studying your own appraiser's detailed report, you may decide to settle out of court. If you believe you have a case, hire a lawyer experienced in condemnation proceedings and carry through.

Laws You (As a Homeowner) Should Know About

We have already discussed your liability for negligence and possible injury to others on your property and for the actions of your family on others' property (Chapter 4). You've learned about the possible pitfalls when buying a home (Chapter 13), and possible faults in a title. Some of the other booby traps to avoid are—

Fences — How, Where, and What — Local ordinances may govern your rights to build a fence and how you build it. For example, you may be prevented from building a fence between the front of your house and the street. Or a front-yard fence may be limited to three or four feet in height. Possibly, it can only be a "property line" fence; that is, one that defines a lot line but doesn't obstruct a view. Deed restrictions sometimes limit fence building activities. Back-yard fences may be no higher than six feet in many localities. So, before you begin digging post holes, follow these hints—

• Check local ordinances, zoning restrictions, and your own deed for any possible limits or restrictions on your planned fence.

• Make sure — don't just guess — you know the exact location of your property lines. Look for iron pins at the corners of your lot.

• Consult with your neighbor. If you agree to share the cost or to place the fence directly on the lot line, commit the agreement to writing and have the agreement witnessed and notarized. You may have no problem with your current neighbors, but if they sell, you need something in writing when dealing with new owners.

• Build your fence back from the property line if you and your neighbor cannot agree. Setting the fence line about two feet back from the property line allows you access to the back side for maintenance without trespassing on your neighbor's land.

• Make sure you don't block a neighbor's view or breeze. Already a considerable body of common law is developing to substantiate a land owner's "air rights."

• Don't create a traffic hazard by erecting a sight-blocking fence around a corner lot. Drivers need to see around the corner at an intersection to avoid accidents. You might be liable for damages if your fence were proved to be the cause of an injury accident.

• Once you build a fence, keep it in good condition — including the side that faces your neighbor.

Drainage — Your Rights and Privileges — Ground water flow affects your property. You cannot, for example, build a dam around your property and change the natural course of surface water.

Property Lines — Don't take a realtor's word, a mowed grass line, a fence, or even a rotting wooden stake as a true indication of a property. Make sure you know what you are buying. Nations are still fighting over dividing lines between countries. Similar bitter disputes over property lines have fueled feuds, turned friendships sour, and led to murders at worst and court cases at best. Inaccurate surveys and inadequate descriptions have led to many disputes. To protect your interests, think about these effects from property-line law—

• Every bit of land is described somewhere, somehow. But, because the earth's surface is roughly spherical, flat pieces which can be measured sometimes are odd shaped — and inaccurate.

• Only permanent markers, such as iron bars or pipes driven deep into the ground or metal markers cast in concrete, can be trusted. Don't depend on stones, wood stakes, or measurements from other, so-called permanent markers. If you are buying property that has not been surveyed for 20 or more years — require a new, legal survey before buying.

• Uncontested public use of land sometimes conveys common law access. The law on this point varies among states. However, if you attempt to block off access to some neighbor's property, you may be sued and will frequently lose your right to deny right of way. Accordingly, if you allow children to use a path across your land, livestock to walk in a path to water, or permit the public to drive in and out of a location, you may be granting public access without knowing it.

• Don't plant trees that are likely to grow tall or spread over your property line. Suppose an apple tree on your lot branches over your neighbor's land. The part of the tree that intrudes into his "air space" can be trimmed without your consent. Also, he can collect any apples that *fall* on his land. While he can't legally pick apples from the tree, you can't trespass to pick them either. Avoid such problems by planting trees well back from a property line.

Tax Effects On Your House And Home

Because of the sizable impact of taxes on home operation

expenses, consider these points—

Income Tax Deductions You Can Take Around Your Home — Almost any homeowner can benefit by filling out the long Form 1040 when filing a federal income tax return. Since state income tax laws vary, these comments apply mainly to U. S. tax laws. Common deductions you can claim include—

• Real estate taxes — Deduct the full amount of the property taxes you pay to your local community, county, and state. If your mortgage company collects a monthly fee and pays your taxes from this account, make sure you ask them for the exact amount of taxes paid. If you own a cooperative apartment, deduct your proportionate share of the cooperative's taxes.

• Interest paid — All of the interest paid as part of your mortgage payments and as interest on assessments (but not the assessment itself) is deductible. Get a yearly statement from your mortgage company that breaks out the interest portion of your monthly payments.

• Casualty losses — Flood damage, windstorm damage not covered by insurance, and earthquake damage are typical of casualty losses you can deduct if you detail the actual loss. The critical point is the suddenness of loss. You can't, for example, deduct termite damage you discover because that loss occurred over an extended period of time. Casualty losses must also be unexpected and unusual — losses that are sometimes blamed on the Almighty as "acts of God."

• Theft losses — A special form of casualty loss results when your property is unlawfully removed with the intent to deprive you of its benefits. You can't claim something you lost as a theft. You must be able to prove that somebody stole the property before you can claim the deduction.

• Use of home in business — If you customarily work at home or dedicate one or more rooms of your house to business use, you can deduct "ordinary and necessary" expenses associated with that business use. If you use a den as an office, deduct a proportionate amount of the expenses according to either the number of rooms or the floor space. Of course, to qualify for a business deduction, you must be using a part of your house in a business — not as a hobby. You may spend a wad of bills on a greenhouse for growing orchids. But, unless you sell the orchids and work at orchid culture as a business and not as a hobby, you cannot deduct the associated expenses.

Tax Effects When You Sell a House — Ordinarily, when you sell your house, you must consider the tax effects as on any long-term investment (if you have owned the house for six months or longer). Any gain is taxed at 25 per cent or 50 per cent of the gain is considered as additional ordinary income — whichever is less. However, there are a number of exceptions and other factors you can use to reduce the tax you must pay—

• You pay no tax on a gain if you buy and occupy another home within one year after selling. Or, if you are building another home, you must start construction within one year of selling and occupy it within 18 months of selling. And the new house, either one you buy or build, must cost as much as or more than the house you sold. Sounds simple, and the inflation effect on house prices means you usually spend as much on a new house as the price of your old one.

• Long-term gain or profit is computed as the difference between the cost and the selling price. However, certain factors affect the cost for long-term gain computation.

1. Capital improvements increase your original cost, but maintenance expenses do not. You can add the cost of finishing a basement, adding on a new wing or carport, or paving a driveway. But, you cannot add to the basic cost the money you spend for painting the house (except as noted hereafter), for refinishing a hardwood floor, or fixing a broken or leaking heating system. If you plant shrubs and lawn yourself, you can deduct the original cost of the plants, seed, and fertilizer — but not the value of your labor or the cost of sprays, dusts, and fertilizer to keep the plants and lawn growing.

2. "Fixing-up" expenses can be added to the base cost (or deducted from the selling price) if you spent the money to improve the chances of a sale or the selling price within 90 days before the sale.

3. Selling expenses can be deducted from the sale price. If you pay a 6 per cent realty fee for selling your house, deduct this from the gross price to determine the net or adjusted selling price. You can also deduct the cost of paying off assessments, tax stamps required to register the sale, and other expenses that you pay — not those that the buyer pays.

• When computing the price of a new house to determine whether it is greater than the adjusted sale price of your old house, add any buying expenses, such as attorney's fees, title insurance fee, mortgage finder fees, etc. Also, if you are building a new house, collect construction costs on your new house during the 30-month period beginning 12 months before you sell your old house and extending 18 months after sale.

• You may not be required to pay any tax on the gain in property sale if you are 65 or older — providing you have lived in the house for at least five of the eight years prior to the sale. You can use this tax-forgiveness feature only once in a lifetime.

Question Rates and Assessments? — You bet! Tax assessors are not super-human; they sometimes make mistakes. If you believe you are being taxed unfairly, don't hesitate to question your property taxes. However, consider these factors—

• Taxes are likely to be higher than expected on older houses whose depreciated value may not be fully reflected in the assessed valuation. A blighted area may still be carrying a tax load reminiscent of better days.

• Know how to read your tax bill. Many of the costs may have been voted in as levies to pay off bonds or special assessments. Also, while you might consider your tax bill extremely high, a reassessment might increase rather than decrease the current value. So make sure you have a case for a lower assessment before asking for a review.

SUMMING UP

Knowing your rights and responsibilities under the law can save you money two ways — by helping you avoid an expensive loss through ignorance and by leading to savings on your income and property tax bills. Wrapped up in a mixed bundle were these ideas for working with the law and getting the tax savings you're entitled to by —

- Learning how to safeguard the title to your house or property.
- Writing a guarantee when you buy a new or used home to get the maximum protection available.
- Protecting yourself against frauds and shady deals.
- Knowing your rights if your property is condemned and how to get the most money when negotiating with a government agency.
- Recognizing your responsibility and limitations on fences, water rights, and property lines.
- Taking advantage of the tax laws to reduce your payments on income and property taxes.

INDEX

Tub repair ?
caulking ?
Plumbing ?